SHRINKS

THE ANALYSTS ANALYZED

SHRINKS

THE ANALYSTS ANALYZED

JAMES PARK

BLOOMSBURY

First published in Great Britain 1992

Copyright © James Park 1992

Bloomsbury Publishing Limited,
2 Soho Square, London W1V 5DE

A CIP catalogue record for this book
is available from the British Library

ISBN 0 7475 0794 5

10 9 8 7 6 5 4 3 2 1

Designed by Geoff Green
Typeset by Hewer Text Origination Services, Edinburgh
Printed in Great Britain by Clays Ltd, St Ives plc

This book is dedicated to my mother, Mary Park

shrink Psychiatrist/head-shrinker, who makes his or her patients feel very small. American slang.
First literary appearance in Thomas Pynchon's Crying of Lot 49, *1966*

shrink Psychotherapist who brings relief to patients by shrinking their inner demons. American slang.
Spoken to author on the streets of Brooklyn, February 1991

Contents

⊙▢
⊙⊙

Acknowledgements

MANY psychotherapists and psychoanalysts contributed to my work on this book, and not a word of it would have been possible if they had not been willing to give me their time and attention. Since they mostly wished to remain anonymous, I cannot thank them individually. I can, however, express my special thanks to Gaby Marks of the London Centre for Psychotherapy, and Jill Curtis of the British Association of Psychotherapists. Also to David Belgray of the Midtown Consultation Center, Anabella Nelken of the National Psychological Association for Psychoanalysis, and Zvi Lothane, all in New York.

Additionally, I would like to thank Albert Appel for putting me up in New York, Clare McKeown for doing the same in Boston, and Barbara and Rafael Carmona for providing a house in the Languedoc where the pages that follow were written. Thanks also to Ondine Upton, who provided invaluable support and encouragement throughout the period of preparation, research and writing the book. The original manuscript was read by Matthew Reisz, Sebastian Cody, Eric Rayner and my editor Kathy Rooney, who all made many helpful comments. The book's faults are all my own.

Preface

⊙⊡
⊙⊙

Psychotherapy is both frightening and dangerous. It is frightening because no one can know in advance what will emerge from an exploration of his or her inner world, and whether the consequence will be beneficial change or a terrifying tumble into an abyss. It is dangerous both for the therapists, who must put their psychological health on the line for every encounter with a patient, and for those who must entrust themselves to strangers in the hope that their problems can be solved, their pathologies changed and their psyches rehabilitated. Given that the process goes so dangerously deep, and that so much can go wrong, it is reasonable to ask whether the potential rewards of undergoing therapy are worth the inevitable risks.

On entering a therapist's consulting room no one can feel confident of finding a safe haven. There have been too many instances of therapeutic malpractice, and of patients enduring much suffering in the false belief that they will thereby come to live happier, healthier lives. One hears of practitioners who sit in silence for months, seemingly unaware that their patients are reliving memories of vicious fathers or persecuting mothers; of patients dragged down into depression by their therapist's gloomy moods; of therapists who deny the truth of their patient's most traumatic memories. One hears also of therapists who sleep with their patients, extort money from them and generally inflict upon them abuses at least as great as anything they experienced in their unhappy pasts; they then compound the indignity by proclaiming the age-old excuse of miscreants everywhere, that the victim asked for it, or imagined it.

Many patients have told of becoming so entangled in the relationship with their therapist that they could find no way out. Although they acknowledged that the therapy long ago stopped doing them any good, they were not able to loosen the therapist's grappling hooks. They paid their first visit many years before, complaining of some minor unhappiness, but now, after spending several thousand pounds on treatment, they believe that they really are sick. Seemingly, the therapist has used his or her knowledge of a patient's deepest fears, anxieties and longings to practise the worst sort of emotional blackmail. Sick themselves, such therapists lock their patients into their own miserable world.

Instead of publicly acknowledging the dangers involved in their profession, and the suspicions that people have of them, therapists have too often simply hurled brickbats at each other. In the therapists' world view, it is the approach of other practitioners that is wrong and misguided. Therapists who think they are radical and free-thinking will dismiss others as dogmatic, rigid, fanatical and obsessive. Those who pride themselves on adherence to 'correct' technique will accuse nearly everyone else of being sloppy and muddled. Both will illustrate their point with tales of the misadventures that befell the patients of a certain analyst with whom they are acquainted. And instead of opening their profession up for examination, practitioners frequently react with paranoia towards those who seek to investigate its workings, and claim that it is impossible for those outside the privileged circle to understand anything significant about it.

This refusal by therapists to countenance their own flaws has helped to persuade many people that psychotherapy is a sinister practice, which should be abolished. Jeffrey Masson, for example, has argued that all therapies put excessive power in the hands of their practitioners. The highly-charged intimacy of the therapeutic situation not only makes abuses against patients possible, it actively encourages them. 'The structure of psychotherapy is such,' he argues in *Against Therapy*, 'that no matter how kindly a person is, when that person becomes a therapist, he or she is engaged in acts that are bound to diminish the dignity, autonomy and freedom of the person who comes for help.'[1] To relieve our emotional pain, he argues, we should look not to some professional cadre, but to normal human friendship.

Many have responded to Masson's rallying call. They are an assorted bunch. Look to your friends, some of them cry. Reform the churches, others demand, so that the priests can again offer themselves as society's main source of consolation. There are those who insist that people should learn to endure their suffering and not look to others for healing. Still others say that families should learn again how to look after their own. Turn away, they all say, from the therapists, for they are not to be trusted. They do not listen. They go to sleep in sessions. They are cold, calculating people. They are only in it for the money. They get their kicks from abusing the power relationship. They lack common sense. They make you depressed. Enter their doors and you are in danger of being persecuted, misused and abused.

Among this babble of voices are some who have suffered from malicious, rude and abusive therapists. Their criticisms are subjective and partial, but rooted in the data of unhappy experiences. They are joined by others whose distorted view of psychotherapy is created only by fear, who would grab at any excuse to avoid facing the exposure that therapy demands. They cannot bear to look into the pain of their past, the discomfort of their present, or the possibility of future change. They abuse therapists because they do not want to consider the possibility that they could benefit from their ministrations.

They will argue aggressively that they do not need therapy, mocking those foolish enough to undergo treatment. Among them might be a man in his mid-thirties who idealizes his mother, has never slept with a woman, still forms adolescent-style crushes on girls, and toils into the early hours of the morning to fill the gaping hole in his emotional life. He argues that family and friends should get people through emotional crises. Another sort of sceptic could be a woman, unable to bear the thought of ever again coming to depend on another person, who regularly gets drunk, screams hysterically at her boyfriend, expresses unhappiness with her work, and declares that anyone who sees a therapist is a wimp. Suffering, she argues, must be endured. It makes us into bigger, better persons.

It never occurs to such people that therapy could enlarge the possibilities of their existence. They are afraid to admit that something hurts inside, that their past was not so rosy, that their parents crippled them at the same time as they gave them succour and comfort, and that they could change aspects of the way they are. There are people like these who come to psychotherapy late in life. For them, what is often hardest to bear is the thought that they did not have to be the unhappy, embittered failure who stumbled through several decades. And then they may think of those others who will endure their whole span without ever discovering what therapy has to offer. However much they toss on their beds at night wondering why things do not run more smoothly, scream and shout at those close to them, or practise abuse on strangers, they choose simply to endure whatever distress and pain comes their way.

The critics are right to say that therapy is a difficult business with uncertain benefits. No treatment, of any variety or intensity, will remove all emotional distress, nor can it be administered without inflicting additional pain. There will be moments in the protracted process when most patients will feel worse rather than better. It is foolish to expect, as some people seem to, that drastic changes in our psychological organization can be secured without severe discomfort, danger and risk. A British analyst has remarked that it is not surprising if some people equate analysis with 'molestation', since the process can so often be experienced as an 'attack on the person's self' that 'emphasizes the person's inadequacy and separation from human life.'[2]

People can deteriorate during treatment, and watching someone do so can be a distressing experience for their friends. There is a joke that therapists tell against themselves. A man has a hundred friends. When he goes into analysis, he starts to lose them. Finally, he is down to the very last one. That friend says to him, 'Look, I have known you all your life. You have always been difficult. But now, since you went into analysis, you have become intolerable.' The man turns to him with a smile and says, 'Yes, that is true, but I feel so much better about it.' But, whatever the immediate negative consequences of therapeutic treatment, its long-range goal is to make the patient better able to relate to others.

For those who contemplate it from the outside, therapy is indeed a fearful unknown. It requires a great leap of faith to put one's psyche into the hands of another. One must trust that the other person is not going to inflict excessive harm, and that one can emerge from such a strange process more whole, more capable of fulfilling oneself. Many people, perhaps most of them, spend the first year or two of their therapy trying to consolidate that leap into the darkness, and to build a trusting relationship with their therapist.

Entering into therapy does make people vulnerable. Through seeking a therapist's assistance at the point when they feel most disturbed and least capable of making clear, rational decisions, they put enormous power into the hands of the healers. One might wish it was not necessary to make that leap of faith, but what is really the alternative? When family and friends can no longer assist, there are few other ways in which people can be helped to adapt to the ever-changing demands of contemporary life.

There was a time when priests and rabbis offered a framework through which people could look for meaning in their suffering, but few are now prepared to simply accept that their afflictions are sent by God to try them. They want to lessen the ache that comes from inside, and expect to find agencies to help them. And the religious values which once held out to people a goal towards which they should aim are no longer of much use when there is so small an area of shared belief available to the vast mass of the population. Destiny is now generally seen as something each individual must discover for him or herself, it cannot be prescribed from above. Sermons and prayers are of little help for the sort of questions that people bring to their one-to-one sessions with a psychotherapist.

To those sunk into depression or driven crazy by anxiety, general practitioners will dispense drugs which will relieve the symptoms. Such interventions may be the only option available for those who cannot afford therapy and have no access to a publicly funded provision. They may also be a useful standby for those confronted by a short-term crisis, such as a bereavement, divorce, or important exams. And they may help to bring other people away from their 'black hole' to a state where they can reflect upon their ills in therapy. But when psychological ills have deep roots, such drugs are no substitute for therapy. They mask the problem, they do not attack its roots. By propping up people so that they can get through their daily round, and giving the impression that they can get better without asking questions about why they feel the way they do, the pills can prevent people from looking for a way out of psychological distress that will lead towards a fuller life.

And it is utopian to declare that friendship or the family nexus could drive the therapists out of business and save people from undergoing that unnatural encounter with a stranger. Those who reach the point of needing therapy do so precisely because their support systems have broken down. It is crazy to expect their parents and others who mostly made them what they are to be of much help. Many seek therapy at a stage when family encounters have become red-hot with rancour, resentment and bitterness over emotional damage inflicted many years before. And while some do learn to grow through their friends, many are too damaged to trust other people; they find themselves repeatedly locked into masochistic, destructive and unsatisfactory relationships. They need therapy because they must learn another way of relating to others.

Men and women live in the chains of their past. Whether their fathers were cruel, kind, or absent; whether their mothers supported them with loving approval, hectored them on to greater ambitions, or lived the double life that alcoholism imposes, these early figures cast an inescapable shadow over their lives. They may have been born with temperaments either lively or placid, gregarious or solitary, but so much of what they do – the goals they follow, the partners they choose, the conflicts they enact with workmates and lovers – follows patterns that they learned in early battles around the crib, the playpen and the schoolyard.

Many find in mid-life that they have set out in pursuit of goals which could never have satisfied them. Others discover that their dreams of happiness at work or in relationships are constantly frustrated by their own behaviour and attitudes. Some feel listless before the challenges of life, unable to find the courage to face up to the tasks they see before them. Some feel at the mercy of contradictory voices from their past, telling them at one and the same time that they are loved and hated, good and evil, that they can achieve great things and that they are always going to be hopeless failures. Caught between these pressures from their pasts, most people feel that they have become much less than they could have been.

Psychotherapists hold out to people the dream that they can some-how remake themselves – that those persecuting parents, or the grand-mother who smothered them with love, or the next-door neighbour who introduced them prematurely to the mysteries of sex will lose the capacity to shape their lives 20, 30, even 50 years after the period when they had them in their power. They offer to help them define the goals more clearly and unlearn the patterns that keep those goals from being attained. They offer to free them from unproductive, pain-inducing patterns of behaviour, to lift their feet out of a muddy past and set them firmly tramping to a more hopeful future.

That dream has become increasingly potent as the pressures on people to change and adapt have grown. The fashionable political philosophies of the last decade or so have encouraged people to take responsibility for their own fate and fortune, and to give up hoping that they will get much help from their society or community. So great has been the stress placed on individuals that people have had to ask themselves where they could find the capacity to bear the weight being placed upon them. Feminism has helped women to articulate their feelings more clearly and to seek an understanding of the social structures that constrain them. It has also, indirectly and more slowly, persuaded men to start thinking about their relationships, and to verbalize some of what they feel inside. Meanwhile, talk shows on television and radio have not only encouraged greater emotional literacy, but also acquainted people with the idea that it is legitimate to seek help.

Therapy, in its many varieties, is an increasingly acceptable option in the Western world. There has been an expansion in the areas within each society where there is no longer any shame attached to confessing that one pays regular visits to a therapist. The stiff upper lip is still the norm in the American Midwest and in many areas of British society, but others have come to accept that the problems of modern life are too great for many people to cope with on their own.

And so it is that therapy has become an issue about which nobody feels neutral. To some, therapists are, at best, dogmatic, pedantic and narrow-minded; at worst, they are corrupt, lecherous and cruel. Others see the therapist as a mother figure, the nurturer who will soothe all pain, heal all distress and put the life of their patients on a new track. 'For or against?' was the question that nearly everybody asked me when I told them I was writing a book about psychotherapists. The notion that I could see therapists as a mixture of the good and the bad, the gifted and the incompetent, the well-meaning and the wicked was beyond their ken. They, it seemed, had made up their minds a long time ago.

As I explored the subject, I became increasingly aware of my own ambivalences. While I would try to cajole into therapy any friend who was in emotional distress, I had heard too many tales of incompetence to allow for complacency and had to admit to having felt profound suspicions of my own therapist. Was it possible, I wondered, to form a true picture of a profession that is at once so idealized and so condemned? I needed to find out why psychotherapy sometimes fails people so badly and whether the abuses and malpractices are inherent in the nature of the therapy relationship, or simply a breakdown in a relatively sound system.

But trying to find out what goes on in psychotherapists' consulting rooms is a little like investigating what happens in other people's bedrooms. When one hears of fantastic experiences, one is tempted to smile and assume exaggeration on the part of the speaker. And simply because it is a fearful process that they would like an excuse to ignore, many people find it easier to be cynical and to believe that the tales of insensitivity, brutality and viciousness contain the whole truth about therapy.

Without solid information to go on, many construct their attacks on psychoanalytic therapy around theories developed in Vienna some 80 or 90 years ago. While it is true that analysts have a tendency to quote Freud, Jung, Klein, or other great theorists as if they were gospel, it is wrong to ignore both the enormous developments that have taken place since that date, and the gap, for good or ill, between what therapists are taught to do and what they actually do. 'What people say or write theoretically,' one analyst said to me, 'often has a very marginal connection with what they say when describing what they actually do in a session.'

I decided that the only way to approach the questions which troubled me was to talk to therapists about their way of working. I started to contact them by following up friends who moved in the same circles, and by writing to the key training organizations in London and New York. Then I asked the people to whom they had directed me for the names of their colleagues. In this way I gained access to people in training and those who were just beginning their careers, as well as to well-known analysts and therapists of repute within the profession. If they appear in the pages that follow under pseudonyms, it is not because they are ashamed of what they do, but because most did not want to run the risk of exposing too much of themselves to their patients.

When I started, I feared that I would find therapists defensive and resistant to my questions. This fear was not groundless. The first person I reached on the telephone spoke ominously of her anxiety that I would 'damage the profession'. When I tried to speak to one analyst about therapies that went wrong, she just kept insisting, 'That is not everybody's experience. A lot of analyses and therapies are not like that.' It had not occurred to her that there might be some value in exploring just why it is that some people become stuck in helpless, untherapeutic relationships. Another analyst, who later explained that he had been unable to 'libidinize' my questions, repeated the old adage that nobody was 'entitled' to write about psychoanalysis unless they had either given it or had it. The clear message was that I needed full analysis. 'Even Aldous Huxley,' he facetiously added, 'took some mescaline before writing about it.'

But I found that most therapists, both in Britain and the United States, were keen to answer my questions. At the beginning, when I was not quite sure where my doubts about therapy were going to take me, I was sometimes confronted by paranoid reactions that I later came to consider a justifiable response to my own uncertainties. Some interviews started a little stiffly, but eased up as my questions revealed more about the attitudes I carried with me. Many seemed to be stimulated by the effort to articulate what they did, outside the rarefied context of their professional societies. They gave accounts of their ways of working that rang true for me.

There is a danger that in talking to 120 therapists I will have been seduced into their own idealized view of themselves. I hope I have treated their words with enough scepticism to give an account of analytic practice that will help those who only condemn to question some of their doubts, and also lift the blinkers from those who cannot quite acknowledge that the profession has warts and defects.

The resulting book is an attempt to tease out the elements of truth and fantasy contained in some of the suspicions people have of therapy by describing the ways in which therapists think and work. The first three chapters explore the reasons why people become therapists, and how they are shaped by their trainings. Is there, as many suppose, something warped about those who choose analytic theory as a profession? If not, what is it that makes them want to spend their days listening to patients' talk about their memories and fantasies? How are their attitudes moulded by the theories that they learn, and is it true that therapists spend most of their off-duty hours squabbling about the finer points of theory like medieval monks arguing how many angels can dance on the point of a needle? Is analytic training anything more than a sophisticated form of brainwashing?

Chapters 4–6 explore the way different analysts vary their technique, looking at how therapists resolve the contradiction between the need to establish natural relationships with their patients and the need to develop an 'analytic' stance that, by its nature, differs considerably from ordinary human relating. Does their training make it more difficult for analysts to console, comfort, or confront their patients? Do therapists refuse to acknowledge the realities of traumatic experience in defiance of common sense?

Chapters 7–10 look at how the match between patient and therapist can determine the success or failure of therapy. Can therapy work when patient and therapist come from different classes, races, or sexes? What makes for a good coupling between patient and therapist? Given how unsettling and psychically dangerous it can be to treat deeply disturbed patients, what equips a therapist for such work? And if it is true, as I would argue, that most therapy is free of serious abuse, what is it that sometimes goes so terribly wrong, and why?

Can psychotherapists be trusted? For the most part, probably yes, but only when those who undergo psychotherapy know something about what it is they should be getting. It is one aim of this book to provide an account of the way in which some therapists operate that will help consumers to tell good from bad. Not that such a process will ever be easy, for nothing is simple in the practice of psychoanalytic therapy. It is a profession in which practitioners must constantly resolve contradictory positions and balance out opposing goals. To qualify as an analyst one must know about emotional disturbance, and yet be well balanced oneself. In the day-to-day work one must be natural and yet analytic, loving and yet distant, flexible and yet firm. In their struggle to do that, psychotherapists probably provide lessons for everybody in their dealings with other people. While reading the pages that follow, one should bear in mind that psychoanalysis is a paradoxical profession.

Introduction

PSYCHOTHERAPISTS work with a limited repertoire of techniques. They can either speak or they can be silent; they can also touch, but most therapists deny themselves this option. How much they listen and how much they talk will depend on their personality, the way they interpret the needs of their clients at any particular time and the model of therapy in which they were trained. Those models divide into two basic types. Psychoanalytic therapies (those derived from Freud, Jung and their successors) use the therapist's silence and attentiveness to create a space which patients can fill with their own material. Most other therapies require the practitioner to be more active, more directive and more obviously involved.

To illustrate the difference between these two approaches, I describe here the methods followed by two therapists, Elinor and Caroline. Both were trained in the psychoanalytic model, but while Caroline has stayed with its basic precepts, Elinor has developed a confrontational style that has little to do with what she learned. Such a development away from orthodoxy is by no means uncommon. Psychotherapy is a profession where, behind the closed doors of the consulting room, everyone does it 'their way'.

I make no apology for the fact that my argument is rooted in my subjective experience of these two women – Elinor, whom I interviewed, and Caroline, who was my own therapist. I describe how I experienced the two of them, and where I thought each could be helpful and where destructive. There are elements in Caroline's approach which brought me relief, but might distress others, as I was irritated in my turn by aspects of Elinor's approach that she considers likely to be of benefit. It is because individual needs are so different that the debate about therapeutic effectiveness cannot be easily resolved.

It was during her training that Elinor came to feel that the analytic approach was mystifying and unhelpful to patients who wanted something more direct and 'normal'. Those who defend the psychoanalytic position would claim that it is the strangeness of the situation it creates which makes for effectiveness. The fact that therapeutic relationships are so different from all other human relationships is what enables patients to learn through them a new way of looking at the world and their place within it. Whereas Elinor tries to help patients by imposing her own view of the things upon them, Caroline encourages them to cast off the hectoring voices of their past and to find their own way.

Elinor is not shy about revealing her impatience with what she learned during her training as a psychoanalytic therapist. 'I have been through the mill and thrown the whole lot into the air,' is how she introduces herself to me. She freely admits that when she occasionally attends lectures on contemporary theory, she does not understand a word. It is all 'hocus pocus' and 'baloney' to her. Nevertheless, she feels that she is a good therapist, who uses her common sense and the wisdom that comes from experience. She does not have time for many others in the field: 'So many of them are terribly mixed up, quite frankly.'

Now in her late fifties, Elinor has her white hair drawn tight across her head, reflecting her direct, no-nonsense manner. There is no couch in her consulting room, just two chairs in which therapist and patient sit face-to-face. For the patient, jammed in between a piano and a bookshelf, the room must feel crowded.

The first indication that Elinor has rebelled against the canons of psychoanalytic therapy are the pictures of her grandchildren sitting on a table beside her chair. Analytic theory requires that therapists should keep revelations about themselves to a minimum, so that their patients' fantasies about them are not cluttered up with too much real knowledge. Therapists cannot fail to give some clues as to the reality of their lives, but it is generally thought that they should try not to force information on to their patients.

Elinor, however, thinks that patients have the right to know anything they want about her. She disagrees also with the idea that therapists should err on the side of silence. 'I ask direct questions,' she says. 'I don't have people just rambling on.' She will ascertain the immediate problem or problems that have brought someone to see her, explore a little of their family background and current relationships, and then offer them what she considers to be helpful advice.

Modern society, she feels, does not sufficiently stoke people's ambitions. Far from being driven against frustrating social norms and constraints, as were the patients seen by Freud, those who come to her mostly lack goals. The absence of social pressures – to form lasting relationships, to get married, to bring up children to a life better than one's own – has left people stranded. 'People do not know what they want from people any more,' Elinor insists. 'They do not make commitments. And because of having so much freedom, there is an insecurity in relationships.'

For such patients, she argues, the silent analyst has nothing to offer; for he or she simply mirrors the passivity of the patients' parents. There is no wellspring of passion to be uncovered. What they need is to be cajoled, guided and instructed. When they do not know what they want to do, Elinor encourages them to take up an Open University course or to attend evening classes and learn a foreign language. If they do know what they want, but lack the gumption to start working towards their goal, she will set them some 'little tasks' to perform. When they have some achievement to feel proud of, she feels, they will start to make progress. Such positive advice is alien to a psychoanalytic approach, which insists that patients should be helped to make their own decisions.

I visited Elinor to interview her for this book, not for therapy, but she tried to give me a flavour of how she works. 'This is the kind of work I would do on you if you came to me for therapy,' she kept on insisting. In my opening remarks I had incautiously revealed that writing books was not, at present, a lucrative occupation. She already knew from a mutual acquaintance that I had been 'properly' educated. When she asked me whether I was married, I confessed that I was not. I had, it seems, given her a theme.

'The way I see it,' she asserted, 'at your age you should be married.' She went on to argue that if only I had been under pressure to find myself a wife as soon as I left university, then the need to become a family breadwinner would have driven me to construct a successful career. 'Certain things play against you,' she said. 'It is acceptable to have one girlfriend, then another girlfriend and so on and so forth.' Too much sex, found too easily, seemed to be the cause of my problem. The nature of that problem, however, had not been defined.

Elinor advanced her views with total confidence. She seemed uninterested in discovering whether they had any relation to *my* reality. I tried to tell her that watching my father struggle to support a family, while also wanting desperately to break free from an academic job and pursue his own creative ambitions, had long ago persuaded me that marriage and fatherhood were traps into which I should not fall too early. In trying to fit me into her universal theory, Elinor was doing violence to a particular, painful reality. For me, *not* being married was a kind of victory.

I might have made allowance for the peculiar circumstance of our 'trial therapy' and assumed that, given more time to build the therapeutic relationship, Elinor would have taken all this on board, but she wrecked the chance of that concession by going on to say that she felt 'sorry' for me. In saying this, she ignored the fact that I had never acknowledged having a problem of the sort she described. She riled me further by comparing me (negatively) to her own son. 'He is really very successful,' she said, 'and what is more, he is a writer too.'

Had I turned up on Elinor's doorstep in need of real help, and had I been feeling more fragile, such implied reproaches could well have locked me into the therapy process, albeit in pursuit of purely masochistic gratifications. People may keep on going to therapy, even when they do not feel it is doing them any good, because the hurt it stirs in them is familiar from early relationships. I might well have found myself going back again and again to Elinor's consulting room, trying to win a place in her esteem and struggling to fulfil her programme for me, as I had in the past sought approval from my grandmother, an eminent scientist and principal of an Oxford college. It worries me that Elinor, unlike the psychoanalytic therapist who attempts to show patients what they are doing to themselves, would seem to be content to allow them to repeat their early patterns.

When I complain about her method in these terms, Elinor offers a response that is double-edged. On the one hand she declares it to be a good thing that I should try to win my grandmother's esteem. Is it not, she argues, through the emulation of powerful, successful figures that we form the ambitions that drive us on through life? But she also sums up my argument in a way that shows she has understood something of my situation. 'What you wanted,' she says, 'is the freedom to be able to express your views and to show what kind of person you are, and to fulfil yourself as who you are, and not what your grandmother is and has expected of you.' As a patient, I would have found that statement reassuring.

However, the mention of my grandmother causes our conversation to take a more worrying turn. She knows something of my grandmother's history and wants me to tell her more. What sort of parents did she have? How did her mother ensure that she received a good education at a time when that was not the natural thing for a young girl? What sort of man did she marry? How did her children turn out?

Elinor, like my grandmother, is obsessed with the sort of achievement that can be measured by the size of one's entry in *Who's Who*. I tend to look more cynically upon the damage that ambition can do to one's children and, through them, the grandchildren. Elinor starts to make me angry. When I point this out to her, she is not diverted.

'Haven't you got an interesting background?' she declares. 'Do you find it interesting? Does it excite you? I do hope it is being made use of. I hope you don't reject it. That is the sort of thing I would say to a patient.'

If I had been such a patient, I hope I would have walked out at this point. Elinor may have been able to give a reasonable account of my inner experience, but her words and manner do not reveal any profound sympathy, nor does she leave any space for me to deepen her knowledge of how I feel. Instead she has an idea to put to me, an idea which she thinks could be the solution to my still undefined 'problem'.

'Is it not possible for you to go and ask your grandmother about her early life?' she asks. 'What a wonderful subject for you! You might say this is not what I want. I want to do my own thing. I would say please yourself. But I have got a good book for you. Here you have this tremendous book and you are not writing it. You call yourself a writer! How can it possibly be that you have not pursued this opening?'

I get the feeling that we are no longer play-acting. We are doing this for real. I tell Elinor that I had recently discussed writing my grandmother's biography.

'I don't think you have,' she replies, 'because if you really had done more than give it a little thought, you would be deep in it. And I don't think you would have the same kind of depression. I personally feel that when people have an enormous goal, they are not depressed.'

I now have some indication of what Elinor considers to be my problem. 'What on earth,' I ask, 'makes you say that I am depressed?'

'I would not say you strike me as deeply depressed. But most people are depressed unless they have a huge project on, or are in a marvellous relationship which is going to lead to marriage.'

'But I am committed to the book I am researching, which is the reason why I came to see you.'

'But I feel you have this other biography you should be doing. I feel that you are missing a great opportunity.'

To anyone acquainted with the principles of analytic therapy, Elinor's attempt to bully me into writing my grandmother's biography is an outrage. Elinor knows something about the complexity of my feelings towards my grandmother, and how these influence my feelings about work, money and relationships, but she chooses to ignore them as she hurries on to fit me into her own theory and its related solution. She has decided that the project which most interests her is of considerably more significance than the book I am currently writing. She has totally abandoned any pretence of helping me to understand myself more fully and to move from there to define my own goals and a strategy to attain them. Her own beliefs tell her that people need pushing and cajoling; and that is what she does to me. She is not open to the possibility that I would not benefit from being treated in that way.

I resent Elinor's treatment of me, but others clearly do respond more favourably. Elinor has a steady flow of clients. Many are women in their mid-thirties, who need to find gainful employment now that child-rearing no longer fills their days. Others are men who bowed down long ago before the parental demand that they should enter the family business, and who now consequently find themselves mired in depression. And there are several women approaching middle age who still look after their elderly parents. As Elinor describes her most characteristic patients, she confirms my suspicion that they would all have a streak of masochism in their make-up. They must respond to Elinor as they have responded all along to many others in their lives – obediently, if slightly reluctantly. Her role, perhaps, is to play the substitute parent whose power is strong enough to wrest them away from the original version. Once pulled free, some may start to fulfil their own destiny.

There was a time when I too was drawn to women who knew exactly what was wrong with me and how I should adjust my life. I clung to those who told me to pull myself together and grow up, even though they made me feel worthless and wrong-headed. In my perversity I felt that they truly understood me and that through them I would become a stronger, more fulfilled person. But I no longer care for people who have programmes for my life, who prescribe solutions without paying attention to the way I define the questions. Although Elinor offered to take me into therapy, I did not take up her offer. I had already learned, through experience of another, more traditional therapist, to expect something different both from therapy and from other people in my life.

During the time that I went to see her, I never picked up any substantial information about Caroline, not even where she did her training. The room in which she received people was smaller than

Elinor's, but the sparse furnishing allowed her patients to feel a sense of space. I would sit with my back to the window. To my right there was a couch, which I was never invited to use. On the table behind me was a vase of flowers, tissues for clients who were inclined to tears, and a clock, so that Caroline would know when to finish the session. If there were any pictures hanging there, I do not remember them. I gazed only at the books which filled the wall facing me, and at my therapist. She was much younger than Elinor, probably in her early thirties, and had long black hair, which she sometimes wore loose around her shoulders.

Caroline believed in analytic silence, and I responded enthusiastically to the invitation that she offered to fill the resulting void with my own story. It could be said that I plunged headlong into that silence and joyously splashed around in it. How could I not, when all my life I had been surrounded by women who tried to fill their own inner emptiness by screaming at me? Throughout my childhood I had sat at the kitchen table, alternatively stunned by the babble of voices, or tuned into my own inner world. In choosing girlfriends, far fewer in number than Elinor imagined, and never lightly discarded, I had sometimes fixed upon women who would repeat my experience of the family home. Finding myself in the presence of someone who simply listened was a truly wonderful experience, different from anything I had ever experienced before.

It astonished me at first that I could speak fluently for 50 minutes, that I had so many words in me. I had no idea where all these memories would lead, what would result from this act of recall. I told Caroline about my father's death some six months previously, and about the house in the country where I had spent my happiest weeks as a child. I talked about my stormy, unsatisfactory relationships with women, and the depressions from which I suffered. I talked about a friend who had died when I was seven, and for the first time in my life I was able to weep for him. In short, I talked about whatever I wanted, whenever I wanted. Given how little of these things I had been able to reveal before, it was an activity that had for me the feel of something forbidden, and I began to compare visiting a therapist to hiring a prostitute. In return for payment, I could pour all the sewage of my memories into her ear. She sat there quietly, taking it all in, and occasionally making some remark to indicate she really had been listening and had understood something of what I was talking about.

Those expurgatory sessions worked magic for a while. I would go in with a headache, and emerge 50 minutes later feeling fresh and revived.

To express my emotions and be listened to was a new, invigorating experience. But there were doubts and suspicions eating at the resolve which took me once a week to Caroline's office. What does she think of me? What does she want from me? Why is she doing this? Should I be doing this? Should I be exposing my past to her? Am I going to get trapped in this relationship? What had at first seemed refreshing now began to appear strange, sinister, unnatural. I began to understand why some people cannot shake off their suspicions of therapy.

On the surface I had been positive about therapy, but as I look back on that time, I also recall that I was continuously attempting an escape. I spent two weeks in Wales writing a book. I applied for a job that would have taken me to Spain for 12 weeks. I almost secured a commission to do a book which would have involved my following a film crew around the South of France for eight weeks. When that fell through, I set off for four weeks in the Moroccan Sahara. A few months later I went on an expedition to the Hebrides. I may have valued my therapy, but I certainly was not going to make any sacrifices to ensure its continuance.

Despite this evidence that my commitment to therapy was skin-deep, or perhaps because of it, Caroline suggested that I start to come twice weekly. I complied, but this shift substantially altered my image of her. She was no longer a prostitute for hire, but an evil seductress who was after my money. My changed perspective was a consequence of her practice of making me pay for the sessions I missed, however many weeks notice I gave of my absences. Caroline's fee was not exorbitant and, in view of my chronic absenteeism, she had some justification for using the fee in an attempt to make me value her time and thereby deepen my attachment to the therapy. But she also touched on a long-standing fear – that the women in my life would drain me of money.

Caroline's increased call upon my time and my purse provoked a crisis in our relationship. The girlfriend I was seeing at the time was not someone to whom I could confess my twice weekly trips across London; she had no time for therapists and our relationship, always fragile, could not have survived the storms that this revelation would have provoked. Further, since I had not talked about this concealment to Caroline, I felt that I was cheating on both the important women in my life. It seemed that I would eventually have to choose between the blonde girlfriend who shouted at me and the black-haired therapist who listened quietly to my words. I had to find out which one cared for me most. My girlfriend's love I confirmed regularly, after a fashion, in bed. How far would Caroline go towards giving me a sign of her concern?

'I would like to be able to meet you outside this room,' I said. 'To go to a café and have a cup of tea. To talk about ordinary things like two friends.'

'That is quite impossible,' I recall her replying. 'It would mean crossing the boundary that separates my work from my private life.'

Caroline's answer may have been right in principle, but it was ill-attuned to the reasons behind my request. She could have asked me to explore why I had this wish to see her outside the consulting room, and we might have come to analyze the choice I was about to make. I might either have learned that I did not need to decide between the two women, or have opted to make a different choice. As it was, her answer shattered my faith in her, and shortly afterwards drove me out of therapy. I had asked, in my own way, whether she cared, but her reply suggested that all that mattered to her was the professional relationship between us. Now I could see only coldness behind the silence, and I was furious. Furious but unable to express the emotions I was feeling. Months earlier I had written in my diary, 'Perhaps instead of crying with Caroline I should shout. It begins to happen. I do get angrier and clearer.' In reality I still had a long way to go before I could articulate such strong feelings during the sessions.

The end of therapy came abruptly. I decided one morning that half an hour in bed with my girlfriend was more valuable to me than 50 minutes with my therapist. A couple of months later that relationship too was to founder. The passion, it was put to me, had gone out of our encounters. And perhaps it was just such an ending that I had unconsciously wished for. By choosing to abandon the therapy, which might have continued for many years, and opting instead for a fragile relationship which was set to self-destruct, I demonstrated my reluctance to embrace emotional commitment.

I do not claim that Caroline or Elinor are in any way typical of analytic or non-analytic therapists. What they do illustrate, however, is the complexity of feelings that therapy throws up. By taking up a posture – demanding, assertive, slightly hysterical – that reminded me of all the women in my life, Elinor aroused in me the desire to do battle with her, to try again to win the contest that I had been losing all my life. If I had been seduced into therapy with her, it would have been an intense, furious encounter but, I suspect, a futile one. I would eventually have left the battlefield exhausted and drained, but without having significantly changed.

Caroline, by contrast, behaved towards me in a way that distinguished her from any other woman I had ever known. She created a space in which I could say whatever I wanted, although my sense of gratitude towards her prevented me from expressing the anger that I also felt. Although I rebelled finally against her silence, the process had already changed me. I was never again to feel the sense of crushing depression that had taken me into therapy. I found the courage shortly afterwards to leave my job and pursue a writing career. And I have never since fallen in love with an hysterical woman.

Most of the rest of this book is concerned with the sort of therapy practised by Caroline. It will already be clear why I feel most sympathetic to this approach. Having myself struggled to throw off the mandates of my parents and my grandparents, I warmed to an approach that would allow me to negotiate a path away from their negative influences. Since I suspect that most people have to negotiate their way through parenting that is in some way intrusive, the psychoanalytic approach seems to have more chance of scoring bull's-eyes and bringing relief from psychological pain. It may be that there are patients who need to be provoked, challenged and jostled, as they never were by their parents, and that for them Elinor's therapeutic style provides much more lasting benefit. But it could never work for me.

Elinor and Caroline also represent the poles between which all therapists have to steer. Elinor's model, with its noise, its bustle and its bossiness, may seem more normal and natural than the psychoanalytic approach simply because it recapitulates aspects of parenting. People may not like it, but they can cope with it. It is what they are familiar with, after all. They are told what their problem is. They are told what they can do about it. The approach seems efficient, dynamic, reliable. Above all, it can be confronted in the open and argued with. The danger is, however, that therapists who are directive, imposing and challenging may push their clients towards places where they do not really want to go, and where they may not find relief from their distress or clarification of their uncertainty about themselves.

The aim of the silent therapist like Caroline is to provide an experience significantly different from any other relationship in the patient's past. For those whose parents were distant and aloof, the analytic therapist's manner during sessions may seem dangerously close to past realities. In general, however, it is the strangeness and unnaturalness of psychoanalytic therapy that people object to. They want their therapists to be more friendly, less cool, less preoccupied with the mystique of the profession. They dislike the notion that the therapist is a magician who will unlock the secrets of their soul, and they look instead for a special friend who will comfort them in adversity. They want to close the gap between therapist and client, to establish a relationship of equality.

Most therapists struggle to find a balance between the two modes of being. Unlike Elinor, they try to create an environment in which patients can speak freely and feel that they are being truly understood. Unlike Caroline at that crucial moment in my therapy, they try to show that they really do care. They aim to be natural and yet also analytic, to combine distance with warmth. They try to be giving without obstructing the patient's need to express hate and anger.

The problem for patients trying to come to terms with psycho-analysis lies in the very fact that so often their only previous experience of love is from someone who is callous, abusive and demanding. In every relationship, including that with their therapist, they look to repeat that situation. That is what they are used to. That is how they understand loving and caring. In the absence of any clear signals about what their therapist is feeling towards them, they imagine that the response is similar to that which they brought forth from their parents or step-parents or uncles or whoever. They send out signals and expect the customary response. When it does not come, they are unnerved.

I might, for example, have been relieved if Caroline had once shouted at me, as other women had; in a way that's what I was asking her to do when I called upon her to leave the room with me for a cup of tea. The dilemma with which I presented her was that, while she could not become a player in my game without depriving me of the opportunity to discover what I falsely expected of her and thus destroying everything that was valuable in the therapy, nor could she simply stand aloof without driving me out of therapy. And I did not give her time to find a solution.

It is because therapists have to walk such a tightrope that the good ones are so much more interesting than the stereotypes depicted by critics of the profession, or those created in our own fears and fantasies. They must allow the patient to set the agenda, but bring forth interpre-tations that will help the process along; they must respond emotionally and honestly to a patient, while also making sense intellectually of what is being told to them; they must seem to be completely involved in the patient's story, while also maintaining sufficient detachment to fit that story into a wider scheme.

It is hard to balance out these qualities. The analyst in training will tend to be cold and distant, pursuing conceptual rigour and fitting the patient's experience into a procrustean bed of theory. Experienced therapists may be too relaxed, too casual, no longer listening with full attention to the twists and turns of the patient's story, no longer distinguishing between actions that help the patient and those that gratify themselves. Only the therapist who can walk the tightrope will hold up an example to patients that will enable them to reveal the different layers in themselves, their own inner richness and potential for growth.

In the pages that follow I show how therapists struggle to define their position on the tightrope. The therapies that I talk about are almost exclusively psychoanalytic. I initially intended to cover the whole field, from behavioural and cognitive therapies to transactional analysis (TA), gestalt and bioenergetics, but it soon became clear that many of the apparent differences between these different modes were also differences within the psychoanalytic field. Psychoanalytic therapy is much more varied than most other practitioners allow for. I met a TA practitioner who implied that all psychoanalytic therapies held that humans were innately wicked, and a psychosynthesist who declared herself opposed to the sort of unbalanced power relationship that a psychoanalytic approach necessarily entails. Both, it seemed to me, were caricaturing their opponents and taking no notice of debates within the field of psychoanalytic therapy. Rather than embark on an enormously complicated and probably futile attempt to distinguish one form of therapy from another, I decided to narrow the field and try to give an account of how psychoanalytic therapy is practised in Britain and the US.

It will also cause extreme irritation to some people that I have not distinguished between psychoanalysis and psychoanalytic psycho-therapy. Psychoanalysis is a term normally applied to treatments of high frequency where the patient lies on a couch. Psychoanalytic psycho-therapy is a less intense process, but it deploys similar techniques to psychoanalysis, sometimes including the use of the couch, and has the same goal – to plumb the depths of the individual's unconscious. The achievement of that goal may have more to do with the patient's attitude than with the frequency of sessions. 'There are people,' said one analyst, 'who work analytically once or twice a week, where others come four times a week, fuck about and do nothing.' An attempt to define psychoanalysis by frequency of sessions is, therefore, fraught with pitfalls. In Britain, for example, three-times-a-week is always called therapy, whereas in the US, many regard three-times-a-week as analysis.

And yet frequency does make possible a different sort of relationship. Seeing someone four or five times a week, with such short gaps in between, will usually deepen the relationship. 'If you have too much of a gap,' another analyst said, 'between one session and another, the sessions get filled up with what happened last week. But with five times a week, you get something different going. Patients exhaust the obvious things about their current life and start to talk in a freer way. They bring out background thoughts that are not focused on telling you about something. They are more willing to get off the track and wander around.' The containment of psychoanalysis gives patients the freedom to explore more deeply their dreams, fantasies and wishes.

Generally speaking, I have referred to people as analysts if that is what they call themselves, but I do not mean to imply that they are radically different animals from psychoanalytic therapists. At the extreme, there is an enormous difference between the two, but the middle area is impossible to define. In such a situation, being pedantic about the difference between analysis and therapy is unhelpful.

1

Healing Wounded

Reasons for becoming a therapist

WHEN I told one acquaintance of mine that I was writing a book about psychotherapists, she was appalled. 'What a dreadful project!' she remarked. 'They all have such twisted minds.' I quizzed her about how she had developed such a view. It turned out that she had been to one therapist. But while she had doubts about the value of the experience, she did not recall him saying anything particularly odd during the six months she had visited him. Some prejudices against psychotherapists withstand all contrary evidence.

'Have you met any really mad ones yet?' people kept on asking me while I was researching this book. I generally had to report that I had not. One kept me waiting for an hour and then charged in with an inane remark about her children's laundry. Several were somewhat manic or made rather eccentric statements, like one who referred to the analytic process as equivalent to sexual intercourse. There were many whom I would definitely not recommend to my friends as therapists. Most behaved with a degree of spontaneity that suggested they would not last long at the top of a major company or merchant bank. But since they were therapists, I judged it healthy that they were, for the most part, open and frank about themselves, showing that they had long cast off the pretence to be anything other than who they were.

What sort of people become therapists and why? It is a complex question. But is it right to maintain, as some do, that the impulse which drives people to become therapists, connected as it is to their own inner disturbance, actually puts their competence in doubt? Does being sensitive to one's own disturbance and engrossed in its exploration mean that one is dangerously disturbed? I will then look at the reasons why people who have already established themselves in one of the caring professions feel the need to move on and train as therapists.

Therapists themselves have embraced the idea that there is something strange about their choice of profession. 'We are all mad,' says

Birgit, somewhat disarmingly, 'in the sense that we have a compulsion to be a container for other people's madness.' But this is not such an extraordinary statement given that many therapists are convinced that *nobody* can avoid a share of madness. 'We can all be psychotic,' says Mary. 'At those times we try to convince ourselves that the way we are thinking is correct, when it is absolutely crazy.'

It is not being mad that drives people to become therapists, but being interested in the workings of the mind generally and sufficiently aware of everybody's potential to become disturbed. Those who control admission into the various training institutes look for candidates who combine maturity and balance with a profound understanding of mental illness. They must be people who have suffered enough themselves to understand other people's pain, but who are no longer controlled by their own disturbance. It is a balancing act. 'We would not want anyone who is too crazy,' says Michael, who is responsible for selecting candidates to join one London training organization, 'but a little craziness helps.'

It is difficult for an applicant to know whether they have the right balance of qualities. For most other sorts of training, those going for interview will have a good idea of the general requirements. To the aspiring analyst, these can be something of a mystery. Owen, a psychologist who applied to join the Institute of Psychoanalysis in London, compared the experience to two Kafka novels. 'How do you get into the castle?' he says. 'How do you beat the rap in a trial, when you do not know what you are accused of? You are led into the presence of two analysts. They sit there inscrutably and occasionally ask you some rather alarming questions. With a normal interview, you would look them in the eye and smile a lot. When you are being interviewed to become a psychoanalyst, none of this applies. You cannot say, "Well, I am a jolly healthy person and I am extremely interested in Freud and have a good track record." What you have to show is that you are sick too. But you cannot say that you are a frustrated paedophile who has fantasies about eating babies. Then you would be too sick.' Owen's candidacy was rejected.

People become therapists as a way of dealing with their own emotional confusions, but that does not mean that the degree of disturbance most of them manifest is anything out of the ordinary. Critics of therapy find the link between the need for therapy and the desire to become a therapist inherently suspect. It worries them that people rest their claim to competence on an acknowledgement that they are sick. But it is not the case that the *most* emotionally disturbed are those who seek therapy, nor that those who stay out of therapy are necessarily more free from disturbance. For nearly everybody, therapy is both a search into their deep past and an attempt to put right those things that cause distress and discomfort.

There are few people who go through life without feeling, at some time, distraught, depressed and in need of help, and those who do would certainly not have the qualities required to work as therapists, nor much desire to do so. Many formulate the urge to train while they are themselves in treatment. And those who start a training in the belief that they are doing so out of intellectual curiosity, an altruistic desire to relieve the pain of others, or a sense that this is a good way to earn a living, soon find in their personal therapy that they have a deep, unacknowledged need to sort out their own emotional life.

There are therapists who endured deep trauma in their childhoods, but many were never much more disturbed than the rest of the population, and few of those to whom I spoke about their early years seem to have had a particularly rough time. Paul, who listens daily to the horrific experiences of the severely disturbed patients with whom he deals, often finds comfort in recalling his own childhood. 'I was not abused,' he recalls, 'I did not break down. I had reasonable relations with my parents.'

What marks out those who take up psychotherapy from the rest of the population is not so much the degree of their disturbance, but their ability to grasp how they construct defensive mechanisms against derangements that affect everybody. Many find themselves undertaking therapy because, at a certain stage, the awareness of their inner turmoil becomes pressing. They feel raw and become interested in why they feel raw. Sensitive to their own disturbance, they are made acutely conscious of the unhappiness endured by others. 'For me,' says Eve, 'one of the most meaningful aspects of practising psychotherapy is that it uses the parts of me that I was always most criticized for as a child. That I was over-sensitive and tended to take things to heart. These negatives became positives. Something that felt authentically me suddenly had value. That was very gratifying.'

All therapists seem to have had early experiences that sensitize them to the complexity of people's emotional lives and create a problem of understanding which eventually, many years later, drives them to seek help. 'What drove me to become a therapist?' asks Jane. 'I do not know how to answer that. Initially what made me become a psychologist was a wish for therapy myself, but I did not know that. Gradually I came to realize that I was trying to give unto others what I was really needing myself. But I could only give them something false because I did not understand enough.' Jane tried a variety of different therapies, but none of them helped. 'My problems were too profound. They did not touch what needed to be touched, or help me to understand.' Eventually she found her way into psychoanalysis and stayed for 13 years.

Jane's difficulties arose from the fact that her father had died two months before she was born. Although this was obviously an event in which she could have played no part, the need to explain it led her to take on an awesome responsibility for what had happened. 'As I conceptualized it, either he was damaged by my birth, or there was something so horrific about me that he dropped dead at the sight. It seemed to me as if he had died on the day I was born. It was as though I had killed him.'

It was the behaviour of Jane's mother which convinced her, as a little girl, that she was to blame for what had happened. The mother drifted into alcoholism and patterns of behaviour which were deeply confusing to a small child. Sometimes she was sensible, kind and nurturing; but under the influence of alcohol she could also be wild and histrionic. In the absence of a real male figure, Jane built out of her experience of the other, drunken mother, an image of men as bogies. When she became an adult, she felt she had to defend herself against all males, whom she conceived as dangerous, intrusive and potentially exploitative.

I interviewed Jane in her apartment. Now in her forties and apparently living alone, she was smartly dressed. Her sitting-room has an old-fashioned atmosphere, with patterned furniture, a music centre by the sofa and conventional oil paintings on the wall. As she talks about being driven into therapy by 'feeling like a child, not feeling grown-up', I have the strange and slightly disturbing sense of being in the presence of that child, perhaps from the way she uses her hands, her restlessness on the sofa, or the slight whine in her voice and the way words get distorted between her tight lips.

The impression Jane makes on me suggests how deep in early infancy lay the roots of her problems, helping to explain why she needed such a long stretch of analysis to comprehend what had happened to her. For others, it is the conjunction between early experience and later events that lays the seeds of their subsequent entry into the profession. As Max opens the door to me, it is clear that something other than my arrival preoccupies him. He hurries me into his tiny waiting room, which has just enough space for a two-seater sofa and a small table supporting some magazines. From there I am later led to his consulting room, where he sits in an impressively large rocking chair. The desk in one corner of the room is disorganized, as is his conversation. Max is interested in what I want to know about, but tends to dart off in pursuit of his own preoccupations. Since his talk is interesting, I am mostly happy to let him ramble.

He says that his own desire to become an analyst began to form during a profound depression that set in after hearing that atomic bombs had been dropped on Hiroshima and Nagasaki. At the time he was stationed in the Pacific, having been just old enough towards the end of World War II to join the navy. 'I became appalled that I had been looking forward to spending my life in the hope of fighting another war which, if it came, would obliterate the world. This seemed to me a ridiculous thing to do. I decided that I wanted to understand why people could do such awful things to each other. It was a slightly grandiose dream, which still sort of bites me.' Max went on to study psychology at university.

But the roots of Max's desire to investigate human disturbance lay deeper than the mushroom clouds over Japan, in the situation that drove him to seek a romantic escape on the high seas. 'My mother and father,' he says, 'were bloody unhappy with each other, and when I was young, I was really scared of the rows that they had. My mother was not happy with my father and was always grumbling about him. I would often think, "Why on earth did my mother marry this terrible man?"'

At the time, Max was perplexed by his father, and worried that he might become a similar sort of person. Now, he finds it easy to identify the man's flaws. 'There was something autistic about him. He was slightly stiff and had to have his routines. He was technically good at the piano, for example, but not very musical. He could remember poems off by heart, but he could not appreciate what they were saying. I used to feel ashamed that he was so uninteresting, and that is what made me sail off on this grand adventure; to fight for King and Country. I felt terribly guilty about that afterwards. I felt that I had to do something for my mother and father. I wanted to make them better, and if I could not make them better, I would make the world better. You cannot make anything better without understanding it, so I had better start understanding it.'

Max and Jane both experienced some lack in their childhood that they felt called upon to fill. Forced to provide *for* their parents the sort of caring, nurturing, supporting and loving that many other children receive *from* them, they both had early on-the-job training as therapists. Jane's situation was the more complicated. Her mother was suffering because her father had died and it was all her fault. How could she repair the damage she had caused? The precipitating factor for Max was his feeling that he needed to make up to his mother for the failings of his father, the man she had married.

Others told me of childhood experiences that had similarly allocated them a therapeutic role in their families. Felix, who speaks with the careful deliberation of an academic and long-time exile from eastern Europe, had an experience similar to that of Max. 'Even as a child,' he recalled, 'I looked after my mother. My mother and father did not really match at all, even though they somehow managed to stay together. She had lots of problems, and since my father did not have any time for her, she had to talk to someone. She talked to me.'

Rosamund, whose warm smile and gentle manner put me instantly at my ease, took on responsibility for looking after her depressed mother, learning skills which her more extrovert twin sister has never mastered. 'It is still going on,' she says. 'Our mother is being difficult now. I can stand up to her and my sister cannot. She gets too emotionally involved and cannot handle it. I tell her to hang up on mother and I will deal with the problem.'

Absent mothers, depressed mothers, dead mothers, aggressive fathers: whatever the family situation, it seems to drive the therapist-to-be into taking on parts of a parental role. At the same time, because they have had to invent it for themselves, they lack a model for it. Antonia refers to her mother as a 'non-mother'. She was, she says, 'very bright, very intelligent, very sophisticated, but sort of absent. It made me very curious about mothering.' Alexa, whose cultivated accent does not quite conceal her sense of wonder at now finding herself in such a satisfying and rewarding profession, was working as a journalist when the experience of having her first child forced her to stop and think about what she was doing. 'I had no idea,' she says, 'about how to be a mother. I was groping for ideas about how to cope with the situation. Everything seemed to go to pieces. I did not know who I was, what I wanted to do, where I was. I was in complete chaos really.' It may be because they are offered no satisfactory figures to emulate that so many therapists make such bad parents.[1] Unable to rely on their instincts, on an intuitive sense of what is involved in bringing up children, they have to learn the role from books and from their own, sometimes appalling, mistakes.

Caught up in an emotional vortex that they cannot understand, aware of deficiencies and absences that need to be filled, the therapist-to-be may start to think of human beings as great mysteries to be fathomed and explored. Where some expect only love and support from their parents and other important people in their life, and others learn in the parental home how to manipulate and use other people, the therapist-to-be feels adrift in the middle of enormous questions about why human beings behave in the way they do. It is the sense that people are mysterious that may drive them into therapeutic work.

Sam, an exuberant and friendly Indian, traces his interest in psychology not to family dramas but to a particularly disturbing event from his childhood. As a young boy growing up in Calcutta, he participated in a demonstration against continued British rule of his country. Policemen intervened to break up the gathering, firing indiscriminately into the crowd and killing one of Sam's closest friends. He realized that the bullet which hit the friend standing at his side could just as easily have been for him.

The protesters were rounded up and Sam was among those put into the crowded cells. He was teased by the adults among whom he found himself, who said that a man on the same block, a mass murderer, would come and deal with him. Sam was terrified. 'I was shivering under a blanket,' he recalls, 'when I suddenly felt this hand over my face. I turned round, looked up and saw the murderer. I just screamed. Everybody ran up. He spoke to them all, saying that anybody who touched this little boy would be on his list next.' The next morning Sam started to receive special treatment from both prisoners and warders.

'It was,' he says over 40 years later, 'a totally mind-blowing experience. That there could be so much humanity in such an allegedly cruel person had a great impact on me. It started me thinking whether I too might not have a dark side and a nice side. It brought home to me that human beings are not what they appear to be.' Sam describes himself as being 'essentially a very boring person' because the only thing that interests him to this day is 'human beings'.

Who am I? Why do I have these feelings? How can I relate to these other people around me? These are the sorts of questions that take people into therapy, and then into training as therapists. They want to know more about themselves. 'You have to know,' said one therapist, 'that the first person you are helping is yourself.' And that process of self-exploration goes hand in hand with the struggle to understand other people.

Rafael is an administrator in a profession where most shun bureaucratic responsibilities. But in his clinical work he likes to deal with more disturbed patients whose material will stretch him. 'I am interested,' he says, 'in my own madder bits. I find the disturbed patients much more engaging. They stretch my own internal images and ideas and thoughts and feelings and hopes and dreams and nightmares. They also oblige me to deal with bits of myself that add to my own development. That may sound one-sided, but unless I got something out of it, I do not think I would be very good as a therapist. Equally, unless I was primarily there for them, I do not think people would come back to me.'

Critics of psychotherapy consider it wrong that people should be getting something for themselves out of helping others, as if it was possible to believe in saintly altruism. Behind the desire to enter the profession, they see only sinister motives and evil intentions. Therapists, they assert, hope to find in the look of love offered by their patients a satisfaction which the rest of their emotional life does not offer. They are loners in life looking for companionship in a professional therapeutic relationship. They have a prurient, voyeuristic curiosity in the private lives of others.

All these are possible motivations for becoming a therapist. They are also, perhaps, a part of everyone's reason for choosing the job. The desire to know other people and to be with other people in a relationship of close intimacy is undeniably part of therapy's allure as a profession. But there can be no easy dividing line between those motives that are sinister and those that are pure. The original intention contains a mix of the good and the bad; it is the balance that is important. Consumers of therapy must rely on the wisdom of the various training organizations to weed out those who lack the maturity to help others while they help themselves, and to tame those elements in each and every one of us that might work against the therapeutic task.

During the first part of our interview Sophie's answers to my questions were a little fierce and rebarbative; only later did she begin to relax. She admitted that a desire for closeness and intimacy with others was one of a number of factors which drew her towards becoming a therapist, adding that this urge was 'duly modified' during her own analysis so that it did not become too pressing. Felix too describes 'meeting people, being with people all day long' as one of the joys of therapy, and alludes to the danger of not having a private life at all: 'One could just work from morning to evening and then go to bed.'

Clearly there is a danger that therapists who do not have satisfactory personal relationships will start to make demands on their patients. Michael, whose dapper appearance and geniality made a strong impression on me, emphasizes the need for would-be therapists to have a stable background, providing some guarantee that they will be able to withstand the pressures of the work. 'We look very carefully to see whether the applicant is getting his or her needs satisfied somewhere else so that they will not have to rely on the patient for strokes and other gratifications. If the therapist is isolated, has few friends and a slightly ivory-tower view of life, then I am not sure that we would accept him or her.'

Nevertheless, intimacy, for both patient and practitioner, is one of therapy's rewards. If therapists choose the profession because they want to know people in a way that one is rarely able to outside marriage and an all-too-rare friendship, that is not so unworthy. Many therapists are not capable of the dissembling, the concealment, the presentation of false personas that are the day-to-day reality for those in most other occupations. It is because they want a deeper form of relating that they become therapists. 'You do get involved,' Alexa remarks. 'One is not just coldly listening to the person. You do get to love the people you see.'

It is equally possible to attribute sinister motives to the therapist's desire to know other people through the therapeutic encounter. Should therapists not live their own life in the world, rather than experience things vicariously through others? Perhaps, but where else could they have such a rich and varied experience? Robert is so keen to convey to me the excitements of his profession that he cannot get the words out fast enough. 'It is not so much voyeuristic,' he says of what he regards as one of the chief pleasures of analysis, 'as being in a kind of boundaryless connection with the patients. It is like the experience you hope for when you go to a really great movie or play, and you lose yourself in it.

'You learn so much,' he went on, 'about different things that you would never otherwise have a chance to know about. I have learned about the way people of the lower classes live. I have learned what it is like to grow up as a princess in India with elephants. I have learned what it is like to be an investment banker, an orthopaedist and a molecular biologist doing cancer research. These are worlds that are not open to me in any other way. And you learn about them in such intimate detail that it is a very enlarging kind of experience.'

But the chief gratification almost every therapist reported to me was that of seeing people become better. Susie, herself a vivacious 40-year-old, recalls the joy of hearing a patient in her forties say that, for the first time ever, she felt that she was truly alive, that she wanted to live for another 40 years and do all the things she had never done before. 'You are so privileged,' she remarks, 'to enter someone's life at this level, especially when they feel that they do not have a life.'

And while many therapists worry about the limitations of what can be achieved, given the slowness of the therapeutic process, Rosamund is sometimes made aware of the way a successful treatment can set a ripple effect in motion. 'It is hard, painful work,' she says with a contradicting smile on her face, 'and I would love not to do it, but the reward of thinking that you have helped a generation of children not to suffer in the way that I have suffered and my children have suffered because of the things I did not know is so great. Helping the mother means that the next generation is not going to have such an awful time. I can help a lot of other people's children in a way that I could not help my own children because I was messed up by my own mother.' Psychoanalysis itself makes one cautious about accepting therapists' claims that they are in the profession to 'help others', but it would be wrong to discount the gratifications that flow from seeing other people gain a renewed sense of their potential.

Psychotherapy is a vocation. It is not a profession that parents hold out to their offspring as a desirable option for their future. While the urge to train for the job may be rooted in childhood experiences, very few people choose therapy as their first profession. The desire first to enter therapy and then to become a therapist is one that people rarely formulate for themselves before their late twenties, an age when the need to sort out emotional problems often becomes pressing. And training courses mostly require applicants to have had previous work experience that demonstrates an aptitude for working with people and dealing with emotional problems. It is true that in the US, where psychoanalysis and psychotherapy are relatively high-status occupations, many become psychologists, social workers and psychiatrists as a way of going on to train as analysts or therapists. Generally, however, the life of a therapist seems too abnormal, too solitary, too strange to present itself to many in their late teens as a natural career path. And their own inexperience in living would in any case not suit them to the practice of listening to the sufferings of others and trying to offer them a way out of their personal darkness.

Medicine, social work, psychology and teaching provide the most common springboards into therapy training. But it is psychiatry which has traditionally been seen as the 'natural' route. This is partly because analysis, the talking cure, did grow out of psychiatry (the treatment of mental illness by physical and chemical means) and partly because of the long-running struggle by psychiatrists, particularly in the United States, to keep analysis as their private preserve. This controversy dates back to the beginning of the century in Vienna, when Freud was called upon to defend the right of Theodore Reik, a non-medical practitioner, to work in the profession. To the authorities such an open policy was fraught with dangers.

In the US during the 1950s psychoanalysis was seen as the treatment of choice for many psychiatric patients; most psychiatrists underwent some form of analytic training and the psychoanalytic profession was jealously guarded by those with a psychiatric background. The American Psychoanalytic Association (APA), until recently the only US organization with links to the International Psychoanalytic Association (IPA), was a closed shop of medically-trained practitioners. Only in 1986, as a result of a threatened lawsuit, was the APA compelled to accept into training a broader range of individuals who had 'achieved a professional identity as human caretakers through therapeutic clinical activities of demonstrated excellence'.

In fact, the closed doors of the APA were only a minor irritant to those who had not undergone medical training. There were plenty of other institutes, including the National Psychological Association for Psychoanalysis (NPAP) set up by Reik himself, which offered them a training. As long as they could boast a psychology PhD or a qualification as a medical social worker, graduates would be entitled to practise and receive payments from insurance companies or other third-party sources.

In Britain psychoanalysis has never had the same hold on psychiatry, and even the leading institutes have long been open to people from non-medical backgrounds. There are few posts within the National Health Service for those who have had a psychoanalytic training, and because drugs and physical treatments are generally preferred to the talking cure, there is little incentive for a psychiatrist to train as a therapist. In fact, most are actively discouraged from doing so. They are told that it will burn up their energy and knock out their ambition. Some are even warned of the risk of having a breakdown if they undergo analysis. This is an acknowledgement that personal problems will often have led people to take up psychiatry. Much better, they say, to leave the pathology that is driving them behind a defensive wall than to run the risk of having a trainee who can no longer hide his depression, or function effectively at work.

It is because psychotherapy can seem to trainees so much more appealing as a form of treatment than administering electric shocks or prescribing drugs that many consultant psychiatrists will do their best to ensure that trainees are not over-exposed to that model. 'They feel,' says Nigel, a retired psychiatrist, about his former colleagues, 'that

35

those who want to take that particular road will be indoctrinated by psychotherapy. It will colour their attitude and take them away from considering the possibility of there being any physical cause to the patient's problem. They can undertake therapy in cases which would respond well to certain other treatments. The patient goes on for years in an expensive, time-consuming form of treatment, without any actual benefit.'

There is a paradox here. Young doctors take up psychiatry because they are curious about people, and that curiosity often has roots in their own emotional distress. It is because they want to talk to people about their lives that they choose psychiatry rather than brain surgery or a specialization in ears, noses and throats. Yet, all too often, they are offered a model of the mind that has nothing to say about the meaning of human distress, and a means of dealing with it that distances them from the other person's pain. 'Being a doctor,' I was told, 'is quite a serious disadvantage in becoming a psychotherapist. The medical training rules out too much empathic contact with the patient.'

Some will be seduced by the neatness of the diagnostic system with which psychiatrists parcel up mental illness. Some will be impressed by the powerful effects of psychotropic drugs. Others will enjoy being the doctor in the white coat who basks in the glory of bringing relief to patients on the ward. And still others will channel their emotional needs into fighting the battles that will take them up the ladder of power and influence within the hospitals where they work.

But there are also psychiatrists who become uncomfortable with the distance between what brought them into that specialization and their actual practice. They will start to think about a training in psychotherapy. 'I was beginning,' Vanessa put it to me, 'to find general psychiatry a bit unsatisfactory, like plumbing. It was a patch-up job. The analytic way of thinking about people seemed to be much more complete.' Keith, who now works in the sort of psychiatric hospital where he can abandon the traditional white coat for a colourful sweater, felt that his colleagues in a more traditional institution where he had worked paid too little respect to people's individuality. He also began to wonder whether there was not some means of helping people out of the terrible distress that brought them into hospital and kept them there. 'These people were being treated with drugs that were not only not helping them to get better, but were also adding to their difficulties by making them even odder through debilitating physical symptoms.' He started to train as an analyst, but kept that information very much to himself. 'I felt that it was necessary to keep it quiet,' he says.

A similar sort of split divides those who choose to remain in the mainstream of psychology from those who break out into analytic training. Some are happy to build careers out of experimenting with rats in cages, or constructing elaborate questionnaires which they circulate to a representative sample of the population and then use to formulate certain limited deductions about human behaviour. Others work with therapeutic systems – behavioural, cognitive – which aim to teach patients how to get rid of their symptoms by giving them tasks to perform and directions to follow, believing that there is no deeper psychological reality that needs to be tapped in order to release people from emotional suffering. All psychological ills are seen as, to some extent, the result of poor education.

But there are others who, finding that the psychology they learn does not answer the questions about themselves that drew them, albeit often unconsciously, into the profession, start to look further afield. As Alice has gone further into her own analysis, she has also become increasingly dissatisfied with the knowledge base provided by her psychological training. 'I have done additional bits of psychodynamic training,' she says, 'but I feel I would like a really solid grounding in one particular orientation. It's not that I am not able to do a competent job with what I have, but there is an awful lot more I would like to do. The quality of the work I do would be greatly enhanced if it was more solidly grounded in analytic theory.' And Max was beginning to become disillusioned with academic psychology when he heard a lecture by the British psychoanalyst John Bowlby. 'That settled it for me,' he says. 'He was talking about real people and their development. He was also saying there was something we could do about it.'

Like the psychiatrist or the psychologist, the social worker may be drawn into the work through a desire to help others that is also at some level a desire to help themselves, but then become involved in activities that limit their exposure to people's emotional needs. They can excel at the management of their paperwork, the organization of home helps and other forms of assistance to those within their catchment area, and they may put their energies into fighting inter-departmentally for their budget. But none of these activities will bring them closer to understanding people or themselves. 'Most social workers,' says Samantha, 'think that you can put something right by doing something, or providing something. They become caught up in a spiral of activity. They do not want to face the level of anxiety that you experience with people and families in difficulty. They discharge their anxiety by doing things.'

37

It is through frantic activity that social workers hide from themselves the unconscious reasons why they were drawn into the profession. Many end up, as a result, profoundly dissatisfied with their work, without knowing why. Others discover through direct contact with those on their caseload that such an approach is not only useful for the clients, it is also enormously gratifying to them. 'I gradually realized,' says Antonia, 'that the longer I was able to give each client, the more beneficial it was for them. Often they needed to talk. And then I began to feel that I knew so little about what they were talking about. I felt I needed to understand.' Exposure to the pain of others may stir them up but, instead of looking for routes of escape, the therapist-to-be feels the need to explore more, to know more, to give more. Such people find their way into therapeutic training.

There are many other backgrounds from which therapists come. Charles had been profit manager for an American airline before he decided to become a therapist. Peter had been a policeman, a sailor and much else besides before starting to train. But such people may find it hard to gain entry to the more highly regarded trainings. The guardians at the gates show a preoccupation with academic qualifications which may drive away many who have a natural gift for relating to people. That, at least, is the view expressed by Edwin, the director of an unorthodox training institute in New York, who claims to have trained housewives, hairdressers and taxi-drivers. 'Before talent,' he said, 'psychoanalysis has to lay down its arms. I have had people come in with all kinds of academic credentials; they cannot do it, they crawl on their faces. I have had librarians come in with a most exquisite sensitivity for other people. I have had bartenders come in, who know the angle, who know about people. I train them, other people will not.'

It is certainly true that those who come from the more established professions will often have quite a lot of unlearning to do before they can complete their training as therapists. Many must abandon the defence mechanisms that insulated them from their clients and patients. The psychiatrists will have to appreciate the pain that brought their patients on to the psychiatric ward. The social workers will have to understand the real misery of the lives endured by their clients. And the psychologists will have to learn a model of therapy which allows for a real interaction between therapist and patient.

There is distance as well as closeness in the encounter prescribed by analytic therapy. Therapists must be sufficiently involved with their patients to know what they are feeling, but they must also have enough objectivity to be able to peer to the roots of their suffering. It may be that many analysts do have something to learn from the housewife, the taxi-driver and the bartender, but they also have something useful to contribute from their own background. 'I do not believe,' remarked one analyst who is noted for being rather cool and buttoned-up, 'it is all to do with feelings and nothing else. Nor do I think it is simply an intellectual exercise. It's a combination of both and they cannot be separated. One is not there to be overwhelmed by horrific feelings. One has to be able to reflect on them intellectually and to understand what they are about.'

The therapist must learn how to be intellectual and empathic at the same time. The training process must enable them to compensate for whatever their past work experiences had neglected. Two women who had previously been academics expressed to me their sense that becoming therapists had enabled them to find parts of themselves that had previously been cut off. 'It involved allowing myself to hear what was going on inside me,' said one. 'I had never before allowed myself to respond at a profound level.' For another, the training process forced her to look at problems from another direction than that she was accustomed to. 'What I found myself doing,' she says, 'was seeing what felt right and then looking at it theoretically. My problem previously had been a tendency to do the opposite. The most important thing in therapy is knowing how you feel, rather than imposing a theoretical framework first of all.'

The psychiatrist, the psychologist and the social worker must all look for the quickest, neatest, tidiest, most efficient solution to the problems presented for their attention. Those who defect from these professions to therapy must learn the art of patience. There are no medicines to be handed out and no surgical procedures to be administered with promises of quick results. No administrative arrangement can at a stroke alter the quality of someone's life. For the analytic therapist there cannot be, as the analysts once hoped and countless Hollywood movies suggested, the single brilliant interpretation, a penetrating insight into a past trauma that will resolve all psychological problems. Instead, there is only listening, attending, interpreting and hoping that the process will eventually bring the patient relief from pain and suffering. 'If only we can wait,' said the British psychoanalyst Donald Winnicott, 'the patient arrives at understanding creatively and with immense joy.'

2

In the Bazaar

Dogmatists and eclectics

'Is she a Freudian or a Jungian?' This question has to be fielded by many who have been foolish enough to admit that they are in therapy or analysis.

Those who move in sophisticated circles may have to submit to further barracking along these lines: 'Or is she perhaps a Kleinian, a Kohutian, a Winnicottian, even a Lacanian?'

Behind such questions lies the assumption that anyone who can submit themselves to the attentions of such a schism-afflicted profession is a prize idiot. Therapists, the argument goes, cannot begin to agree among themselves about what happens to little boys and girls, and what is the source of our psychological ills. Most of their energies outside the consulting room are given to perennial squabbles about when to date the Oedipus complex, whether little girls envy their brothers' penises and other such arcane questions. Their patients are unfortunate victims of these conflicts, who will be cajoled into providing the raw material that will support the case being put by the embattled analysts, and brainwashed with the idea that their therapists hope to have accepted as the new gospel throughout the psychoanalytic world.

Luckless patients might try to get themselves off the hook by saying, 'I do not know,' or, 'She says she is a Freudian, but she does not behave like one.'

To which the questioner might very well riposte, 'In that case you are an even bigger fool than I took you for. You really ought to check her out. You cannot let her pull the wool over your eyes.'

And what if the patient comes back the following week and says, 'She is an eclectic. She says that she has read widely in many theories and that she uses whichever seems appropriate at the time.'

Would that silence the questioner, or would he say that 'eclectic' means 'muddle-headed'? 'She has to believe in something. You cannot have a therapist without a core theory.'

A quick-witted patient might suggest at this point that there was some confusion in the questioner's mind. For, while his enquiry about the therapist's doctrinal orientation suggests a fear that he might become a pawn in a theoretical argument, with his symptoms fitted into an ideological box that has nothing to do with his reality, he also wants to believe that the therapist has access to a reliable system of thought which can be applied in a standard manner to bring about a successful outcome.

The diversity of theories causes considerable anxiety to those contemplating entry into therapy. Why can therapists not develop a single system, as medical doctors managed to do in the late 19th century? Why can the therapists not sort themselves out? Why can they not form a clear picture of what causes emotional disturbance, and the techniques that are required to bring relief from distress? Should patients not say, 'Hands off!' until the therapists can develop a coherent, consistent body of knowledge to justify their strange technique?

The demand for a single system is based upon a reluctance to accept the degree to which psychoanalysis is a subjective science. Analytic theorists cannot help but see the world through the distorting spectacles of their own inner vision. They are all, in some sense, writing about themselves, as well as their patients. And while there may well be a single human substrate which they are inspecting from various angles, it is something that can never be distilled. At different periods, in different social contexts, with different analysts, different aspects of the human mind come to the surface. A string of similar cases might seem to prove a universal rule, whereas they are in fact particular to their time and place. The human subject, it turns out, is too complex, too recalcitrant and too idiosyncratic to be easily categorized.

I met someone while I was writing this book who declared, 'It is OK now to say you don't believe in God. But you cannot say you don't believe in Freud.' For therapists to call themselves Freudian is the easiest way out of what one analyst described to me as the 'scandal of schools'. The labelling is simple, it is clear and it indicates that one is a follower of the true faith. But we live in a post-Freudian age. 'It is not often appreciated,' writes the American analyst Stephen Mitchell, 'how different from Freud's initial vision psychoanalysis has become.'[1] Freud's single-system model of the individual whose inner world is created by the play of almost biological drives has been largely pushed out by theories which trace the organization of the psyche back to the influence of real events and the ways in which people relate one to another. While all therapists owe an immense debt to Freud for having first charted the territory of the unconscious, and many speak with wonder of the way in which later ideas were anticipated in his 24 collected volumes, there are very few analysts who would now subscribe wholesale to the Freudian system, with its eccentric baggage of drives, and its concept of oral, anal and phallic stages. When one meets those who do, it is like talking to people who have wandered in from another century.

The establishment of Freudianism as the orthodox line has compelled many original thinkers to argue that they were simply adding to the master's work and developing his approach. Melanie Klein had done work with pre-verbal infants, Heinz Kohut had gathered material from 20th-century narcissists; both argued that the conclusions from their researches required only some modifications to the Freudian picture. And Jacques Lacan in France launched a call for a 'return to Freud', challenging those American analysts whom he felt had diluted the Viennese master's greatest discoveries.

But to these theorists one has to ask, 'Which Freud?' Each writer takes a part of Freud's teaching – a suggestion here, a proposal there – and emphasizes it above all the others. And how far can one go without doing such violence to the original concepts that it would be far simpler to admit that one has fundamentally different beliefs? Would Freud have understood very much of one of Lacan's seminars if he had dropped in during the summer of 1968? Probably not. And is it not more honest to emphasize the differences in outlook between Freud and Klein or Kohut or Lacan than the similarities? While it may be possible for practitioners who follow divergent schools to find common ground at the level of practice, the points of conflict between the theories themselves are irreconcilable.

The contemporary climate is one that encourages many flowers to bloom. Instead of embarrassing dogmatism, there is the embarrassment of diversity – a dazzling, dizzying, proliferating array of theories and schools, each of which attracts adherents and opponents. Any attempt to assert the superiority of a single approach seems doomed to failure. As the American analyst Robert S. Wallerstein has remarked, 'We all seem to do reasonably comparable clinical work and bring about reasonably comparable clinical change in the (comparable enough) patients that we deal with.'[2] And for the outsider, it is sometimes difficult to work out what the differences are all about, to disentangle real conflict from divisions that have to do with history, personalities and faction.

But barely hidden in the squabbles of psychoanalysis and the proliferation of schools are fundamental, irresolvable disputes about human nature. Is the infant eaten up with inner rage, or simply searching for a gratifying environment? Is it our fantasies that make us suffer, or the realities of what people do to us? Are human beings condemned to a state of continual unhappiness, or is a real sense of inner fulfilment attainable? Between these different outlooks there can be no easy resolution.

In Britain and the United States Freudian analysts and Jungian analytical psychologists long ago decided to go their own way, with separate institutes, congresses and journals. Just as the clash between the Viennese Jew and the Swiss Gentile, who had formerly been as close as teacher and star pupil, rapidly became irrevocable so, it seemed, there could be no meeting of minds between their successors.

Others subsequently quarrelled with Freud and set up their own organizations, but as long as he lived, the Freudian movement remained essentially one under the banner of his writings. However, during World War II the British Institute of Psychoanalysis was split by controversy that centred on Melanie Klein and Freud's daughter, Anna. In the absence of Freud himself, it was for the first time possible to ask, 'Who is the true Freudian?' The outcome was a very British compromise that left Freudians, Kleinians and the so-called Independents (followers of Object Relations theorists such as Donald Winnicott, who emphasized the significance of real events in forming mental structure) acknowledging each other's very significant differences, but still trying to stay together in the same (Freudian?) boat. And to this day they still gather at meetings, to talk about their cases, present their ideas and lob insults at each other. The Freudians call the Kleinians 'fanatics', and the Independents are dubbed 'wishy-washy' by the Kleinians.

'We thought it would all blow over in time,' says Max, a prominent Independent who seems irritated and a little perplexed by the continuing contention within the Institute. 'We thought that we would work it out. But it still goes on. The battles are about technique, about people accusing each other of doing bad analysis. There is a nasty tradition of saying that if you are doing something different, then it is not proper analysis. When you are really engaged with a patient, and then a third person comes along and says that you are failing to pick something up, you just go crazy. People say, "Why didn't you do this?" or, "Is it not obvious the patient is really saying that?" To be told you are not doing proper analysis really hurts.'

To Max, the solution is for each side to admit that it is 'floundering' and that its dogmatism reflects a fear of acknowledging the uncertainty inherent in a trade. Each side, he feels, should accept that there are different ways of doing analysis, and try to learn from other schools. For others, too, the endless battles have begun to seem tedious. 'We have created the kind of mentality,' says Nancy, a Kleinian, 'which is much more appropriate to a football club, where if you support Tottenham Hotspur you are against Arsenal. It is boring and personally I have had enough of it. It stifles people who do not feel free to think, free to change.'

Given the passion with which the followers of different theories sometimes defend their chosen line, one might imagine it would be easy enough for would-be analysts to discover the theory they wish to follow: they simply have to hit upon the view of human nature that most accords with their own. But people are not so simple. They are split and pulled in all directions. They have parts of all human experience written into their individual script and, in any case, the theories themselves can be read in different ways. Making a match between theory and personality is, in fact, no easy process. Many look back and conclude that they stumbled on to their particular path by chance. 'My choosing the Freudian frame,' says Irene, 'was sheer accident. I did not know anything about Freud or Jung when a relative referred me to a therapist. What that therapist's orientation was did not worry me at all. It was her ability to reach out to me with understanding that mattered.' One cannot know whether Irene's therapist happened to belong to a congenial orientation, or whether, as she herself supposes, the orientation did not really matter at all.

Paul was a health worker in a mental hospital when he first became interested in psychoanalysis. He speaks hurriedly, quietly, almost conspiratorially, so that I worry whether my tape recorder will catch any of his words. He tells me how the more disturbed, psychotic and schizophrenic patients touched something in him, forcing him to read analytic thinkers as a way of getting to know more about the thought patterns of those he was attempting to help, and about himself. When he decided to go into therapy, as a preparation for training, his strong prejudices against Freud, whom he had learned to consider reductionistic and sexist, persuaded him to undertake a Jungian therapy.

His analyst helped him sort out his emotional life and was very 'nice', but as he began to work with patients, Paul found that this was not such a useful model to work with. 'I was unambitious with my own psyche. I thought that if you just provided a framework, sat there and facilitated what went on, the terrible things that the patient brought with him would be put right by some sort of healing process. From my experiences, however, I began to understand that it is as important an emotion to understand hate as love, if a really loving relationship is to be made possible.'

A particularly disturbing patient brought Paul's anxieties to the surface. She became extremely dependent on him, and then turned on him for failing to give her the love which she thought he had promised. Paul became convinced, as a result, that he needed not only more training, but a different training. 'I began to realize that I needed to be a negative figure as well as a positive figure.' He decided to opt for a Kleinian training, one that promised to be very different from the Jungian approach and to provide him with the rigour he felt he needed.

There are aspects of Kleinian technique that Paul still finds difficult to accept, particularly the way it encourages the analyst to interpret everything that the patient feels or does as a source of information about earliest infancy (an issue covered in Chapter 6). In his views on the relative importance of interpretation and the provision of a warm, supportive environment for the patient (topics discussed in Chapter 4), Paul admits that he is much closer to the position taken by the British analyst Donald Winnicott, who saw the analytic relationship very much as a two-way process between therapist and patient. And he still feels comfortable with some of Jung's ideas. Nevertheless, he admits that his Kleinian analysis taught him much about himself that was important and valuable. 'Things have been interpreted for me,' he says, 'in a way that tackled areas which the other approaches couldn't reach.'

Paul's experience illustrates just how difficult it is to disentangle the various theories from each other in terms of what they indicate about practice. Everybody, after all, modulates the theory through his or her own character. For Paul, it seems, Jungian theory played up to his own weaknesses and left him feeling somehow incomplete. Others might find that the same approach enlarged areas of their personality that had previously lain quiescent. It may also be that Paul's Jungian analyst was deficient, rather than anything in the theory itself.

What, one wonders, would observers conclude about his theoretical orientation from watching Paul at work? Would they detect an essentially Jungian outlook, but feel perplexed by his preoccupation with infantile fantasy? Would they see a Kleinian who was much more affable than the stereotype of a Kleinian analyst normally allows for? Or would they feel that he was muddled, confused, all over the place?

For Paul, the decision to opt for a second training as a Kleinian was associated with his need to do penance for a patient whom he had been unable to help, and upon whom he had inflicted unnecessary suffering. Several other people I spoke to associated Kleinian therapy with chastisement, and acknowledged that this was part of its attraction. Patients, they said, who had been through the pain and punishment Kleinian analysis is thought to involve reach the other side with a much deeper understanding of their inner world than those who have undergone a less thorough analytic process. 'Lots of people,' says Alexa, 'do imagine that they will be put through a tougher time, and that the Kleinians really do know how to make the patient suffer. Some Kleinian analysts do have a way of interpreting which keeps the patient in a rather enclosed world of punishment, aggression and hatred. So people who want to suffer are happy with some Kleinian analysts.' Alexa clearly has doubts about whether Kleinian analysis ever resembles the fantasies people have of it.

Discipline is a word that is often used to describe Kleinian technique. Max, whose relaxed informality suggests the distance between himself and the Kleinian position, declares that they are 'very unsloppy, very conscientious. And they are on to something, but they do get to a point which, to someone like me, seems to lack humanity.' Supporting this is the impression given by many consulting rooms, which appear zealously tidy. In fact, some Kleinians choose to work in a completely antiseptic environment, free of pictures, books, carpets and any other clues to their personal tastes and foibles. Mary, who is not so extreme, nevertheless confirmed my suspicion that the sense of order is an important part of the Kleinian mentality when she revealed that she enjoys cleaning the house as relief from therapy sessions.

Klein's focus on the very early months of life provides a corollary to domestic neatness. If everything can be accounted for in terms of infantile fantasy, the tide of envy and love felt towards the mother's breast, then the analytic task is circumscribed and tidy. By tracing the patient's later feelings to the patient's early experiences, they have explained enough. It is this indifference to later experience that accounts for the charge that Kleinians lack interest in other work being done in psychoanalysis.

'What attracted me to Klein,' says Mary, 'was that she went back to the earliest stages of our creation. It meant going deeper, earlier and getting a much deeper understanding. It was an interest in what makes us the kind of people we are. There is something in me that is very interested in foundations. If I do a garden, I like the preparation. I spend a lot of time preparing the ground, sowing the seeds and getting them off to a good start. I have a pretty good idea of what is going to happen after that.'

To some patients this interpretation of present pain in terms of infantile fantasies around the mother's breast carries profound insight. The British Kleinian Nini Herman has written of how her Freudian analyst 'had simply no idea that he had been entrusted with the pieces of a splintered child', whom she goes on to describe as 'a very frightened urchin, who bit and hissed and screeched and spat at anyone who came too close'.[3] And Owen, a psychologist who did not realize his ambition to become an analyst, similarly found that his Freudian analyst, preoccupied as she was with his desire to kill his father and sleep with his mother, left whole areas of his inner experience untouched. 'She had no feeling,' he says of his analyst, 'for early infantile functioning. I was aware of having a lack of identity, a lack of a sense of self, not knowing who I was, what I wanted, why I wanted it. I would be lying there, floating, feeling an incredibly primitive sense of inadequacy. She could not make any sense of that.' Like Nini Herman, Owen turned to a Kleinian to have his more primitive fantasies explored and explained.

But the neatness and the discipline can also arouse rebellion. Klein encouraged analysts to make deep interpretations from the start of the analysis, 'to open the door to the unconscious' and 'to prepare the way for analytic work'.[4] As a result, Kleinian analysts can be experienced as very invasive. 'I was getting floods of interpretations,' says Owen, 'a tremendous amount of intervention. You could not stay silent for 30 seconds without the analyst saying, "What is going on here?" '

Such invasiveness can be all the more distressing because the patient finds it difficult, confronted by interpretations that relate to their earliest fantasies, to make any sort of comeback. Those early experiences, preceding speech and full self-consciousness, are necessarily lost to memory. One non-analytic therapist I spoke to often asked his Kleinian analyst whether he could provide some help to relieve the depressions from which he suffered. The analyst replied to this with a question about why he wanted to be 'fed'. 'I think it is a waste of time,' says Nora, 'saying to an upset and angry patient, "You are angry with me because I have got the breast, and you are envious towards me for having the good thing." '

Andrea has a highly intellectualized approach to her work, and one can easily imagine her protesting against anything that happened in her analysis which she did not understand. She contrasts her Kleinian experience with a subsequent analysis from a follower of the abstruse French theorist Jacques Lacan. 'With the Lacanian,' she says, 'I had the means to defend myself. I could articulate why an interpretation upset me, or seemed to miss the target. With the Kleinian, how could I respond to the statement that all my problems were due to my mother's breast? I could not say, "No, it is not true." How could I say that? I could only be passive or defiant. There was no position in between. I felt suffocated by that.'

Kleinian technique encourages analysts to see themselves as the expert guide to the unconscious. It is they who will unlock the secrets of the inner world to which patients have no access. Such an approach infuriates independent-minded therapists like Henrietta. 'The Kleinian analyst,' she says, 'tells you what happened to you as a child. I think that is outrageous, actually. I think it is absurd to say you know what the other person is thinking and feeling. It is infuriating, to say the least, and therefore impedes the development of the patient's capacity for productive thinking. And it reinforces the idea that the analyst is the one who knows, which is precisely what has to be given up as an ideal. There's a sense in which the analyst does not know a thing.'

Kleinian analysis is not always practised in the way depicted by these critics, but insofar as it is, one can see its attraction to some analysts. It is much more comfortable to feel that one knows, that one has knowledge to which no one else is privy, and that everyone else is misguided. To those of a perfectionist disposition, Kleinian ideas are intensely beguiling. 'I think personally,' Birgit remarked, 'that there is a certain fundamentalist attitude in Kleinian thought, as in Catholicism or Islam. I wonder whether people who have a need for this absolute certainty tend to be drawn into the Kleinian frame.'

Speaking very generally, one can say that Freudians and followers of Object Relations theorists differ from Kleinians in the extent to which they see the analyst as controlling the therapeutic process. Since they see their function as being that of enabling patients to discover things for themselves, they tend to limit the amount of interpretative activity they consider appropriate, especially during the early stages of an analysis. 'It is no good bypassing the conscious ego and talking about primitive fantasy,' says Nora, 'when the patient has not got a clue what you are talking about. It is too big a jump. The more classical stance is that you have to work down slowly through the layers until what you are saying makes some kind of sense to the patient.' Also, they conceive of the therapist's position *vis-à-vis* the patient as much closer to a position of equality.

Frederick was analyzed by Anna Freud and regards himself as a defender of the classical tradition. One of his colleagues describes him to me as a 'devout, old-fashioned Freudian'. His consulting room has a timeless feel, with the red leather chairs and mahogany book cabinets evoking the aura of the Faculty Club at Harvard, where Frederick taught many years ago. The bust of Abraham Lincoln behind his chair suggests that he is proud to be an American in a country where psychoanalysis has been hijacked by Kleinian ideas, against which his colleagues still in the United States have largely protected themselves. He is relentless in his gentle mockery of Kleinian attitudes.

'It is interesting,' he says of Kleinian theory, 'and I can understand why some intelligent people might find it interesting, but I am sort of immune.' Accounts of Kleinian analyses leave him unimpressed. 'The patient will say some everyday things which are not very interesting on the surface. The analyst sees what is behind them and makes something fascinating out of it. Every sentence is interpreted. And no matter what the patient says in response to such a brilliant interpretation, it confirms its accuracy. We call it "fireworks" analysis. It appeals to the intellectual part of everybody.'

Frederick suspects that although such an approach is immensely reassuring to the analyst, it does very little for the patient. His own method involves standing back from the patients' material and encouraging them to grapple for their own interpretations among their memories and fantasies. What is being explored is not the almost unfathomable drama of earliest infancy, but repetitive patterns that work their way through life. These may indeed come out of infancy, but Frederick's approach is not centred on an attempt to describe infantile fantasies. 'Analysis,' he says, 'is the experience of going over and over some very important, rather traumatic periods of childhood and various life experiences. Exploring their ramifications and looking at them from many different angles.' Whereas Kleinian patients, he feels, tend to talk about their analysis in terms of conveyed insight, Freudian patients should feel, he argues, that they have analyzed themselves.

Freudians and Kleinians both emphasize the primacy of interpretation as the curative factor in psychoanalysis. They conceive of inner fantasy as being the motor to psychological disturbance, and analysis as aiming to bring what is unconscious to consciousness. Object Relations theorists and followers of the American analyst Heinz Kohut focus rather more on the real experiences of the child in

growing up, surrounded by mother and significant others, and suggest
that an important part of therapy lies in the way that the therapist is
experienced by the patient. By being with someone who can endure
their anger and support their rage, patients learn that their wants can
be satisfied without repressing their deepest needs and formulating
a 'false self'. To enable this to happen, the analyst has to provide
the love that mother, father or others failed to offer. Understanding
what happened is only part of the psychoanalytic cure; experiencing
something else is also important. (This topic is explored in Chapters
4 and 5.)

To all these therapists working in the Freudian tradition, whether
Kleinians, Freudians, Kohutians, Winicottians or whatever, the unconscious is seen as a more or less dark place where the mechanisms
can go wrong in an infinite variety of ways. To this the Jungian adds the
idea that the unconscious is also a resource of great richness, producing
fantasies which, when made conscious, can help individuals to heal
themselves. Whereas Kleinian analysts work to formulate insight about
the unconscious, and classical Freudians try to remove the obstacles
to self-discovery, Jungians try to facilitate what they see as a natural
self-regulating function.

Jungian ideas appeal to those who feel that their inner world needs
awakening and bringing out, who are less concerned to calm a storm
than to stir a breeze. For Shelagh, who still carries with her some of
the common-sense manner of the psychology researcher she once was,
it was this view of the unconscious as something other than a 'cesspit
of repressed nasties' that drew her into Jungian analysis. Her problem
lay not in her relations with people, but in a hunger for a different level
of being. 'I was someone,' she says, 'who needed to discover my inner
world, and my own experience of analysis was of discovering a much
deeper sense of my own three-dimensionality.'

But like most generalizations about the various psychoanalytic
orientations, that which suggests Jungians are so concerned with
nurturing their patients' unconsciouses as to neglect the need to untie
emotional knots is misleading. Alice, another psychologist, responded
to the stereotype by feeling some initial reservations about seeing a
Jungian analyst, even after a less than satisfactory experience with
a Freudian. She feared it would be a 'cop-out' in which she, as a
patient, would be instructed in various semi-mystical concepts, so that
the darkness and fury raging inside her would be left untouched. 'What
I encountered, in fact,' she says, 'was somebody who was immensely
rigorous and thoughtful. He looked at presenting problems as being a

signal that some kind of different pattern of growth was needed, and he saw the self as having a self-healing function.' It was an outlook, she felt, which 'encompassed the spiritual without ever becoming a way of not looking at what is really going on'.

Those analysts who are attracted to Jung's ideas range from those, like Paul, who are looking for a serious alternative to what they see as Freudian reductionism, to oddballs who are fascinated by astrology and flying saucers. Because of the association between Jung and followers of the New Age, many in the Freudian camp view Jungian ideas as 'mystic' or 'wacky', and this prejudice acts as a restriction on dialogue between the two groups. Jungians tend not to suffer from the absolutism that afflicts many Freudians and Kleinians, and this can make it difficult for them to see the problems others have with their ideas. When John, a Jungian and an enthusiastic advocate of dialogue between the schools, was about to present one of his cases to a group of therapists from different orientations, he took the precaution of canvassing the views of a colleague on his paper. She advised him to leave out a planned reference to the patient's 'hyperactive, near-psychic sensitivity to the atmosphere' between patient and therapist. That, she told him, 'would be like a red rag to a bull. The Freudians cannot stand anything paranormal or psychic. Their minds close up.'

The attempt to fill their patients' emptiness does encourage some Jungians to see themselves as guides and teachers, albeit in a very different way from the Kleinians. After the immediate crises that brought a patient into therapy have been resolved, the therapist will start to talk about Jungian concepts – the shadow, the animus, the anima and suchlike – and to educate the patient in the Jungian way. 'Jung himself said that analysis is an education,' comments Abraham. 'There are times when an education comes out of it.' In their own way Jungians can become as directive as Kleinians. For some patients such an approach can seem to miss their deeper levels and avoid their problems. Nini Herman has written about how her own Jungian analyst, like the Freudian, evaded the real experiences of the agonized infant struggling within her. In the Jungian case it was through searching for 'higher truths and transcendental nourishment' rather than going after 'deeper understanding'.[5]

But thinking as rich as Jung's can be read in many different ways. For Rosamund, who works almost exclusively with very disturbed patients, it is precisely the deeper areas of the mind to which Jungian thought gives access. 'Jung,' she remarks, 'was madder than Freud, and maybe all the Jungians are madder than the Freudians. He himself went through a psychotic period, and he dealt with psychotic patients. He worked at a deeper level.' Such an image of Jungian thought has nothing to do with its depiction as a way of providing strait-laced members of the middle classes with an answer to the problem of meaning in their empty lives.

It was 5 November, Guy Fawkes Night, when I visited Rosamund's consulting room. As I walked through West London to the smart street in which she lives, I saw bonfires being built and parties being prepared. I knocked on the door, was warmly received and then led into her room below floor level. As I sank into the comfortable leather chair and looked at the objects around me, I had the sensation of sinking into a deep chasm. I felt as if I had strayed into the presence of a long-lost aunt with whom I was immediately able to establish an intimate relationship. For a moment I wondered whether I might ask to lie on the couch and start pouring out my thoughts. Somehow I managed to recall myself to the interviewing task and start asking questions.

I had the sensation that this Jungian would take me to a place deeper than I had ever been before. But if Jungians dig deep, they do not always dig in the same place as the Kleinians. Looking back, Nini Herman felt that her Jungian analyst had been excavating an area a long way from where her pain and suffering lay. To Rosamund, however, it seems that followers of both theories are talking about the same thing, only in a different language. 'The Kleinians and the Freudians that I know,' she says, 'are not that different from what I am. It is just that we use different words.'

Some Jungians have made an effort to relate Jungian thought to Kleinian terminology, thus linking the two approaches. They argue that the Kleinian notion of unconscious fantasy fits well with the Jungian concept of 'archetypes', inherent images that do not depend on actual experience for their formation. 'We are all on about the human mind,' says Esther, 'and we cannot really be so far off from one another. We are not talking about Earthlings and Martians here.'

But while this attempt to link Kleinian and Jungian ideas might seem common sense from one perspective, from another it is an intellectual outrage. 'The actual similarity is skin deep,' one British therapist has written, 'since the source of the phenomena, how they are spotted in the clinical setting and how they might be dealt with therapeutically are radically different.'[6] There is, in the end, no escaping the fact that fundamentally different perspectives on humanity and therapeutic method are embodied in the Kleinian and Jungian belief systems. It may be simplistic to characterize Kleinians as emphasizing the dark, cruel and vicious aspects of human make-up, while Jungians focus on the positive and uplifting, but there is nevertheless an element of truth in the caricatures.

Yet, while it may be true that there can, on a theoretical level, be no happy assimilation between such disparate approaches to the human mind, it is possible for individual therapists to make use of seemingly contradictory theories in practice. Each finds an echo in a different part of themselves, and each has a use in dealing with patients who bring up different sorts of material. It was Paul's experience that, while Jungian ideas matched his kindly nature, he needed Kleinian theory to equip him as a therapist who could be useful to all his patients. Given how divided we all are, this sort of eclecticism might seem to be the natural position. Dogmatism, after all, runs the risk of bringing out only one part of the analyst's character and rendering him or her inflexible. 'The aggressive person may become a belligerent analyst,' writes the British analyst Patrick Casement, 'the insecure either dogmatic or passive, the indecisive exaggeratedly open-minded, the narcissistic too often insistent that they must be right and so on.'[7]

There was a time when William, who trained as a Kleinian, believed that if only he could make the absolutely correct interpretation in every case, he would be able to cure all his patients. Those who knew him 25 years ago describe an obsessed ideologue seeking to propound the true faith. But age and experience have dulled his conviction, and increasingly he finds it difficult to square his clinical experience with the theoretical ideas that most attract him. The man I met was a quiet, slightly perplexed pipe-smoker. 'I was,' he said of his past self, 'always hoping to make sense of what I thought I was doing intuitively by referring to all the theory I had been learning about. But I still find myself in the position of being able to make sense of what I do in only a very piecemeal fashion. There are important ideas I have taken from many sources, but that has not necessarily led me to adopt the rather elaborate theoretical constructs in which those ideas were embedded and which sought to offer an account of the whole of human development.'

Although the absence of open discussion between Freudians and Jungians, the stand-off between Kleinians and Freudians in the British Institute, and the various schisms that have resulted in members of various London and New York training institutions going off with their disciples to set up on their own can be used to illustrate a state of implacable hostility between the various psychoanalytic schools, there is a considerable interflow of ideas between them. I spoke to many so-called Jungians and Freudians who acknowledged a deep debt to the work of Object Relations theorists on the mother-child relationship. And I spoke to a member of the American Psychoanalytic Association, an institution deeply hostile to Kleinian ideas, who acknowledged that Kleinians have taught him and other American analysts a lot about envy. When therapists talk about themselves as Kleinian, Freudian or anything else for that matter, it is often just a question of emphasis.

And there are some therapists who become so removed from any single orientation that they dub themselves eclectic. Edwina, whose display of pots and figurines in her consulting room initially give me the false impression that she is a Jungian, applies her philosophical training to the argument against dogmatism. 'Being an eclectic for me,' she says, 'means having a rational, empirical view of so-called truth.' She had initially been drawn to the Kleinian model, but then realized that what attracted her to that set of ideas were the same things that had alienated her from a fundamentalist Protestant background. 'I had been there before, I thought. I have spent years of my life getting out of this. Am I really going to embrace it in other forms?'

Edwina, like William, feels free to pick and choose from a variety of theories, without swallowing any of them wholesale. She approaches analytic theory as a supermarket from which she can pick and choose whichever items seem most persuasive. 'I find Freud amazingly fascinating,' she says, 'but I do not accept the theory of infantile sexuality. Klein's account of paranoid-schizoid behaviour is clinically useful, but I do not accept her paranoid, schizoid and depressive positions as an account of infantile development. And I think the death instinct is nonsense. I find the Object Relations theorists the most useful, but Kohut's theory of the self has lots to offer that is missing from them. I play around with a multiplicity of strands. I want to preserve my own capacity to think without having anything imposed upon me. I do not think anyone has the final word. And I may change my mind tomorrow.'

But where does this leave someone about to enter therapy? All this talk of arcane theories and the arguments for them is unlikely to ease the anxieties of those who contemplate putting themselves into the hands of therapists. They want to know where their therapist stands and what he or she believes. They want to know whether they are going to be in safe hands. Are they going to be better looked after by a Jungian, a Kleinian or a so-called eclectic? Who is best equipped to help them resolve their problems? How can they make sense of such a disparate, diverse and fragmented field, characterized by what one therapist has described as 'a shifting and amorphous mosaic of apparently differentiated, incompatible and mutually hostile bits, exhibiting neither coherence nor direction, full of unease'?[8]

A possible answer to these anxieties is to say that when it comes to work in the consulting room, the theorist's orientation is not the most crucial thing. Whatever the stereotypes suggest, being a Jungian or a Freudian or an eclectic does not automatically prescribe the way therapists respond to individual patients, nor say anything about their ability to treat particular conditions. Patients should be much more interested in the therapists' temperament and personality than in their theoretical orientation. Can the therapist understand what I am saying? Do the interpretations offered ring true? Do I feel comfortable with him or her? These are the more important questions to ask. (The problem of determining the suitability of any particular therapist is explored more fully in Chapter 8.)

Mastering theory is an important part of any therapist's training, but its significance in the consulting room has often been misunderstood. On the one hand, the therapist needs some theory with which to structure the material offered by patients. Without theory there would be no way to respond to the memories and fantasies and stray thoughts that are presented. How would one organize and assess, interpret and question? 'The analytic process,' writes Stephen Mitchell, 'entails a collaborative, slowly emerging and painfully won three-dimensional understanding of the patient's experience. "There's this, which underlies that, which leads to that, which infuses that with meaning."'[9] The therapist without a core theory would not know how to start exploring the material offered up by the patient.

But theory should generate questions; it should not be expected to yield answers. Where theory becomes obstructive, where patients hear the analyst talking too much about breasts or Oedipal wishes, or the shadow or self-objects, they should ask whether what is being talked about has anything to do with them at all. The analyst must draw on theory but use it and present it in such a way that it makes sense to patients' knowledge of themselves. Here it may be that the depth of the unconscious and the impossibility of ever fathoming its depths is the therapist's greatest ally. Thus, whatever framework therapists bring to the consulting room, as long as they have a listening faculty sharp enough to pick up something of their patient's inner history, they will be able to present an interpretation that is 'good enough' to register with some part of that patient's experience. In an important sense interpretation is metaphor. 'The patients learn to understand and accept these metaphors, and if they provide a good fit,' writes Robert Wallerstein, 'then they will be effective.'[10]

For the therapist struggling to understand the patient, it is important, in a certain sense, to forget theory altogether. 'Theory,' says Frederick, after years in practice, 'is hardly a conscious factor in anything I say or how I talk to my patients, although I certainly know classical theory very well.' Nora, another veteran, describes theory as a 'prop' to the most important thing, which is 'the relationship with the patient'. Slightly ingenuously for someone who lectures on the development of the structural theory and the subsequent expansion into Object Relations, she says that she has never been interested in theory. 'I suppose I know quite a lot but it has sort of sunk down into the depths somewhere. I use it without knowing half the time now what it is.'

Such an atheoretical way of thinking can only be a distant ideal for trainee analysts. As they struggle to understand their patients' material, it is impossible not to look at the patient through theoretical spectacles. One described feeling 'as if there was no patient there; it was just you and your theoretical concerns'. And whenever therapists are made anxious by a case, unable to grasp or understand the patient's experiences, they will have recourse to the library that almost all of them keep in their consulting rooms. 'It is quite comforting,' says Laura, 'to find that other people have come up against the same problem.'

But most acknowledge that this attempt to find the patient in the theory is riddled with dangers. 'Some patients,' says Samantha, 'make one feel terribly at a loss. It is very hard to bear that feeling. You rush to the theory in your mind and try to get the patient to fit into that. I am sure I do that a lot, and that is not good therapy. We need to be in touch with the patient. If there is something compelling about the real person, the theory can never be as good.' And Gavin describes the 'rigid, lifeless' quality of those interpretations delivered with one eye on his textbooks. 'It is only if one is having one's own original thoughts that what one says feels alive.'

That is all very well, the cynics might argue. It sounds fine, but what about these training institutions and the relationship that develops between trainees and their analysts? It is just a brainwashing operation, after all. Things are organized so that the minds of these disturbed people can be tenderized, and have theories dunned into them. There is no way therapists can emerge from that process with their listening antennae unskewed, open to the real experience of their patients. It is the training process that turns decent people into monsters, isn't it?

3

Mind Control

Therapists in training

OO
OO

THE aim of a psychotherapy training is to enable students to understand and master their own psychological problems, to gain a broader
grasp of the sorts of emotional knots that others tie around themselves and to bolster their powers of empathy and intuition so that
they can help their patients. Such a training usually comprises three
parts: trainees must go into therapy with a practitioner who has
been approved by their training organization; they must undertake
a certain number of training cases under supervision; they must also
attend theoretical seminars and write a number of papers. Of these
three elements, it is the training analysis that most judge to be the
vital part of the process, and upon which critics of psychotherapy
have directed their sharpest attacks.

'It is scarcely to be expected,' wrote one commentator, 'that a
student who has spent some years under the artificial and sometimes
hothouse conditions of a training analysis, and whose professional
career depends on overcoming "resistance" to the satisfaction of his
training analyst, can be in a favourable position to defend his scientific integrity against his analyst's theory and practice.'[1] And it has
been suggested that 'a psychoanalysis from an analyst of a kindred
orientation' constitutes part of a 'recipe for disaster'.[2] The training
analysis has been depicted as the arena in which psychoanalysts are
transformed from open-minded people into pedants who lack any
capacity seriously to examine their basic beliefs.

For several years, several times a week, aspiring therapists must
expose their innermost secrets to someone who comes to know much
more about them than anyone else. That knowledge of their charges'
sensitivities and susceptibilities is thought to give analysts a special
sort of power. Through homing in on their weak spots analysts can
put trainees into a raw, vulnerable condition, so that they can drip
into their psyches all their prejudices, hang-ups and most eccentric

theories. In such an encounter, it is thought, there can be no room for scepticism, doubt, or freedom of thought.

There is an unbridgeable gap between the critics' view of the training analysis as a sinister form of indoctrination, and the practitioners' view that it is the means not only to resolve the trainee's personal problems, but also to give him or her the ability to offer deep understanding to a wide range of patients. This happens through the enlargement of what Patrick Casement has called their 'empathic resonance', the ability to empathize with every level of patients' experience. He has written of the possibility 'that each person carries the potential to feel all feelings and to resonate to all experiences, however strange or alien these may be to their conscious selves', and argued that the aim of a training analysis is to expand the capacity to respond to others by removing areas of 'repression' and 'disavowal'.[3]

The enlargement of one's capacity to tune into what others are feeling is something that normal methods of teaching cannot achieve, and the need to achieve such a state is part of the justification for the sort of discipleship that a training analysis inevitably becomes. Such a process does have its dangers, but these are the dangers of analysis generally and it is the ultimate aim of analytic training to overcome them. Analytic training is not, in reality, as sinister an undertaking as those who argue purely from theory often conclude.

The training analysis is sometimes written about as if it were no different from the indoctrinating procedures practised by the Moonies and other contemporary sects. But while there is a risk that some analysts will exploit the therapeutic relationship in that sort of way, taking the dependency needs that it puts into play as an opportunity to inculcate sinister doctrines into the patient, trainee or otherwise, no one has ever said this is desirable, or demonstrated that it is really common practice. Good analysts are never interested in cloning patients; they help them to find out about themselves and who they want to become. According to Alex, who really did think that I should be in analysis, not interviewing analysts, 'You should go to the person who can catalyze you to reach your full capacity as yourself. I do not think that the patient who talks like his analyst and looks like his analyst and behaves like his analyst is an analytic success.'

It is a likelihood in all therapeutic relationships that patients will come for a while to idealize their therapists, and therefore seek to follow their example. Mostly this is a healthy part of the process of reliving one's earliest experiences in order to understand them, and then go beyond them. But there is a danger that trainees, once caught up in this process, will tend to swallow ideas from their therapists without giving them serious consideration. And there are reasons for thinking that they are more likely to develop an idealization for their analyst than their lay counterparts. This is certainly worrying.

Although trainees are likely to be less 'sick' than many patients, entry into training tends to render them 'infantilized'. Having risen up the hierarchy in their chosen career to establish themselves as psychiatrists, psychologists, teachers or social workers, they are now flung back to the bottom of the career ladder. There they find that they are surrounded by reminders of their junior status. At the Institute of Psychoanalysis in London, for example, there are separate toilets for students and members. It can be a galling, painful and difficult experience in which the trainee's self-esteem sinks to an all-time low. 'It is easy,' says Shelagh, who gives me the impression that she is more career-orientated than many of her colleagues, 'to get persecuted and feel a bit paranoid.' Those pitched into such a condition cannot hope to communicate with their analysts as equals, even though their early grasp of analytic theory might be thought to give them an edge over the lay patient.

During analysis the patient should feel free to behave spontaneously and to talk about anything that comes up, but there are reasons why the trainee might feel inhibited. Whereas lay patients can happily unspool their most absurd memories and most outrageous fantasies in the confidence that nothing will penetrate beyond the consulting-room walls, the trainee can have no such confidence. There are many institutions where the analyst has an important role in deciding when trainees can take on their first patient. Trainees, anxious to graduate as soon as possible, must be keen for that moment to come soon. To that end, they may try to present themselves as more mature and more stable than they truly feel inside. Being in training may inhibit their capacity to expose their most primitive feelings in analysis.

In theory, those institutes where the analysts have less authority to determine the course of their patient's training should provide a more liberating environment. Of her experience at one such, Shelagh says, 'I did not feel that I had to be a good girl in my analysis. I did not feel inhibited with her.' But fantasy can still create a link where there is none in reality. 'I have often regretted,' says Rachael, by her own admission a somewhat cerebral and controlled person before her analysis, 'not having had a great deal of analysis before I went into training. There is always the fantasy that your analyst is watching you and thinking what kind of therapist or analyst you are going to make.

I was trying to be good and I was trying to be theoretically correct. It can inhibit you. You cannot be as messy and childlike as you would like to be. That will be analyzed, but it still changes things.'

There is no outside sanction to stop lay patients from deprecating and scorning their therapists if that is where their emotions drive them. For trainees, however, that freedom is curtailed. They are very likely to start looking up to the analyst as someone who has attained the status that they seek and has realized the image of what they too want to become. In such circumstances it is difficult not to hang on his or her every word, attending sessions in the hope of absorbing true wisdom and viewing the analyst as a wonderful person. As they struggle with their own patients, many trainees must wish they could bring just a smidgen of that wisdom to bear. 'You really idealize your therapist,' says Rachael, 'and you think that what they are doing is wonderful, so you want to be like them. When you start out, you fiercely subscribe to whatever your analyst or therapist believes in in a really defensive way.'

Clearly, the training analysis presents many potential pitfalls. The problems created by the trainees' desire to make of their analyst a fount of wisdom will become serious if the analyst actually wants to be seen in that way. The position of training analyst, usually one handed out to an institute's members after several years of practice, brings with it many satisfactions. The appointment provides a flow of patients looking for a full-blown analysis, when most of the rest of one's caseload may be asking for only once-a-week psychotherapy. More importantly, it indicates that he or she has been acknowledged as a leader in the profession, judged fit to hand on wisdom to future generations. This could lead people to feel that they had the right, even the duty, to ram pet theories down the trainee therapists' throats.

Much rests on the trainees' ability to make the right choice of analyst. There is a danger here that they will opt for the senior figure with a solid reputation over someone with whom they can establish a real rapport. There are good reasons for doing so, since the identity of one's analyst marks one's whole career. Rebecca holds senior posts on the committees of her institute, but she often finds herself under attack on the grounds that her own analyst had been expelled from the organization for unethical behaviour. To make matters worse, one of her supervisors had gone mad. It reveals something about the difficulties analysts have in judging each other's work behind the closed doors of their consulting rooms that such significance can be attached, many decades later, to the identity of one's analyst. That increases the probability that they will sacrifice intellectual freedom for an attitude of veneration.

If they choose to be analyzed by well-known analysts and leading figures in the analytic 'movement', students may put themselves in a position where it is hard to throw off their analyst's shadow. This reveals itself in the concern that many therapists feel to establish their place in an analytic family tree traced back to one of the historical founders, and the way in which several tried to impress me with the fact that they had been analyzed by an analyst who had herself been analyzed by both Freud and Klein. One of them, perhaps seeing that I was a little sceptical about the significance of this revelation, then quickly added that 'there is something childlike about our obsession with lineages'. But those who had touched the hem of Melanie Klein could not mention her name without stunned reverence.

My interview with Alex was not a success. I had been told that he was generous, open-minded and witty. I had looked forward to meeting him, but he admitted early on that he did not approve of my project and that he did not want to answer my questions. He kept on reiterating the rather old-fashioned view that those who have been analyzed are part of an elect group with access to wisdom that is not accessible to those who have not.

'What did I do wrong?' I asked, as he looked at his watch for the third time in 45 minutes.

'You started off by treading on one of my corns.'

'What was that?'

'You said you had read *that* book.'

He was referring to Phyllis Grosskurth's biography of Melanie Klein,4 an excellent book that examines the detail of her life in a sympathetic and far from muck-raking way, but which has been universally reviled by the Kleinians.

'I feel,' he insisted, 'that it was a travesty.'

'I never said that I considered it to be gospel,' I retorted.

'Certainly somebody did. The person who wrote that play about her. I was one of her patients. There is the Topolski print.'

He pointed to a picture of Klein hanging prominently by the door, although he did not really need to tell me who had analyzed him. The grounds on which he based his hostility to me, and his evident reverence for his analyst several decades after her death, worried me. Despite his recommendation that I should find an analyst who would not seek to clone himself in me, I wondered whether anyone so much in awe of his analyst could really examine her views with any degree of objectivity. I suspected not.

Those who establish schools of psychoanalysis might seem to have an interest in inculcating their ideas in every forum that becomes available. But the vast majority of analysts do not have the desire, nor possibly the capacity, to establish such a hold over their patients. And those who do not want to be viewed as founts of wisdom and human perfection can work to minimize the chance of their being seen in that way. When I went to see William I knew that he had been analyzed by Wilfred Bion, a formidable theorist and a follower of Klein. There, I thought, would be a figure from whose influence it would be hard to escape. Perhaps William's transition from dogmatist to liberal indicated that such a battle had taken place. If so, he denies it. 'It so happens,' I was told, 'that he did not care to be viewed as an imposing figure, as a man of authority, as a guru. Any inclination shown by an analysand to treat him in any of those ways would become the subject of analysis. He made it easy to maintain and preserve one's individuality.' If it could be shown that most analysts behaved in much the same way as Bion, then the criticism most commonly expressed of training analysts would be shown to be largely without foundation.

The main argument Robert wanted to get across to me was that analysts who sought to impose their views and attitudes on patients were simply bad analysts. 'There are some analysts,' he remarked, 'who try to get people to be like them. This is obviously some sort of narcissistic exercise on their part. For myself, if I find a training patient in analysis with me who reports on making interventions that sound too much like me, I will say there is some sort of identification going on which needs to be analyzed. Why are they sounding like me and not like them? Why is the person not developing a style of their own? Are they inhibited, too closely identified with me, or just really shallow people?'

Analysts play such an important part in the lives of their trainee patients, that they cannot help but influence their views on analytic questions. But most want to encourage their charges to make up their own minds. When Rafael went into analysis with the wife of Donald Winnicott, he started to move from the liberal end of the analytic spectrum towards a more classical stance. I put it to him that this must have been the result of his analysis. 'My view,' he replied, 'would be that it was the way I chose to interpret my experience with her. I know other people who have had just as traditional an analyst as I had, but who have not moved in that direction.' He went on to observe that two friends share the same traditional analyst. While one has taken up a classical position similar to Rafael's, the other has gone the opposite way. 'He is very political, wanting to work in the community and to adapt his training to a broad spectrum of society.'

It does seem, therefore, that a spirit of intellectual freedom is far more common in training analyses than sceptical observers usually suspect. Most of the therapists I spoke to said that they could argue with their analysts, challenging them on issues of theory and technique. 'There was always room to differ,' Irene remarked. 'It was not ever a question of "This is the only way to do it." The principal thing I learned is that the way to do it is my way. The purpose was for me to find out who I was, and how I could use the space offered.'

There may be a tendency, in the early stages, for trainees to ape their own analysts. Confronted by their first patients, it is easier to imitate than to innovate. But imitation may still be the seed from which the mature analyst develops his or her individual line. Nora worked with a classical analyst who interpreted much of her experience in terms of penis envy. 'She had a tendency to push the classical stuff at me. At the time I thought, "Oh dear, you really swallowed that one and believed in it like the coming of the Holy Ghost." I had to pick and choose later. There are many areas where I have since thought that I am not going to do what she did.' Nora was never bludgeoned into submission, she just gradually discovered what it was she truly believed. It was through taking on board her own analyst's perspective and assessing it in relation to her own instincts that she hit upon the path that reflected her nature.

If the trainee's idealization of his or her analyst remains strong, that process of separation may be very hard. But there are aspects of the training process, including exposure to the analyst's real-life persona, which can turn reverence into realism. Reading your therapists' books and articles, hearing their lectures and gossiping about them with other patients might, of course, only increase your elevated view of their wisdom and insight. For Jeffrey Masson, however, seeing his analyst in action at a scientific meeting was an important element in his disillusion with psychoanalysis.[5] And one analyst told me how seeing one of his teachers break down in class helped to shatter any illusions he retained. 'There was a woman in the class who was a royal pain in the arse,' he recalls. 'The guy had a fit. He said, "Either you stop talking and leave this class or I am going to leave because the two of us cannot be in the same room together." It was a very rude awakening to see one of my heroes fall apart like that.'

This process is a strong argument for bringing analysts and their trainee patients together in shared activities within their training institutes. Eve joined an establishment where it was not required for her analyst to be a member. She initially welcomed this as giving her the freedom during sessions to explore her inner world without inhibition or anxiety. She could say what she wanted in the consulting room because there was no danger that her revelations would influence the course of her training. Later, however, this created problems. Never having seen her analyst in any guise other than that of analyst, it was difficult for her to work through the idealized feelings she had for him. There had been no arena in which she could challenge him, or witness his fallibility. 'I felt guilty,' she says. 'I thought, "Who am I to think I know a better way? I must not earn more than he does. I must not do anything different and imply that his way was not the correct way."'

I spoke to some therapists in New York who had found another way of protecting themselves against the dangers of indoctrination and idealization. They had gone into analysis with someone who was not a follower of their own favoured orientation. Robert clearly enjoys having such a training analyst on his caseload, someone who has chosen Kohut's 'self psychology' in preference to his own classical Freudian orientation. He claims that this makes for an interesting and productive encounter. 'She chose being a self psychologist,' he says, 'for her own internal reasons. As much as I would prefer her to be a Freudian, I would not think of trying to alter her therapeutic stance. I am aware of feeling that she would be a better therapist if she were practising a different orientation, and if it were within my power to change her entire life and personality, there is some level at which I would prefer that. But I would not give in to that any more than I would give in to punching a patient who annoys me.'

It is difficult, however, to imagine a British Kleinian being allowed the luxury of a Freudian analysis. 'A candidate,' says Frederick in continuation of his gentle campaign against the Kleinian cause, 'who goes into a Kleinian analysis has a Kleinian stamp for life. You have to present in seminars as a Kleinian. You are always being judged on whether you are doing Kleinian analysis correctly. Technically, they could take a Freudian supervisor, but it would be like a Jesuit saying, "I'm going to attend a Holy Rollers study group." The elders would shake their heads in dismay.'

Individual analysis is an important part of the training, but there are other significant inputs in the trainees' formation. The most significant of these are their training cases, taken under supervision. Through their supervisors, trainees pick up a model of how to practise which will almost inevitably differ significantly from that of their own analyst. The benefit of this is increased in those trainings which encourage students to work with supervisors from different orientations.

For trainee therapists, starting with their first patient is anxiety producing. 'It can be quite crippling,' says Nora. 'It can stop you hearing. It can make you speak too much out of anxiety, when you need to be silent and wait. It can push you up the wrong creek because of the desperate need to say something rather than nothing. You can follow some hare so that you and the patient can have some pseudo-analysis for quite a long time. You both collude in something out of a desire to relieve anxiety.' At such times the trainee is looking for dogma, not terrifying freedom.

The anxiety is both the natural result of trying to apply what one has learned in practice, and of the need to do everything to ensure that the patient stays the course. If the patient gives up the treatment, it is like snakes and ladders – the trainee must go back to the beginning and start again with someone else. Under these pressures, therapists are bound to start questioning their own capacity for the job. What have I got to offer this person? they will ask. Am I any good? 'You have got to bear with that,' one therapist said, 'and sort out your own anxieties from those that the patient may be evoking in you.'

In such circumstances, the trainee, so vulnerable and so afraid of failure, may come to see the patient as an enemy to be conquered rather than as an unhappy person to be helped. 'I think,' says Rachael, 'that some of our teachers did not help us to maintain a sense of compassion. It is sometimes very easy to lose it when you feel so persecuted. You want to be perfect. You want to look grown-up. But when you ask someone to come into your consulting room for the first time, your knees are shaking. The one thing you must not sacrifice is your sense of compassion.'

Working with this level of anxiety, training therapists are likely to hang on every word pronounced by the supervisors who must guide them through their first cases. 'Early on,' says Robert, 'you use the same language as your supervisors. The supervisor says I might say such a thing to a patient. The next thing the supervisee comes in and says I said this to the patient and it did not work. That is because it was not their language. They have to learn their own language for things.'

But often the rules handed down by a supervisor can be in irreconcilable conflict with the behaviour of the student's own analyst, and also the student's own inner sense of what is right. Frederick, for example, found his first supervisor had a very different model of analytic technique from his analyst, Anna Freud. 'I immediately got into trouble with my supervisor,' he says. 'She said you should not ask questions for clarification and you should not show any feelings of sympathy, even with a depressed girl who was crying a lot over her father's death.'

The discord between the respective styles of their analyst and supervisors forces trainees to make choices and to start steering their own path between the alternative routes on offer. That this process sometimes becomes quite sticky is largely due to the way in which supervisors tend to emphasize orthodoxy over spontaneity. In part this is a necessary caution because a patient's sanity is at stake and it may be better for the analyst to learn the 'right' way before starting to do it their way.

Once trainees start to work with a second patient and a second supervisor, they may find themselves having to process three conflicting inputs. 'You are not only dealing with your own problems,' says Peter, 'you have got a whole bunch of other people looking in on you.' Such discord can be useful in that it forces the training therapists to make a choice and to start on a search for their own way.

But the discord can become so intense that it forces trainees to censor material, to present cases in a way they think will please the supervisor, while in reality continuing to follow their own instincts. 'In supervision,' says Peter, 'you present the work that you think they want to hear. It is what is left out that is important. You doctor your evidence to make sure you come across as a nice guy. In reality the anarchistic and non-conformist bit of you is still functioning, but you edit it out. You have to conform overtly to the system. It is very tragic.' This process obviously runs parallel with the tendency for trainees to paint out their own warts during their analysis, which supposedly should be a plunge into the darkest depths of their unconscious.

In Barbara's case, one supervisor put her into a position that went beyond mild self-censorship into lies and concealment. She was 'petrified' of her supervisor, whom she experienced as rigid, orthodox (and Kleinian). The patient, whom she had been seeing for six months, rang up one evening to say she had taken an overdose. Barbara's response was to phone the local hospital poison centre in order to inform them about the situation and then to contact the woman's husband. 'My supervisor,' she recalls, 'was appalled that I had spoken to her on the telephone, let alone followed up on what she had told me. He said to me, "Now she will blackmail you for ever." I sat there feeling absolutely terrible. But when I went home I realized that I could never not respond to someone phoning me up and saying they had taken an overdose. In the next five years the patient made two further attempts. I intervened, but I never told the supervisor. No way!'

Students with a narcissistic analyst whose views they are expected to absorb, and who have a dogmatic supervisor with whom they cannot discuss the issues, are clearly in a horrible position. And if the analyst and the supervisor ram home essentially the same disagreeable message, the situation is even worse. Is it possible for the third element in their training, the lectures and seminars, to help them resolve their difficulties?

Much will depend here on whether they have chosen an institute which teaches a single system, or one that offers a variety of theories from which the students can form their own idiosyncratic mix. Within the former model, trainees may find that the message of orthodoxy is again rigidly upheld at the seminars and that any off-centre views are held up for mockery by their fellows. They may be encouraged on the one hand to follow their own instincts, but then find that they are judged harshly when that leads them to a place outside the general consensus. I asked Judith what would happen within her institute if I kept on bringing up existential ideas while in training to become a Freudian therapist. 'I do not think,' she said, 'you would be very happy with the course, and I do not think the course would be very happy with you either. Because if this came up whenever there was a clinical workshop, it would really get in the way of what other people were trying to do.'

Judith's view may be that of a teacher over-concerned to lay down a single theoretical line. While many of the therapists I spoke to acknowledged that they felt inadequate as students to challenge their teachers, few said that they were forced to conform. And Nora reported that the students at the Institute of Psychoanalysis in London discussed theory and technique in a climate of freedom. 'There is,' she says, 'a lot of exchange of ideas and views, and an acceptance of the idea that we do not always think alike and that we are not all alike.' She feels that many of the analysts who teach make allowance for those differences, but also acknowledges that 'a vulnerable and youngish student' might find themselves stuck with the search for a single method. 'They could suck in ideas and come to believe that they were their own without having deeply reflected upon them.'

It might seem common sense that therapists should be taught the whole of psychoanalytic therapy, and that their education should, as

B. A. Farrell recommends, 'be absorbed into the organization and ethos of university life'.[6] But this overlooks the fact that trainee therapists cannot approach analytic theory with the detachment that a philosopher brings to the study of Aristotle, Wittgenstein and Hume. They have to learn a method that they can use in the consulting room. Confronted by a range of theories, student therapists do not have the luxury of agnosticism, they have to choose. Otherwise they will go naked into the consulting room and find themselves unable to process their patient's communications in a context where every gesture and word is potentially filled with meaning.

When I visited Ian, he was dressed informally in blue jeans and red braces. He broke off our interview for an adjournment to the stairwell of his apartment block, where he kept a fat cigar behind the water pipe, which he proceeded to smoke. But while his garb and behaviour might suggest he saw himself as a naughty schoolboy, what he described to me was the search for an institution propounding precepts in which he could believe. 'They spoke of themselves as Freudians,' he says of the eclectic training institute he first attended, 'but as I went from class to class, I found myself getting very confused. I kept on asking myself, "How is what I am hearing here going to help me help people feel better about themselves?" I really was not able to answer that question. I could not see myself finding any way to use all this information. To be honest, I was scared.' After four years, he dropped out of that institute's programme and shifted to an organization which propounded a clearer line.

Many students want clear guidance from their teachers as to how they should deal with their patients. This does not necessarily mean that for the rest of their careers they will accept received truth. It does mean, however, that a traditional psychoanalytic training is best suited to those who know how to conceal their real thoughts in order to win the approval of superiors. Those who genuinely believe in freedom of expression within the training context simply will not survive. 'You do see very competent therapists,' says Peter, 'who are determined not to conform. They make their trainings very difficult for themselves. Often they fail their trainings. That is because of their personality structure. Why cannot they just bite the bullet and do their own thing when they have got to the other side? The profession does lose some free spirits because they cannot buckle down.'

The power that the institute has over trainees goes beyond its ability to prevent them from completing the training. It can also limit their capacity to earn a living once they graduate. This is the so-called 'mortgage factor'. Most newly graduated therapists build their practice out of referrals from their analyst, their supervisor and the clinic run by their institute. Having spent large sums on their training, and sometimes got themselves into substantial debt, most will want to secure as many patients as possible as quickly as possible. But if they have been disrespectful and rebellious throughout their training they may find that the telephone does not ring.

There is, therefore, something constricted about analytic training, and this may or may not have baleful effects on the capacity of the newly graduated therapist to be natural, spontaneous and truly responsive. What justification there is for such an unfree approach to teaching has to be found both in the enormity of the responsibility which therapists must undertake with every patient, and in the dizzying freedom that they enjoy once they have broken free of the shackles of their training. They may continue as adherents to a dogmatic line, or they can, like Elinor, ignore everything they have been taught and do their own thing. They may continue in supervision, but with a supervisor who supports their own prejudices or they may decide they no longer need someone else to overlook the management of their cases. They may continue to be involved in the intellectual life of their training institution, or they may have nothing to do with it. But within the boundary of the consulting room, they work under cover of secrecy. Their competence can never be judged as can that of a lawyer, a banker or a surgeon. They are essentially on their own.

The good analyst will be one who sees the day of graduation as the beginning of studying rather than the end. It has often been said that it takes 10 years of practice to become a fully competent analyst. It takes that much thinking, talking and listening to stop working from the book and to cease being anxious about not doing it right. 'For the first eight or 10 years,' says Nora, 'I was very anxious a lot of the time. It was only when I began to notice that I was not any longer worried at the approach of a patient for his or her session that I felt I was truly an analyst. You develop all sorts of increasing depth in your technique, using your own feelings more fruitfully, and not just saying what you think theoretically ought to be said.'

However powerful the message that they receive from their analyst, their supervisors and their teachers, students have to learn that the only right way to do therapy is their way, but drawing on everything they have been taught. They must look upon every encounter with a patient as an opportunity to explore ways to use their personality in order to assist those who come to them for help. 'For a while,' says

Adam, 'one is really trying to apply what others have learned. But then one has to have the courage to use one's own experience as a patient and a therapist to formulate one's own flexible but coherent model. That determines how one hears what people say, how one phrases one's interventions and what one thinks it necessary to focus on.'

4

Masks in Armchairs

Silence in the consulting room

○□
○○

Many people have the impression that seeing a psychoanalytic therapist resembles a visit to the sort of funeral home some gothic writer might describe. The therapist, they understand, will greet you with a blank face, shun a proffered handshake, refuse to acknowledge your uncertainty as to which chair to sit in, fail to laugh when you tell her the funniest joke in your repertoire and say not a single word.

Such tales are often recounted with amusement. Do they perhaps constitute a modern myth with few roots in reality? Can therapists really be so austere and inhuman? With so many reported sightings of such unnatural beings one perhaps has to accept that some are like that. Clare, now a non-analytic therapist, says of her first meeting with an analyst, 'It was a ghastly experience. This monosyllabic person came out of the lift and then fled. I had the nous to follow her. We went along this corridor full of open doors. Then we stopped in front of one. She still did not say anything. I had the sense to go into the room. She then waited until I had chosen one of three chairs. Then she sat there and looked at me. She said nothing. Not even "What can I do for you?" Nothing. So I started to tell her why I thought I had come. But the tension was unbearable. I left with a severe headache.'

The first session with a therapist is a time when patients are at their weakest, caught up in the trauma of entrusting themselves to another. A half-smile goes a long way towards easing the attendant anxieties. A silent and distant stance seems a particularly cruel opening gambit. People come to therapists with many doubts, hesitations and suspicions. They want to know about this person. Can she help them? Will she be kind, tolerant and understanding, or cruel, cold and insensitive? To these questions the expressionless face provides only the most negative answer. 'By being silent,' says Edwina, 'you can be phenomenally intrusive because people get worried about the silence and the lack of response. They cannot think because they are worried about you.'

72

And when that silence continues, week after week, it can be the hardest part of therapy to bear. Some patients want feedback and a form of relating that feels normal. They want to know who the therapist is, what she is feeling and what she cares about. They want to be able to laugh, to hear stories as well as tell them and, above all, to know what the therapist really thinks of them. In rebellion against the strangeness of the therapeutic process, some clients ask their therapist to meet them outside the consulting room. Others beg for the therapist to go to bed with them, as if that is the only way in which one human being can show care for another.

When silence evokes sensations that are too painful to endure, it can drive people away from therapy. I met a woman who had been referred to a therapist shortly after the death of her husband. That therapist never uttered a hello, just summoned her into the consulting room from the end of a long corridor. There he said almost nothing. When she had asked him many times why he was behaving this way he finally said that he was offering himself as a receptacle for her rage and aggression. What he actually made her feel was guilt at her own imagined responsibility for the death of her man. And his passivity also convinced her that he was useless and unable to deal with her, reprising her experience as an enraged child whose parents could not cope. There was nothing that therapist could offer her, and she had the sense to leave.

Others stick with it, even though the therapist's manner arouses anxieties and seems to prevent that healing process which it is meant to ensure. June, for example, stayed in three-times-a-week therapy for seven years. She is grateful to her therapist for bringing back the memory of being sexually abused as a child, but not for a subsequent stance of impassivity that forced her painfully to relive those years in which she failed to get through to her mother. 'I have a feeling,' she says, 'that she was not competent to deal with my material. She became more rigid because of her own fears of what could happen. I was vulnerable to anything that savoured of rigidity. No matter how I tried to communicate that, I could not get through. It was a rerun of my early experience and it left me with feelings of anger and despair. Could she not see what was happening?'

June had a particular reason for finding her therapist's distance unnerving. Others, as a result of their very different early experiences, find silence one of therapy's greatest boons. Charles told me of one of his patients who, having been sexually abused as a child, had a lot of anger to work off. At each session he would work up a fury, threatening to tear off the office door and perpetrate some violent deed upon his therapist. When the time came for the session to end, he would stand up and say that he felt great. Asked what had helped him, he would reply, 'I feel able to say everything here.'

For some people, then, it is the willingness of the therapist to be silent, to allow them a space to speak of a sort they never enjoyed before that is central to the success of therapy. Harold believes that 50 per cent of what helps people in therapy is just having somebody to listen. 'It is the most therapeutic thing in the world for people just to be given an opportunity to be themselves, to talk and say whatever is on their mind. I can go for several hours at a time without saying a word. A lot of people get much better for just having a friendly listener.' He insists that the stereotype of the silent therapist is totally wrong. Most therapists talk too much. I did, in fact, several times hear it said of therapists that they were too chatty. And Paul, who talked 20 to the dozen during my interview with him, admitted that his patients sometimes tell him to shut up.

Silence is the favoured mode of psychoanalytic therapy because its practitioners believe that, in most cases, it starts the healing process. But how do they justify such a strange approach? Why is so much faith placed in such an unnatural form of human interaction? Why should therapists not talk about themselves, what they believe in, their likes and dislikes, their passions and convictions? Why should they not give advice? Why cannot patient and therapist just talk person-to-person about the things in life that make them suffer? Is there not something wrong with people who practise such restraint, who hold themselves so aloof?

It is silence that distinguishes therapy from friendship. When two friends meet, the emphasis is normally on mutuality. What therapists intend their silence to indicate is that they bring no agenda of their own into the consulting room. They respond only to what patients draw to their attention as they talk about whatever comes into their head, rambling around the store cupboards of their memories. Behind the apparent disorder they may come across something significant, some clue to their pain and unhappiness. 'Silence,' says Jo, 'is not just for the sake of frustrating the patient; it is also giving them an opportunity to bring their life into the analytic situation, to let the analyst know how they feel, what they think and where they have come from. To begin with, each patient has to tell the story of their life in their own way.'

Through silence therapists assert that they are not the motivators, and that it is for the patient to do the work. 'I do not see myself as conducting the analysis,' says Stephen. 'I see myself as providing the patient with an opportunity to analyze himself. If the patient is truly willing and wishes to be analyzed, he will do it. All I can do is clear away what I see as blocks in his willingness to do this work.'

Further, the therapist's silence is an acknowledgement of ignorance and of not knowing at what point in the patient's life to start the investigation. The therapist waits, hoping that the patient will use the silence to allow memories and fantasies to force themselves into consciousness. As ideas then suggest themselves to the therapist, he or she will start to point the client along particular pathways, offering interpretations of the material that has been offered and putting stray pieces of information together with others of a similar kind. 'I think,' says Molly, 'that while people may complain about the silence, they rapidly find it useful that you keep your mouth shut until you find something useful to say.'

Silence, then, has an important function within psychoanalytic therapy. It is not dead time, as it might seem to many outsiders. To them, nothing could be more stupid than one person paying another to sit with them in a room and say nothing. But that is not how therapists experience silences, especially not when these occur long after the initial relationship between therapist and patient has been established. Then the silence may be an expression of anger and fury. The patient may be punishing the therapist for a clumsy, stupid interpretation. Or it may be a time of quietly and usefully reflecting on what has been said and understood.

Is it really justifiable to charge someone to sit in silence for 50 minutes? Within the structure of an evolving relationship, therapists claim, such periods can be extremely valuable. Molly, whose intensity when she speaks hints at something wild in her nature, recalls the strong impression that her first completely silent session made on her. 'It was enormously powerful. What stunned me afterwards was to discover that the patient had plotted the whole session in a way that completely corresponded to my own understanding, including her triumph at the end that she had not spoken.' At other times her patients' silences have been the cover for their growing anger. 'You usually get some indication of that in the silence, a feeling that the room feels like a time-bomb, that there is a tornado building up. It is silent but you feel the energy.'

Silence has its greatest value as the guardian of the therapist's relative anonymity. The therapeutic relationship aims to bring to the surface the patients' characteristic way of relating to others, the patterns of misapprehension that cause them pain and distress. The therapist's anonymity assists that process. By his or her relative absence, the therapist provokes anxiety, compelling the patient to start asking questions about the limited information available. Is there coldness in that statement? Is there mockery in that question? What is this person thinking about me? Does she like me or think me a lightweight?

Patients' answers to such questions reflect their experience of those figures in their life who had previously made them anxious, curious, unhappy or whatever. By keeping themselves relatively anonymous and neutral, by doing nothing to justify the answers their patients come up with, the therapist shows them how they misconstrue the actions of others. The therapist says I am neutral. I am not guilty as charged. You think I am mocking you because you think everybody mocks you. That is the root of your difficulties in the world. All the problems of the patient's past and present are manifested in the here and now of the sessions. The therapy hour becomes the place where what goes on outside is repeated in a heightened form and then examined.

In exploring the way that patients respond to them, therapists pick up indications of how patients experienced figures from their past. Vanessa has a patient who regularly expresses anxiety that she is going to reject him. In doing so, he reveals that he expects her to behave as his mother had – a woman who was generally depressed and spent most of her time with her nose in a book, taking no notice of anyone around her. One of Jane's patients takes her hand movements, which are continuous and very enigmatic, to indicate that she considers him to be a 10th-class member of the human race. He also feels the same way about anybody he passes in the street who touches their nose or sniffs. These are, as Mary describes them, 'interpretations without evidence'. Until patients see the falsity of their position, they will continue to suffer. 'They will do that with other people, misunderstand the signals they are getting and cause themselves pain.'

There is, therefore, some justification for those who argue that the therapist must keep silent, however much it infuriates or enrages the patients. Those who cannot bear not knowing about their therapists, who fire a never-ending flow of questions in an attempt to winkle out the truth and become furious at the therapist's evasive answers reveal important information about themselves and the anxiety that others provoke in them. When the therapist turns back a question to the questioner, it can indeed be infuriating. Why won't she answer? Why won't she provide me with the reassurance I seek? But it is often true that there is no answer other than 'It is not me, it is you.' The therapist may want to answer the question, to deflect the intensity of the assault, but to do so would be to put a stop to the analytic work. For the patient to understand that he or she is imagining it is the beginning of the end of treatment. 'It can feel like persecution,' says Mary, 'and it often does, but you need to know the meaning.' Finding out what really happened in her patients' past is Mary's constant aim.

Mary had one patient who strained to the limit her ability to refrain from answering questions. 'She was extremely demanding,' Mary recalls. 'She came in for one session feeling absolutely murderous, lay on the couch and said in a ferocious tone of voice, "Where did you go for your holiday?" I was really taken aback by this. I had to stop and think. I did not want to say something stupid like, "Where do you think?" I had to work out what it meant. Why was she so angry with me? She needed to know where I had been. It was related to her mother having gone away when she was little and her husband working abroad.' Therapists argue that once the patient comes to understand why the question is so important to them, they will not need an answer; they are not being cruel when they refuse to answer, they are being kind.

But although silence has a justifiable place in the therapeutic armoury, it is sometimes used in ways that are defensive, misguided and cruel. If silence gives therapy its potential for effectiveness, it also gives therapists their power. It is through the anxiety, the anger and every other variety of emotion stirred up by the silence that patients come to learn how their lives have been disfigured by their misunderstandings of others' words and deeds. But it is also in the manipulation of these 'false' emotions that therapists have the potential to abuse their patients. They can pretend that there is no reality behind the patients' apprehension of them, when in fact they are behaving in a vicious or mean-spirited manner. They can allow the patients' reliving of their earliest pains to reach a point almost beyond endurance, without necessarily bringing any greater understanding to their situation. Silence may be portrayed as the therapist's declaration that there is nothing in this process for them, whereas in fact it is the vehicle for their covert sadism.

Compelling patients to suffer through silence may be an inadvertent effect of an analyst's inexperience or ineptitude. Faced with patients' deep distress, their outpourings of complex emotions and violent feelings, the incompetent therapist may be terrified into silence. An American analyst has written about the flaw in trainings which leave many graduates convinced that silence is the centre of their technique rather than one device among many to achieve their 'deeper goals'. It is a sorry plight the analyst falls into, 'sitting silently behind the couch, unable to help his patient explore the new, strange situation in which the patient finds him or herself, because the budding analyst is afraid that breaking his personal vow of silence will mean that he is not doing analysis'.[1]

It concerned me that some of the people to whom I spoke were unwilling to acknowledge that there were dangers as well as benefits in therapeutic silence. 'There are certain therapists,' says Robert, evidently sharing my concern, 'who cannot be human. They work very mechanically.' While many therapists felt evident compassion over the pain which their mask of anonymity could cause their patients, others could not accept that their patients' discomfort was a serious illness. They seemed to have hardened themselves against the distress for which they were responsible. When I put it to one analyst that the mask can be very disturbing for some patients, she gave a flip answer: 'I sit behind my patients, so I do not have to wear a mask.' As if somehow the fact that the patient never got to look into her eyes made what she was feeling less opaque rather than more so.

Sarah struck me throughout our interview as someone whose diffidence might cause anxiety to those who visited her regularly. I asked whether patients were ever frustrated by not knowing who she really was.

'Yes and no,' she replied. 'It is not really a huge element in most people's relationship with me.'

I commented on the fact that she seemed not to like the question. 'Do you think,' I asked, 'it is a silly one to ask?'

'As I say, it's not an important question. No more important than a million other questions about what goes on in the relationship.'

'But people worry about it. People want to know where their therapists are coming from, what they know about, what experiences they have had, what opinions they hold upon various issues.'

'We do not know an awful lot about what we are caught up in. It matters to patients that you understand what they are trying to tell you and that you can say something that helps them to put things together. That is what matters, not where you came from, whether you are married, whether you have got children, whether you have done this or that. Patients are like children who want to know about their parents. They think their parents are not ordinary people until they find out that they are. We are as muddled and messy and confused as anyone else.' I was left feeling like a child who had asked a silly question, and I wondered why the issue I raised had touched such a nerve.

There are some creeds of psychoanalytic orthodoxy which treat the frustrations bred by the analyst's silent, impassive, unrevealing stance not as a possibly unfortunate product of the analytic process, but as the very centre of treatment. Therapy is meant to be arduous, difficult and frustrating. If it isn't hurting, it isn't working. According to such theories, the analytic encounter brings to the surface a patient's infantile wishes and fears. The analyst must do nothing that will gratify those wishes or pacify those fears in case that deprives the patient of the opportunity to fully experience his or her primitive feelings. The analyst must stand as a pillar of rationality and complete objectivity. Painful as this stance may be for both parties involved, it is believed to be in the best interests of the patient. The frustration must be experienced so that the infantile wishes can be renounced.

When such an approach is taken to an extreme, it carries enormous costs both for the analyst, who must practise considerable detachment, and for the patient, who must endure deep frustration. A point is reached when the analyst is no longer pretending to be inhuman, when he or she becomes so. Barbara, whose own analytic training has not diminished her sense of horror at the unnatural behaviour of her teachers and colleagues, is still appalled when she recalls an experience she had with one of her supervisors. She suffers from an illness which results in her occasionally and momentarily losing control of her muscles. On one occasion she collapsed in front of this supervisor. Far from reaching out a hand to help her up, he simply stood there and waited for her to do it herself. Reflecting on that incident some 15 years later, she still shakes her head in angry despair. 'I just think it is so inhuman, quite extraordinary.'

Birgit first met her supervisor at a party and formed an impression of her as a relaxed, jovial human being. She could not have been more wrong. 'The minute I came to supervision there was this different person there, a monster really.' Nor was her analyst's manner any easier to accept. She saw him five times a week for nine years. It was a process so intense that she could not at the time reflect upon what was happening. But her doubts about his approach were fostered by three sessions she had with him some time after the end of the treatment. 'They were played by my analyst,' she recalls, 'as though we were two people who had never met before. The interpretations he was going to make would serve as the sole vehicle for conveying that we had a long, close and intimate contact over a long period of time. I found this so distressing that I broke down after each one of those follow-up visits.'

In her own practice Birgit has tried to follow the Kleinian model to which her analyst adheres. Her experience of analysis had, after all, been a powerful one which touched those parts of her childhood that no previous therapist had been able to reach. But she found it very hard to be a 'sphinx' who did not answer questions and did not respond to the patient's expressions of emotion. By her own account a 'warm and trusting person', she doubts whether she ever really achieved the sphinx-like posture held out to her as a model. 'For example,' she says, 'I do not just stand there like a marble stone if patients give me a hug.' Whether it was because she did achieve what she understood to be the Kleinian ideal, or because she felt guilty at not living up to her own analyst's example, the work began to take a physical toll. She developed hypertension, began to feel constantly exhausted and became very bad-tempered with members of her family. 'I was simply going against the grain of my simple, natural being,' she says.

Her own experiences suggest to Birgit that some Kleinian analysts find so much anger in their patients because their blank, impassive faces stir fury. Others have expressed the same view. 'It is debatable,' writes Patrick Casement, 'how much of the paranoid material that emerges in the course of such an analysis is necessarily a primary expression of the patient's internal world: some of it at least is likely to be a response to the analyst's manner of working.'[2] And it has been suggested that the rage which the American analyst Otto Kernberg (whose theories developed out of Klein's) sees in narcissistic patients is a consequence of his approach, so that he is 'continually creating the monster he is perpetually slaying'.[3]

My interview with one Kleinian strongly suggested to me the truth of these theories. The woman who came to the door was dressed in a neat suit, with her hair gathered tidily around her head. The room at the front of the house into which she showed me was slightly characterless, but its varnished floorboards gave off a feeling of warmth. She offered me a cup of coffee and was unfailingly courteous throughout the 90 minutes we spent together.

But something was going on beneath that courtesy which made me feel that shards of glass were being pushed under my skin. I eventually left the house spitting with anger. Days later, I would wake up and bash at pillows in order to exorcize my fury. It was not until I had talked the experience through with an analyst friend that I could begin to understand what had happened, for the process had been a subtle one.

The impact of the session derived from the way that the analyst attempted to impose on me her own ideas as to what she wanted to talk about. Instead of listening to my questions and responding or not, as she chose, she constantly interposed her own agenda. She could not accept that we were involved in a two-way communication. She, it seemed, had to dominate our exchanges and undermine me in the process.

I had pitched to her the same line as I had to nearly everyone else I interviewed – that I wanted to discuss the suspicions people had of psychoanalysis and how far the stereotypes differed from the reality. We started by talking about the factions within the training institute of which she is a leading light. Since many people conceive of psychoanalysts as of a religious bent and consequently impermeable to rational argument, this certainly seemed to me a question coming within the brief I had described. She, however, evidently did not see it that way.

'May I ask you? These were not the things you wanted to talk to me about. You said you were writing a book on popular misconceptions of psychoanalysis. This is a tiny little area.'

'You cannot see the whole without taking a look at the parts,' I replied.

She responded with a series of seemingly irrelevant questions about what the book would be called, my age and my own experience of therapy. Without, I think, my saying anything to suggest it, she became convinced that I had experienced my therapy as wholly negative and that I was out to do a demolition job on psychoanalysis as a whole. Despite my protestations that this was not what I was trying to do, any question I asked subsequently was seen as an attack on analysis.

'Your experience must have been extremely disturbing and painful. That does happen, but it is not typical.'

I tried again to explain that my own experience of therapy had been neither disturbing nor, for the most part, particularly painful. But she had already decided that what I had undergone disqualified me from writing my book.

'I think it is difficult,' she said, 'for you to talk about these things, given your personal experience. You are not looking at it as a broad issue. How does this happen? Why does something go wrong?'

This seemed to me an extraordinary remark for an analyst to make. 'I am surprised,' I said, 'that you raise that as a problem. I would have thought an analyst would understand better than anyone else that there is something personal in the questions I have set out to explore.'

'But it is a problem,' she insisted, 'because of your vulnerability, your sore patches, your hopes that were not realized. It is as though in your more general, impersonal discussion there is also this very personal history of yours that is running alongside.'

'Did you detect a suspicious undercurrent in my questions?' I asked. 'Did you feel under attack in some way?'

'No,' she replied. 'But as we have been talking, I gather that this has been your experience. You know what I thought about you. I thought, ha, good, a writer who wants to expose the misconceptions about analysis and therapy. Good! This is what we need. People who can write and get it right.'

The interview did not improve much from that point. She answered my questions, but in a textbook fashion. Her answers did not quite ring true, as if she had learned them by rote rather than through spending decades in the practice of analysis. It was because of her insistence on finding a single, sinister motive behind my much more complexly motivated questions, her desire to bend me to her purpose rather than to discover what mine was, and her assumption that she understood my feelings that she provoked my anger. I could not help attributing the subtlety of the process with which she penetrated my skin and deranged me to her years of practising analysis, and wondered whether she did not secure reactions from her patients similar to those she elicited from me.

Psychoanalytic theory emphasizes the value of silence as a technique for exploring the patients' inner world. It is not necessary to argue from this that analysts should aim to become blank screens or empty containers into which patients will project their infantile wishes and fantasies. 'An intelligent patient,' says Frederick, when I ask about analysts who try to present a blank screen to their patients, 'will know that this analyst has problems and that he had better get to someone more experienced.' Frederick, who clearly looks on the behaviour of his more purist colleagues with wry amazement, is himself no maverick. He believes very much in boundaries and in the basic principles of classical theory. For example, if a patient asks him whether he has children, he will answer along traditional lines, saying something like: 'This is a relevant question, but in analysis it is important that we do not get into reality. What are your feelings about whether or not I have children?' But he also believes in being natural, spontaneous and friendly. He tries not to distance the patient by 'going up in smoke and not saying anything' when asked a question. He refers me to a classic textbook which declares that 'neither smugness, ritualism, timidity, authoritarianism, aloofness, nor indulgence have a place in the analytic situation.'4 Silence, in short, should not be taken as a licence to cruelty. The analyst should aim to make the patient comfortable and relaxed, while developing a relationship that accords with the rules of analysis.

Like Frederick, Samuel attempts to combine a classical approach with relaxed spontaneity. There is an air of relaxed good taste about the adornment of his rooms. On the low, green marble-topped table that divides us stands an art nouveau vase on which is represented the crowned head of a woman. The picture above the couch shows Odysseus exhorting Achilles to come out from among the women and join in the war effort against Troy. I wonder what meaning it has for Samuel who had fled Poland as a child to escape from Hitler, and found himself in New York via the Soviet Union and Israel.

I have come from lunch and welcome both the comfortable chairs and the tea with macaroons which I am offered. Samuel is short and his complexion is pale, but there is a passion in his eyes and a kindliness in his voice, with its inflexions that are neither quite English nor altogether American. 'Analysis,' he tells me in a voice of determined confidentiality, 'is a cure through love.' I am not sure quite what he means, but I know at once that I am not in the presence of a follower of Klein or Kernberg.

'All mental disorders,' he elaborates, 'stem from problems in relating. They can be cured by a good relation with your therapist. The analyst has to bring the idea of compassion to the task. Love is a principle that should inform everything.'

In Samuel's formulation, anonymity does have its uses. The analyst may sometimes take on the appearance of a blank screen as a way of enabling patients to learn about themselves, but that must not be at the cost of a loving, caring relationship. If they ask him, 'Are you married?', he will tell them. 'I do not think,' he says to me, 'that matters which are in the public domain should be made into an unnecessary secret.' He will try not to reveal other details about himself, unless that seems to be called for. 'I do not play a stereotypical role of the deadpan analyst. I am very much alive. I interact with people here very much as I interact with people outside, except that everything is directed to meeting their needs and not mine.'

Those therapists who try to keep their personality completely opaque deny an essential reality of the therapeutic relationship – that it *is* a relationship. However different it may be from normal modes of human relating, therapy nevertheless operates through a series of exchanges involving two people. If therapists are to achieve their goal of enabling patients to relearn the way in which they form relationships with others, they must be, at some level, participants in the process, not just distant observers. Some measure of distance is essential, but absolute distance is not at all desirable. This is one of the key paradoxes of therapy.

Total self-effacement is, in any case, not a particularly realistic ambition. Analysts may be able to keep certain facts about themselves hidden, but anonymity is an impossibility. They cannot conceal from patients their essential nature, whether they are cruel or kind, calm or manic. And the patient who wants to know will observe whether the therapist is, during any particular session, happy or sad, tired or alert. It is ridiculous to claim otherwise. The analyst who is always silent and impassive will be reasonably read by the patient as cold and indifferent. The analyst who refuses to answer questions will often stir negative feelings. And the analyst who puts no pictures on the wall, uses functional and not particularly comfortable furniture, and always wears black is screaming out information about what sort of person he or she is.

Robert described to me a case in which he inadvertently became irritated, leading to a breakthrough in understanding. He means to suggest that his emotional outburst helped him to know better what was going on, but I don't fully grasp this at first and suggest that what helped his patient was his humanity showing through in his emotional reaction. My remark riles him. 'Your humanity,' he asserts, 'shows through all the time. Part of your humanity is that you really care about their getting better. Part of your humanity is your genuine interest in them. Part of your humanity is how you dress, what kind of regional accent you have, whether you are young or old, what you have on your walls. That is all part of your humanity which shows through.'

And it is true that most of the people to whom I spoke revealed so much through the way they decorated and adorned their consulting rooms that any claim to being 'blank screens' would have been laughable. They did not proclaim the details of their personal life by putting up pictures of their spouses, children or grandchildren, but there was evidence of distinctive taste in the furniture, the pictures on the walls and the assortment of colours around the room. Some, indeed, were scattered with clay figurines, pots and other objects, much as Freud's had been.

Although Mary's room could not be described as bare – it contained a desk, a couch, three chairs, a small bookcase and some plants – its white walls and overall tidiness did leave me with a feeling that something was being withheld. She explained this not in terms of theory but as an expression of her own personality. 'I do not like clutter,' she said. 'That comes from growing up in a large family. I must have experienced my siblings as clutter. I like peace and quiet and clear surfaces and warmth and silence. I can work comfortably in that environment and hopefully it is the kind of environment that will not disturb my patients.' Nick, by contrast, keeps a room that feels like a seaman's cabin, with two great barometers, charts, photographs and ancient clocks ticking away the time.

In the layout of their rooms therapists have to choose between adherence to the precepts laid down in their theoretical manuals, which generally emphasize the need to distance therapeutic practice from 'normality', and doing what 'feels' right and natural. Most, in the end, choose to work in an environment that is comfortable for them. Given the number of hours they must spend in their consulting rooms and what is demanded of them when they are there, this seems only common sense. But many then feel anxious about putting their own desire to be at ease before what the textbooks have told them will benefit the patient. Although Molly, for example, spoke of the sense of relief she felt upon escaping from 'a strange, funny room that was bare, where I hated the colours and everything else' into the comfortable consulting room she had built in the basement of her house, she immediately added that she was worried in case she was becoming 'too cosy'. Many others would justify stamping their personality on to the room and then go on to express anxiety about being too revealing. Several articulated a desire to work in a more 'neutral' room.

The persistence of these anxieties says a lot about the way in which orthodox attitudes become impressed on the minds of therapists, continuing to shape their perspective long after their formal education is over. But the loss of some anonymity is hardly detrimental to the analytic task, since the fantasies provoked by a relative absence of information will be strong enough to reveal how the patient misapprehends others. The relative concealment of the analyst's true personality will provide enough of a backcloth to screen out fantasy from reality and enable the analyst to learn something of the patient's characteristic way of viewing other people. 'If the analyst knows himself well enough,' argues George, 'he will know when the patient is distorting. He does not have to maintain a false self in order to catch the distortions.' To deny that is to deny the capacity of therapists to distinguish between what is being done to them because of what they have revealed about themselves – that they drive a BMW, holiday in the Canaries and read lots of books – and what is being done to them as proxies for other people in the patient's life.

It is strange that therapists have ever attempted to deny this, since anonymity is an impossibility during their own analyses. A trainee analyst will usually know other patients of the same analyst, and have the opportunity to compare notes on his or her method. They will pick up pieces of gossip from colleagues and teachers, and possibly read papers and books the analyst has written. If they can survive such exposure to the reality of their analyst's personality and achievements, why cannot the ordinary patient do the same? Or should one conclude that their own analyses are always unsatisfactory because they are polluted by information from outside? (Several commentators, it should be said, have argued just that.)

There are some therapists who, if they accepted the principle of anonymity, would have to withdraw from the profession. Susie Orbach founded the Women's Therapy Centre amid much publicity, is known as the bestselling author of *Fat Is a Feminist Issue* and is frequently quoted in the press on a number of women's issues. Those who come to therapy with her will mostly know these facts before they enter the door. They can easily find out that she has an American husband and two children. They may have read about her own unhappy childhood. There is a chance that they will share the experience of one woman who went to interview her and felt 'threatened by the model of Superwoman'.[5] Or they may feel pleased to model themselves on such a prosperous, successful female. Whatever attitude they present, Orbach tries to deal with it on the basis of her knowledge of what they are reacting to – her public persona. She recognizes that the image of her which people bring to her sessions can provoke idealization or jealousy, and that is the point from which the therapeutic process begins.

She does, however, try to ensure that her presence is not unnecessarily forced on to her patients. She curtails her public exposure to some extent. She gets very angry when she is misquoted in newspapers and does what little she can to see that this does not happen. And she tries not to become too much associated with causes. 'There are certain public activities that I do not partake in,' she says, 'even though, being quite a noisy person, I might wish to.' Other therapists, starting off from a less publicly exposed position, are happy to wave banners and declare their political position. I interviewed Mitch a few days after the start of the Gulf War. He had been signing petitions, joining demonstrations and generally putting forward his views. 'Does it present problems?' he asks himself. 'It did come up last week. Patients saw I had signed a petition and said, "What is going on?" That is something I have to work through with them.' As he sees it, such actions only confirm the impression that a patient would necessarily form about his basic orientation to life – from his hairstyle, his clothes and the music he plays in his waiting room. 'Some people,' he says, 'see me as too flower-child, too optimistic about things and not cynical enough. That comes up and you deal with it.'

There can also be physical realities which intrude in such a way as to render anonymity impossible. Barbara's illness means that her state of alertness during sessions varies quite considerably. If a patient says that she looks tired and unwell, she can only acknowledge it. And there was no way, in the long run, that Rachael could avoid admitting that she was pregnant. Apart from anything else, there were going to be four months when she would not be there for her patients. Most quickly picked up her situation, even though they would only raise the matter indirectly – by relating a relevant dream, for example, or telling her that a friend was going to have a baby. But one patient did not provide her with such an opening to raise the issue. Her 'bump' grew bigger and bigger, but still he did not make any reference to her condition. Finally the time came when she could no longer put off telling him. 'He was quite hurt,' she remembers. 'He felt that I should have said something. If I could see that he was having a problem, then I should have picked it up.'[6]

Therapists cannot, in the end, control how much their patients come to learn about them. A variety of factors are in play, not just what therapists are willing to reveal in answers to questions, but also the degree of information they are simply unable, by their nature, to conceal; not only the patients' desire to know, but also their sensitivity to gesture and nuance, and the way in which their disturbance mixes in true and false perceptions of the therapist before them. Each therapist's capacity to be anonymous is, to some extent, independent of their desire to be so.

Sophie, who was initially resistant to my questions, finds that most patients get her wrong. Their attempts to penetrate her mask are not generally successful. 'The patient,' she concedes, 'is sometimes right. If they say you are clumsy, you may have made a clumsy remark. But I recall one patient saying that she thought I was a very shy person, which does not happen to be true.' On one occasion she hurried from her mother's deathbed to be ready for her first analytic session of the day. She was 15 minutes late, but otherwise the session carried on much as usual. The patient, Sophie claims, noticed nothing untoward in her manner.[7] I might have been more suspicious about the truth of this claim had not somebody reported discovering that she had seen her analyst only hours after he had been told he had terminal cancer. 'I did not notice at all,' she says. 'Therapy is such a self-centred thing. You are not bothered about the other person, except in their relation to you.'

Antonia was more revealing during her interview than her opening statements had suggested she would be. Her experience is the opposite of Sophie's. She is often impressed by just how sensitive patients are to her moods. When *her* mother died, there was no question but that she should take some time off work. That put her in a quandary, however. How do you announce your mother's death to patients? Such information is bound to stir up powerful, disturbing, possibly overwhelming feelings in them. But you cannot just take a two-week break out of the blue without giving a reason. And you cannot, surely, tell a lie and call yourself a psychoanalyst. Eventually she decided that telling them the whole truth would be the least damaging option, even though she then had to deal with the strong feelings evoked by what had happened. 'I was given the most enormous love and support,' she recalls, 'but that did not block out the anger they felt as well – about their own parent's death, or the possibility of mine.'

Therapists have to walk a fine line between frustrating patients' desire for information which it does little harm for them to know, and providing them with an excess of detail, smothering their ability to fantasize and to produce material for the analysis. Rachael's patients all now know that she is a married woman with a young child. Nevertheless, she will not respond to personal questions about her family. 'I might pick and choose with some people if it seems appropriate,' she admits. She knows from her own therapy how important it is for the patient to be allocated imaginative space.

Rachael's first therapist had a consulting room in the house of another therapist, and sometimes she would meet that other woman at the door. As she was led to the consulting room, she would often hear the sound of children playing. The fantasy that she developed around these observations, that her therapist and the other woman were sisters, proved very important in exploring her own material. 'I would not want to intrude my own facts on someone before I know what their fantasies are,' she concludes. 'They are crucial to revealing how you see the world. It may be that eventually I will say, "Well, actually, this is the case" or "that is the case". Sometimes it is important to say, "This is the reality which is so different from the fantasy." In that way you show them the strength of their fantasies. But in general I do not reveal things.'

Samantha's anxiety about her capacity to help patients is evident in everything she says on the two occasions when we meet, and is mirrored in the care she gives to answering my questions. She is often astonished by the wide divergence in the way patients interpret the noises in her house. She has one patient, deeply disturbed but very intelligent and intuitive, whose fantasies about the various sounds coming through the walls and the debris scattered in the hallway are extremely accurate. Another patient always gets it completely wrong. He does not want, she concludes, to think about the possibility that his therapist is a married woman, who sleeps with her husband and has several happy children. He has decided, instead, that the house is full of psychotherapists. It is a fantasy that, in Samantha's view, saves the patient from 'thinking about all the other forbidden activities that may go on in the house'.

There are other ways in which therapists' openness about themselves could inhibit the patients' fantasies. An overt expression of their political or religious views might prevent patients from articulating an outlook that was directly contrary, or encourage them to pick away at that area with irritating persistence to the exclusion of everything else. Barbara, for example, although happy to talk about the state of her health, would never confess to being a Catholic out of concern not to limit her patients' freedom to attack the Catholic religion, if they so wished.

Therapy is a process of change. It would be impossible for the therapist's values and attitudes not to enter into the process. Nevertheless, most therapists aim for a neutral stance. Molly, whose sense of how much she gained from her own therapy colours all her statements, speaks of not wanting to impose on patients her own idea of what would be a nice life for the patient. 'My task is to understand their own experience and thereby deepen and enrich it.' And John describes his aim as being that patients 'should at long last become themselves. At the beginning of therapy,' he says, 'that is an unknown thing. One works towards taking away everything that distorts and conceals this mysterious thing. It is a question of the patient getting more and more comfortable with the person they gradually discover they are.'

The therapist cannot fail to let the patient know what he or she believes. The patient who comes to look to the therapist for approval and commendation will tend to imitate aspects of the therapist. Should one conclude that critics who accuse analysts of perverting the minds of those entrusted to their care are right? 'It is perfectly possible,' concedes Alexa, 'to indoctrinate and brainwash people. There are moments when it would be possible to exploit this position mercilessly and to let them have the idea that the only way they can keep on coming here is if they drop from their vocabulary anything that sounds racist or whatever. You can make it very clear.'

Antonia describes with some pride her experience of having a Trotskyite in therapy. 'At the end of seven years,' she declares, 'he was no longer a Trotskyite.' Given that she lives comfortably in a smart area of London and probably does not hold beliefs of a particularly radical nature, one might wonder whether she is not taking an illicit pleasure in wearing away at political beliefs that she does not find congenial. But she describes not a desire to convert the patient but to bring him relief from the stridency, anger and venom that lay at the root of his political convictions. Robert Lindner, who was an espouser of radical causes, gives a similar account of treating a 'Communist' whom he cured of his politics, in his classic book, *The Fifty-Minute Hour*.[8] Both Antonia and Lindner sought to heal their patients' emotional distress; the shift in their politics was a by-product.

Most of the therapists I spoke to were far more concerned that their patients should end the treatment happier people, with a sense of inner purpose and fulfilment, than that they should become more congenial company. And several described patients who, as their situations improved, started to take up positions that became less and less congenial, not as a reaction to their therapists but because of their backgrounds and the values that had been inculcated into them long before. Myriam had a patient who, while making positive changes, also became increasingly materialistic and conservative politically. 'She was growing into an adult role that involved being able to identify with her parents. It seemed to be very much what she wanted. It was not as if she was becoming sadistic or really awful.' And one of Eve's patients, while becoming better, developed an arrogance that really grated. 'I did not think it was my job to say, "I do not like the way you are turning out, let us shift a little." It came from her. She liked herself. It is a weird feeling when a patient turns out a little more psychopathic or opportunistic than you would like people to be.'

Therapists can no more avoid influencing some of their patients than they can make themselves into blank screens upon which fantasies are projected which have nothing to do with the person who has invited them. Nevertheless, what draws most therapists into the profession is not a desire to preach, but the hope that they can repair emotional damage. For them, what makes therapy an interesting and involving occupation is the discovery of the infinite variety of differences between people. That is what motivates them to do the job. But what is the best way to do the job? What is it that cures in analysis? Is it the insight that the analyst offers the patient, or is it the relationship that develops? How loving must analysts be if they are to heal?

5

The Human Face

Shaping the rules

'THERE is no such thing as psychoanalysis,' I was told by one American professor of psychiatry. 'I had two analyses. They were completely different experiences. The only thing they had in common was the frequency of visits and the fact that they both used the couch. When people ask me whether they should go into psychoanalysis, I ask them "Which one?"'

There are certain other factors common to all analyses. Sessions take place at a fixed time in the day for a certain number of minutes (only Lacanians vary the length of sessions) and on particular days of the week. Analyst and patient each settle into a particular place in the room, whether couch or chair. Holiday breaks are established by the analyst. Unless working for a charitable or public body, the analyst will submit a bill for payment at regular intervals. Beyond that, however, nearly everything is a question of personal style.

Some therapists are happy to hold their patients' hands and offer other forms of consolation, which many others would consider ethical breaches. Some allow themselves at times to express the anger or irritation that the patient makes them feel; others label that 'acting out' and think very poorly of those who do it. Some consider that it is often better to be warm and supportive than eagerly interpretative; others feel that *everything* should always be analyzed. To members of the latter group, the 'analytic stance' has to be held solid against whatever storms rage around them. Otherwise, they argue, what is being talked about is no longer analysis but 'supportive therapy' (which makes patients feel better for a while, but does not touch their deep, long-term problems). The analyst must be seen as a figure of quiet reserve, somehow distant from the patients' turmoil, and able to analyze what is going on for each patient with a measure of quiet objectivity.

But, repeatedly faced with calls for warmth and affection, some therapists find that such aloofness is too hard upon their patients.

They cannot simply reiterate, for example, that patients experience the therapist as cruel and depriving because of something that happened in their past, and that it has nothing to do with what the therapist has done. They look for some means of softening their impact and demonstrating their essential kindliness. Analysis is always an immensely frustrating experience for any patient. Sometimes, when a patient finds that too hard to endure, analysts of a beneficent nature feel that it is right to descend from their pedestals.

Getting therapists to focus on this issue was difficult. Some would refer me to various writers – Wilfred Bion or Patrick Casement, Merton Gill or some other theorist – even though I was clearly asking about how they behaved in the consulting room, not the theoretical position to which *they* aspired. I thought there would be some relationship between an analyst's orientation and his or her practice – Winnicottians, for example, being more 'liberal' than Kleinians or classical Freudians – but I could not assume that the theoretical labels would have the same implications for everyone. My main problem was that, beyond setting themselves apart from the stereotype of a 'classical' analyst – rigid, unresponsive, insensitive – nobody seemed to have any other comparative scale from which to work. Yet analysts clearly do vary in the ways they respond to their patients. What follows is an attempt to elucidate those variations.

Analytic training tends to encourage strict adherence to certain technical principles. In the day-to-day reality of the consulting room, however, many start to question the virtue of sticking by what they have been taught when it does not seem to be the most helpful approach for particular patients. 'I have worked with people for whom therapy would have ground to a halt and terminated if I had not been able to make myself accessible to them in a certain way,' says Henrietta. 'The most important thing,' says Antonia, 'is the therapeutic relationship. A patient may need something more. One is always told that one should not reassure patients; they should leave with their anxiety heightened. There are some people who can cope with that and there are others who cannot. There are some things that I would say or do with one patient that I would not dream of doing with another. I think one has to be very careful that one is not using one's parameters in order to hide one's sadism.'

At some level or other, consciously or unconsciously, all therapists will respond differently to each and every patient. However much they try to stand aloof from the emotions they are trying to examine, it is impossible for them to stay uninvolved. Michael's courtesy towards me is such that I cannot quite imagine him raising his voice, but that is not how all his patients experience him. 'I am very influenced,' he says, 'by the emotional make-up of the patient. There are some patients where I feel it in my voice that I am screeching and I am trying to get through a brick wall, and my mind gets all twisted and the words do not come out. And there are other patients who facilitate the process of taking in information and giving it back.' And the British analyst Joseph Sandler has written that 'any analyst worth his salt will adapt to specific patients on the basis of his interaction with those patients. He will modify his approach so that he can get as good as possible a working analytic situation developing. To achieve this, he needs to feel relaxed and informal with his patient to an appropriate degree, and at times he might have to depart quite far from "standard" procedure.'[1]

But how much should therapists seek to change in response to individual patients? On this question there is considerable disagreement and much scope for misunderstanding. Patrick Casement, for example, acknowledges that people bring different needs to the analytic situation. Some who, as children, failed to secure the strong parenting and discipline required to negotiate their early years with some degree of security, will need to find 'structure'. Where those who cared for them were cold and distant, they may be looking for 'responsiveness'. Where what they felt was intrusion and a lack of privacy, they will require 'space'. One might initially understand Casement as saying that the analyst should constantly tailor different responses to individual patients, according to their individual histories, but the thrust of his argument is to insist that psychoanalysts can never know in any individual case which need requires a response.[2] They cannot decide to be strict with one patient, kind with another, because they cannot know, almost until the treatment is over, what sort of response would be most helpful.

Far better, he says, for the analyst to retain a classical pose of neutrality and let the patient secure their satisfaction from that than to put on a different mask for each individual who comes through the door. For while the analytic encounter may be filled with frustrations, it does provide a set of responses significantly different from any that the patient will have experienced from others in their life. The analyst must listen attentively, always be there for the patient and maintain a non-judgemental pose. Just doing that, it is argued, will provide a corrective to most people's experience of other people, from childhood onwards. 'On the part of the analyst,' Casement writes, 'the meeting of unmet needs in analysis is usually more incidental than deliberate. The analyst, by sticking to his/her analytic task, provides the patient with opportunities for finding what is needed.'³ If the analyst holds to the neutral stance, the patient can use that for whatever it is that they seek. In his books Casement provides some moving examples of how this is achieved.

Jack's position has some similarities to Casement's. He does acknowledge that he treats patients differently according to the feelings that they arouse in him. 'Sometimes,' he says, 'one will respond more assertively. Other times you will take a back seat and keep your mouth shut. If a patient comes and clearly has difficulty with a sense of boundaries, then obviously you become aware of that. You will be far more careful with them over that issue than you might with someone else. Sometimes it is instinctive, at other times it is calculated in relation to a particular patient.'

But that is not, he insists, to imply that he works from an assessment of a central deficiency in the patient's upbringing. The analyst, he feels, simply cannot know what the patient needs. Unlike a doctor who can decide whether a patient with cancer requires surgery or chemotherapy, the analyst has no straightforward set of cures to choose between. Instead, he or she must work towards increasing the patient's understanding. 'How can you be sure,' he asked me, 'that a patient needs distance or structure or responsiveness? How the hell do I know what the patient needs? And if they do not get what they need, what is the implication? Will they die? Will they be dissatisfied? Will they be angry?'

Jack feels strongly that analysts should not respond to their patient's clearly articulated *wants* as if they were *needs* which have to be taken into account. As I struggle with my own confusion about how a therapist distinguishes between what a patient desires – space, structure, responsiveness – and what he or she needs from the therapeutic relationship, he becomes increasingly vociferous. 'Maybe,' he says, 'a patient would be better with structure. What happens if I don't provide them with structure? Will they tell me, "God damn it, give me structure! I need it! Give it to me!" Will they fight with me? Will they get angry? If they do, I analyze that. I say, "How do you feel about my not giving you the structure that you feel you so desperately need?"

'Need implies they are going to die if they don't get it. If you don't feed the baby, it is going to die or be so terribly disrupted or agitated that there will be dire consequences. If you don't hold or kiss or touch a baby, the consequences are dire. I do not think that is the case as long as you attend to the patient's wish for this to happen, and their agitation if you do not provide it. It is not that you are being a cold son of a bitch by design so as to secure a particular reaction. You are doing what you do, and if it is not really what the patient wants, the patient will let you know. Then you respond to that. That is what the analytic experience is all about.'

Where some analysts view their patients as children, Jack sees them very much as adults. He does not believe in 'gratifying' his patients' needs because that would be to 'infantilize' them. He also likes to ensure that his analytic relationships are confined to the consulting room. He will not tolerate patients intruding into his private life and he discourages phone calls to his home. Outside the analytic session, he does not feel any particular responsibility for the sense of despair and helplessness that may come over his patients. I wonder how much of Jack's own reluctance to tolerate his own needs is reflected in the way he approaches his patients. I notice that in one of his articles he writes with admiration of an analyst who could be 'revealing about his feelings' and expresses the view that 'many analysts wish that they too had the courage to acknowledge such sentiments'.

But it is not only Jack who is aroused about the distinction between needs and desires. The issue has divided the psychoanalytic movement ever since Freud discovered that one of his colleagues, Sandor Ferenczi, was hugging his patients, offering to see them at all hours of day or night and arguing that an analyst should only really have one patient to whom he or she should offer sufficient care, affection and love to make up for the lack of emotional nurturing in their early lives. Subsequently, Franz Alexander coined the term 'corrective emotional experience' to describe his own approach, and earned himself the reputation of a heretic. To mention the term to analysts is to see them shiver, as if they fear the Inquisitor is about to come knocking at their door.

Many arguments have been gathered to defend the analytic stance from proponents of the 'corrective emotional experience'. What most frightened Freud about the concept was, perhaps, the danger of malfeasance and the possibility that such unconstrained treatments would bring the whole psychoanalytic movement into disrepute. The emotions stirred up in the consulting room were quite powerful enough without therapists pursuing a course that would increase the dangers of therapeutic abuse. Others have suggested that, while patients might enjoy the 'corrective' experience and feel much better for it, any changes secured will not be long-lasting without the application of analytic procedure. The positive feelings that are generated may also prevent patients from ever expressing the rage and anger they also feel. And some patients, it has been observed, once they see the door opened to gratify their wishes, will never cease asking for more, locking the analyst into a spiral of increasingly urgent demands.

And it is impossible, anyway, for patients who are now adult truly to relive their childhood experience. Therapists cannot make up for rejecting mothers, absent fathers or deficient lovers; they can only offer deeper understanding to the patient who has been damaged. The effort to rectify emotional deficits by assuming the antithetical stance to those earlier figures would, in any case, be at too much cost to analysts, who would have to adopt a position that was calculated and contrived, lacking naturalness, authenticity or spontaneity.

Harold was the only analyst I met who embraced the term 'corrective emotional experience' as a description of what he offered to his patients. 'You are enacting a certain role with each patient,' he argued. 'If somebody has had a very indulgent past, for example, and has been taught to see himself as a prince, and is angry most of the time because the world does not treat him in that way, I am going to be very careful about being too indulgent with him. This is the kind of person, for example, with whom I would bring it up if they did not pay me at the end of the month. I would behave very differently towards someone whose father was very stingy and who felt he was entitled to next to nothing.'

Harold has two pictures on his wall. One is of Freud, the other is of his follower Theodor Reik. Both are images of kindliness matching the impression made by Harold himself, with his warm smile and gentle gaze. He uses the heavy black shoes he wears to push back his hard wooden chair to the point where he seems about to collapse embarrassingly on to the floor. Everything he says reveals the pleasure he takes in what he does. At the beginning of our interview he expresses concern about other analysts who do not permit themselves to enjoy their work.

Unlike Jack, Harold views his patients as grown-up children. He compares his role to that of a parent. 'In both cases you are helping someone mature. One of my major convictions is that you should always be working with the child in the adult. The more that the adult can show me the child, and the more that I can relate to that child, the more comfortable I am working with the patient.' He admits that he is not very good with people who find it difficult to talk about their fantasies and dreams. He wants patients to feel free to play in therapy, 'to divulge the most embarrassing, shameful and hostile material, and to be at their angriest, their sexiest, their most bizarre'. By his choice of adjectives, Harold reveals his view of the psychoanalyst's function as being to enable patients to break through taboos and get down to deep material that he assumes will be messy, dark and far from conformity with an idealized vision of humanity.

To illustrate the way he adapts his approach to fit particular patients, Harold describes the case of a woman who seemed from the outset inhibited and afraid. He had proposed for the first time that she lie on the couch. 'Within a few moments she was screaming and yelling. It is the last thing in the world she would do.' The discussion of why his proposal so enraged her brought up the fact that she had experienced all kinds of sexual abuse from her father.

Harold discussed the resentment she felt against both her father and, by proxy, the threatening analyst. But exploring the roots of her feelings was not, he felt, enough. 'You can explain something, but it will mean nothing unless you really show her by your behaviour. I have to show the woman who was frightened I was going to exploit her and force her to lie on the couch that she does not have to do what she thinks I am insisting that she do. I want her to talk about all the ways she feels I am going to exploit her and show her how she is turning every man into an exploitative father. But I do that more by my conduct, by showing interest and understanding.'

It strikes me that, although Harold bravely embraces the term 'corrective emotional experience', what he offers his patients may not differ all that much from what more overtly classical analysts could be expected to provide. They too would reveal by their neutrality that they were not about to leap on the patient and abuse her, and the sort of response that Harold described stands well within traditional boundaries. To find out from other analysts how much, if at all, they would vary their stance in response to a particular patient, I presented them with an account of the case described by Harold – the timid patient seemingly afraid of molestation by her therapist.

Robert has a consulting room in his own apartment. His wife, who is in the same profession, works there too. When I arrive, I accidentally press her bell rather than his. Having pushed my way through the main door, and taken a look at the screen that separates the private areas of the house from the waiting area, I am summoned by the disembodied voice of a woman. I turn to explain my mistake but, of course, there is no one there. Is there any way to communicate my error? Should I open one of the two doors in front of me? Where should I go? Fortunately, a man comes to the door and introduces himself.

Robert sits me in a chair on the other side of the large room in which he works. I have never before sat so far away from anyone to do an interview, and the distance between us seems to represent the metaphorical space that Robert likes to put between himself and his patients. The couch, however, is in the traditional position, close by his chair. My eyes are drawn to the disparate, cluttered array of art Robert has on the wall behind him: Indian carvings, a garish painting in oils and no less than four pictures of Freud.

An 'orthodox Freudian', Robert conforms to the stereotype of an analyst by wearing a beard and smoking a pipe. Describing himself as naturally 'reserved and somewhat detached', he follows a model of analysis in which patients conduct an exploration of themselves, rather than being instructed by the therapist in their inner world. He jokes that reformed schizoids make the best analysts. 'You have to have a kind of capacity for detachment while being involved simultaneously,' he says. Analysts, in his view, should say very little and intrude their personality hardly at all into the analytic process.

Asked about how responsive he is to different patients, he says that he will change his approach, but insists that these are only 'micro-changes'. If a patient is at a stage when a lot of infantile material is coming to the surface and starts to ask questions, he might choose to give an answer to him or her. 'Not because I think that the question is so much more valuable than the ones I did not answer before,' he says, 'but because I know that not answering the question will promote more regression. I may decide to be un-analytic, but it is the tiniest possible departure from the analytic stance I could make.'

As for the behaviour I describe to him, he cannot see that it would affect his technique. The way I put the question implies that I know what might motivate such behaviour. He would not be so sure, and this refusal to accept an easy correlation between symptom and meaning, holding to the position that behind every attitude and action is a deep mystery, marks his overall approach. 'You are saying,' he says, ' "Here is a behaviour, what is your tactic?" ' The trouble is that the same behaviour might mean different things with different people. Let us say that this woman who seems to be in such terror is actually quite masochistic and deriving a secondary gain from being so frightened. She may be somebody who is essentially quite deceptive and not at all frightened, but uses that form of behaviour as a way of neutralizing anything you might do. You could take five patients and say here is the same behaviour, but each behaviour may serve a different place

99

in the dynamic economy of that person.' Those who do not practise psychoanalysis may share my initial reluctance to accept that people are quite so complex. Psychoanalysis is built around a recognition that they are, and that it takes many hours of exploration to uncover what motivates a person's behaviour.

To Robert, it is that search for understanding which distinguishes analysis from other therapies. He dismisses analysts who think that what happens in the relationship between analyst and patient is part of the cure, asserting that they have a need to think themselves important to their patients. An analyst, in his view, must always analyze. Say a patient tells him a joke. His job is to find out what the humour means for the patient and the function it has in his or her emotional armoury. 'I had a patient,' he says, 'who was very funny. He always used some kind of joke to disarm the process. I said to him that despite the fact that I had no choice but to laugh, it was disturbing to me that we should end the investigation of what was going on with that. I wished I could resist the laughing because I was sure that if I did that, it would not be as easy for him to be funny instead of serious. Eventually he was able to become more serious about why he had to be funny.'

Robert notices that his account leaves me somewhat sceptical – not so much about the possibility that laughter could perform the defensive role he describes, but about whether it really would benefit the patient for his analyst not to laugh at the jokes he tells. The aim of such self-control is to force the patient to look at why he needs people to crease up around him, but the failure to secure a response to one's thoroughly honed comic technique could be deeply hurtful. Robert insists that his restraint is important because it would open the gateway to understanding. 'Suppose,' he argues, 'you had a patient who was hysterically funny because that is the way he or she defends against deep feelings of humiliation. When you realize that, the jokes are no longer funny to you, even though they were the first few times the patient told them to you, before you understood their deep sense of shame.' I can see the point he is making, but I do not feel completely happy with the principle of self-restraint that he espouses. Bringing the patient to self-understanding must be the goal, but I wonder whether it really has to be pursued so remorselessly at the price of deep distress.

Stephen too is a classical analyst. His room feels more like an office and he is dressed in a formal suit. Most of our interview is conducted against competition from a noisy air-conditioning system. Like Robert, Stephen disapproves of the idea that the analyst is a wise person who can divine what is happening in the unconscious, then straighten things out by presenting that information to the patient. The aim of the analytic process, as he sees it, is to enable patients to understand themselves. Stephen describes his aim as being to teach patients to do their own analysis. 'I want the patient to learn how to do what I do, so that they can take over for the rest of their lives. I do not control the process for them, I let them do it. The whole strategy is to help the person to become what you know how to be, which is a self-analytic person.'

I asked Stephen whether he would respond differently to a patient who seemed excessively compliant and one who was fearful, like the woman whom Harold had described. Having developed an interest in Wilhelm Reich's analysis of character types, Stephen has more of a system within which to fit the patients he sees. Perhaps because of this, he seemed less unwilling than Robert to draw provisional conclusions from the way patients presented themselves and to build the analytic process out from there.

'With the compliant patient,' he says, 'I would say, "You seem quite resigned to the idea that I am asking you to lie on the couch. I wonder if you have any thoughts about that and about the feeling of heaviness you are giving off." To the second patient I might say, "You seem quite fearful, and I wonder whether you do not think that something terrible is going to happen to you if you lie down." That will become the starting point for the analysis. If the second patient can talk about the burden of life, feeling always the victim, only pleasing others and the kind of relationship she had with a parent that made her feel so frightened to allow herself to be in somebody else's hands, fearing disaster, catastrophe and terrible disintegration, that will take us to the area of her central conflicts.'

Stephen is also keener than Robert to concede that there are times when the analytic stance has to be abandoned in order to minimize discomfort. Even so, it is not a step that he would take lightly. 'If I evaluate that the patient needs something from me at a particular time,' he says, 'and I think that the patient will probably suffer more damage if I do not provide that gratification than if I did, then I will make that gratification. I will then have to work on that with the patient.' He emphasizes that what analysts must be careful not to do is to act in their own interests – because, for example, it is too painful watching the patient suffer.

He tells me about a patient who, towards the end of a session, had described a night when, walking down a street with his young daughter, he had a heart attack and collapsed in front of her. As the man spoke of the awful experience he had forced her to endure, he began to cry. He imagined his daughter in a panic, dumb with terror, not knowing where to turn for help. 'He could not stop crying,' Stephen recalls. 'We were at the end of a session. I fetched him a glass of water and offered him my office for as long as he needed it. He spent another five or 10 minutes there. When we talked about it later, he was very grateful to me for that.'

Like Robert and Stephen, Jo considers that interpretation is the defining activity of psychoanalysis, but he puts more emphasis than Stephen does on the healing role played by a consistent analytic stance, characterized by 'patience, tolerance, regularity, predictability, reliability and empathy'. When I present him with the two cases I had described to Stephen, his answer initially emphasizes his responsiveness to their behaviour rather than the maintenance of an analytical position. The positive impression this makes on me is mitigated by his habit of using the plural pronoun, as if I had asked him to speak for the whole psychoanalytic community rather than for himself. Meeting him at his home on a Sunday morning, he impresses me as a strong personality, ambitious and successful.

'I think,' he says, 'that someone who is very anxious and timid may make us a little bit more cautious, even tempt us to be a bit more reassuring, a bit more careful about what the situation is, and perhaps more cautious about not arousing more anxiety by premature or too rapid or too deep an interpretative process. With the patient who is more compliant, one would probably be more attuned to following their responses to interpretations. One would have to watch that they are really absorbing the insights that are offered. There would be variations in how silent one is, how talkative one is, the range and depth and rapidity of interpretations. That does not mean one abandons the analytic stance.'

Having said this, Jo worries that in his self-appointed position as spokesman for psychoanalysis in New York he has conceded too much. 'If the analyst were to speak carefully, softly and delicately because the patient was very anxious,' he continues, 'the patient might become more so. They might feel that the analyst had become afraid, sharing the patient's own anxieties that they were too fragile. One has to push a bit more. One must not avoid threatening ideas and issues. The best position in my opinion is to remain relatively neutral and to deal with the anxiety by clarifying it.'

However different the emphases placed by Jo, Stephen and Robert when they describe their analytic technique, their basic position is that analysts, while acknowledging that they will inadvertently be influenced by the different characters of their patients, should otherwise change hardly at all in response to individual patients. Such change is dangerous both because of the likelihood that they are doing it to relieve their own discomfort, and because it is impossible to know prior to the conclusion of the analysis what sort of modified approach will be most useful. As human beings, they will modulate their response to particular patients, but as analysts they must offer themselves as a firm rock against which their patients' waves of emotion can splash and break. To do otherwise – to decide that the timid patient needed a special sign that the analyst would not intrude and impinge, or that a deliberately playful approach would help to bring out the compliant patient – would be to pre-empt the analysis and limit the possibility of leading the patient to self-understanding. There is something about this approach that seems to me a little timid and over-cautious. I feel they may be playing safe to the detriment of their patients and wonder whether they are as abstemious in practice as they claim to be.

Although himself classically trained, George is no longer completely happy with this model of analysis. Classical analysts, in his view, act in a rigid and rehearsed way because they are afraid of making themselves too vulnerable. He offers a somewhat caricatured description of their behaviour: 'They really believe you can help your patients by never shaking their hand, not calling them by their first name and crossing to the other side of the street when you see them coming towards you.' Analysts who behave in such a way and emphasize their need to keep a distance between themselves and their patients are, he says, ignoring 'the utter aloneness of being human, the fear of abandonment'.

There are people who respond to the classical method, George says, but they are not the majority of patients. He sometimes jokes with his students that he knows when he has such a case because he starts to feel guilty that he is not doing anything. 'In the course of 20 years,' he claims, 'I have had four or five such cases. They were clearly Oedipal. They were clearly able to use the couch. They needed some help from me to get going, but then they were able to do it on their own. They were able to experience loving me and hating me without terrific swings either way. It is nice when it goes that way.'

But an experience very early on in his years of practice convinced George that many patients might need something else. The analysis had been 'limping along'. In fact, it was going so badly that George, in desperation, asked the patient why he felt they were getting nowhere.

The patient replied, 'When you are silent, it is just like how I grew up. My father never talked to me, he only gave commands. And my mother was also very quiet.' George was very impressed by this response. 'This man had always lived with flatness and deadness.' When George kept on saying, 'How do you feel about that?', or not responding, the patient was, in fact, perpetuating his childhood experience. He became a much more responsive, talkative therapist with such patients. This reflects, it may be said, his lively nature.

On another occasion, also early on in his practice, George suddenly stood up and whisked his patient out of the consulting room – an event unheard of in the experience of any classical analyst. The young man was very thin and often complained about headaches. The idea came to George that he should take him around the corner for a cup of coffee and a doughnut. When they returned to the consulting room, the patient's headache had disappeared. The cause, it turned out, had been basic hunger, as this patient had never learned how to feed himself. The roots of this inadequacy lay in the fact that the patient's mother had taken hours every night to prepare dinner. When the meal arrived, it was always very scant. A typical meal would consist of one veal chop, a single vegetable and a potato. Each gathering at the dinner table was accompanied by furious rows between husband and wife. By a simple, instinctive act, George had unearthed information which it might otherwise have taken many sessions to reach. He acknowledges that it would have been better if they could have reached the same point through words alone. On this occasion, however, a spontaneous action brought enlightenment.

George's tale suggests that analysts who cannot follow any instincts that lead away from analytic orthodoxy miss out on opportunities to shift the treatment process when it becomes stuck. Holding to the analytic stance may be an ideal, but there may be circumstances when it is counterproductive, or just not particularly useful.

Like maintaining one's anonymity behind a blank screen, holding to the analytic stance at all costs is unnecessary, and for much the same reasons. Analysis is a rule-framed encounter, and is perceived as such by the patient. Therefore, a small infraction of the rules can have an enormous impact, without leading on to a form of anarchy in which analytic work comes to a stop. When I asked my own therapist if I could meet her outside the consulting room, at a coffee shop perhaps, that was not a request to which she could have sensibly acceded. Nor do I think it would have served much purpose. Had she, however, proposed out of the blue that we have a session in a café, I would have been bowled over. Recognizing the strangeness of the proposal, I would have been grateful for the fact that she had agreed to infract the rules in order to show me at a stroke that she knew what I was feeling. I would not have expected her to repeat such a strange act, but my attitude to her and the therapy would have been transformed.

Many of the analysts I spoke to were struggling to find a workable balance between warmth and coldness. They acknowledged anonymity as a goal, but as one that must never be attained. They thought it was probably necessary to establish different sorts of relationships with their patients in response to their needs and past experiences. They felt that they should reveal information whose concealment would seem callous, but not so much that the consulting room ceased to be an arena for fantasy and replaying early life. Warmth, compassion and sympathy had to be balanced against coolness, deprivation and frustration. Analysis could not, in the long run, be all analysis. It is sometimes important simply to show oneself as a natural and spontaneous human being.

William used to be convinced that the success or failure of an analysis depended on the analyst making correct interpretations, and that anything which imperilled analytic accuracy put the whole process in jeopardy. 'At the time I believed that who you were, how you manifested yourself and how you expressed yourself was of little or no consequence.' But he has come to recognize that such purism may work against relief of his patients' suffering. 'As time has gone on,' he says, 'personal chemistry has come to seem increasingly important to me. I am less and less inclined to write it off.'

Older models of analytic theory posit a situation in which patients have emotional reactions and analysts remain impassive. More recent thinking derives from, and seeks to capitalize on, the idea that therapy is a complex, multi-faceted and flexible relationship. Sidney, whose gentle manner belies a physique suggestive of an army general or tough union negotiator, is one of those who conceive of analysis as an 'interpersonal' process. It was the experience of his own analyst which ensured that he never tried to assume a distant and aloof stance. He recalls going to see him after a period of military service. The analyst stood at the door with his pipe in his hand and said, 'My God, you look wonderful.' The genuineness of that reaction, Sidney feels, provided one of the most significant lessons in his eight years of analysis. He also remembers a time when he made a critical remark about the analyst's wife. The reply came back, 'You do not have to be with her, I do.' Sidney was, he says, 'both appalled that he had become angry with me, and at the same time pleased that I was able to reach him on a human level so that he responded as a person, as a man, not just as an analyst who would hear everything and react in an intellectual way'.

In general, analysts who work with very disturbed patients will be more likely to respond to the pathology, the background and the expectations that each patient brings into the consulting room. The struggle that such treatments involve forces therapists to develop every tactic they can to help their patients. In the presence of great need, some therapists feel called upon to modulate their behaviour. Cathy is one of several therapists who made clear her distress at the suffering sometimes caused by misguided adherence to orthodoxy. She has a patient who wants her to sit in a position where she can see her. 'I always do,' she says. 'I do it because it is comforting for her, but I make sure that she knows why she needs me to do it. We have talked about it. She wants to be special to me. She wants somehow or other to distinguish herself from the other people that I see. She has always felt incredibly unspecial and terribly deprived. With me she has been able to recognize that she is quite greedy.'

'To be a good therapist,' Edwina insists in a clear challenge to the concept that the analytic stance should be maintained at all costs, 'you must become a chameleon, although hopefully with a core self.' She observes that the pauses and silences that some people have learned to expect of a therapist are considered rude, cruel and depriving by those less well-prepared. In a similar vein, the American analyst Michael Eigen has written, 'I do not have a party line, a dogma about just how I am supposed to be with every patient. I am willing to shift ground, try different styles, try to locate some way of being/experiencing that might work. I do not like getting boxed in to any particular version of myself.'4 The testimony of these analysts seems to put the analytic purism of their colleagues dealing with less disturbed patients into serious question. Perhaps the flexibility which the severely damaged require would also benefit those who are only slightly wounded? The classical analyst might reply that less disturbed patients don't need that sort of response. Those of their patients who feel frustrated by the analyst's distance and aloofness might disagree.

Of all the possible departures from the analytic frame, none terrifies classical analysts as much as the suggestion that they should touch their patients. Many fear, as Freud did, that such a concession would cause the whole profession to be written off as a disgrace. They see touch as the road to countless horrifying abuses. The British therapist Peter Lomas writes, 'The fear that those who need help may manipulate the helper into undue permissiveness haunts the mind of the therapist.'5 After all, most therapists are already considered unclean in the eyes of the public. Have not American movies, such as Robert Altman's *Beyond Therapy* and Marshall Brickman's *Lovesick*, played, albeit in somewhat facile ways, with the idea that therapists almost invariably sleep with their more attractive patients? Why give that idea any additional credence?

Others are terrified at what they might do if they once allowed themselves to break the rules against touch. For Benjamin, those ordinances are there to protect him from wrongdoing and his patients from abuse. He insists on maintaining two yards distance between himself and his female patients. 'I am heterosexual,' he declares. 'I have some very attractive female patients. And they often have fantasies about me that have nothing to do with who I really am. When they start lusting after me, I lust after them. We live in a primitive body. This drive to reproduce our genes is so strong. If a male therapist gets chatted up by an attractive, intelligent and sensitive woman, and he gives her a cuddle because she is crying bitterly, that can be very dangerous. The realization that you are not, for example, the man she is going to marry, that your hug was pure compassion and not lust as well, that can kill her.' With touching frankness, Benjamin admits at the end of the interview that he is looking for a new wife. 'It is not very easy if you are a therapist, but you do not give up.'

But is it really wise to keep such a natural and normal part of human relating out of the analytic encounter? 'There is so much anxiety about sexual contact in the therapeutic interaction,' says Sidney, whose interest in the subject may reflect the fact that he does not look like the sort of man who finds it easy to give or receive physical affection, 'that we have neglected the fact that touch is one of the most important aspects of human relationships. We do not know how to integrate it into the process so that it is not part of the therapist's own personal gratifications, but can be helpful to the patient. There is a taboo on discussing the subject, but we need to know when to touch patients and when to allow them to touch us.'

The strength of this taboo was brought home to Sidney during an international conference in Helsinki when he was having a few drinks with the British analyst Herbert Rosenfeld.

'Do you ever touch your patients?' Sidney asked.

'No. That is not acceptable,' came the reply.

'But look, you work with very disturbed patients. Are you really telling me you never have any physical contact with your patients?'

'That is right.'

Sidney let the matter drop for a while. The two men stayed at the bar. Each had two or three more drinks. Finally Rosenfeld came back with a different answer.

'Of course I touch my patients,' he confided. 'There are times when it is absolutely necessary. But you know you really should not talk about this.'

One suspects that there are many other therapists who say that they would never touch a patient but who will in fact do so under certain circumstances. Where a severely psychotic patient repeatedly begs for a hug, they will perhaps offer an outstretched hand to hold. Donald Winnicott argued that a well-placed interpretation could be more 'holding' than being physically held, but one of his patients describes an experience of analysis with him in which 'through many long hours he held my two hands clasped behind his, almost like an umbilical cord'.[6] Antonia says that, despite the rule against physical contact, 'there may be a patient for whom a hand on the head at moments of great distress is more important than anything I could say'.

Analysts can respond to a patient's call for touch without bringing the analytic process to a grinding halt, as long as their response falls some way short of the demand. Having their wish only partially gratified leaves patients frustrated at not getting what they want, and they are left to think further about the strength of their need, searching within themselves for the inner strength to contain its destructive force. They do not stop experiencing the original deprivation which left them feeling hurt and damaged. Despite touching them, the analyst makes it possible for the patient eventually to learn to do without that touch. Antonia makes this point when she describes working with a woman who had been sexually abused as a child. She begged her therapist to hug her. Antonia responded by placing a hand on her shoulder. 'It's true,' she says, 'that what that did, by relieving the pain, was to stop her going through what she should be going through. But doing that was the most important thing at the time.' One day, towards the end of the therapy, the patient revealed her fantasy that at the end of her last session she would finally get her hug. 'She turned her head and smiled at me,' Antonia recalls, 'and said, "The point is that by the time the last session comes, I will not need you to hug me. I know you will have hugged me the whole time."'

Some therapists take it as axiomatic that patients will only come to understand their needs if their wants remain completely unsatisfied. But for some patients it may only be through receiving a response, however partial, to their expression of desire that they can learn to trust the analyst enough to start the process of inner exploration. Jack argues that a firm line has to be drawn between wants and needs, lest the satisfaction of the former puts a stop to the exploration of the latter. But the impossibility of the therapist ever fully satisfying the patients' wants means that it will always be possible to go on and analyze their needs. And since the two are inextricably intertwined, responding to one may assist understanding of the other.

The British therapist Roderick Peters has described the case of a middle-aged woman whose need was so great that he could not refuse her demand for physical holding, something he had never done with any previous patient.[7] She lived in complete isolation, having no contact with family or friends. She came to see him five times a week, but constantly complained that this was not enough. Her demands were overwhelming. She wanted him to hug her day and night, eat with her, sleep with her and give her his undivided attention. He responded to her sense of deep despair. For a year, patient and therapist held hands throughout their sessions together and he looked into her eyes.

'I incarnated the good mother with her newborn baby, just as much as anyone could with an often mad, 45-year-old, red-haired bundle of trouble,' he says. 'Whenever I frustrated her, which was a daily inevitability because I refused to hug her, quite apart from a host of other frustrations, I abruptly became the cruellest object that ever existed. I was a spider, a Nazi, a scorpion, and was treated accordingly. Within a space of 10 minutes I might see her eyes gazing at me with pathetic, searching appeal, then see them dim over with terrible uncomprehending, incomprehensible hurt and bewilderment. Then see her fury gather in her brows and her eyes lancing me with hatred.' Gradually, after a series of tempestuous battles in which clothes were torn, blows were exchanged and the patient was sometimes physically pushed out of the room, Peters weaned her from her need for physical touch.

It is, as this case illustrates, the patients who call out most desperately for physical affection who are also those most likely to turn on their therapists and attack them. Having idealized the therapist as the good parent they never had, they will also turn on that same therapist as the bad parent they had to endure. They will spit and threaten, conveying hatred, mistrust and fury with every word and gesture. How should therapists respond to such an onslaught? Should they simply endure, calm and impassive, for as long as the storm lasts? Should they endure up to a certain point and then say stop? Or should they join in the slanging match?

For the classical analyst the position is clear. Listen to what the patient says, then formulate a view upon it that will help the patient understand why he or she feels so angry. 'Say the patient is being tremendously provocative,' says Robert, 'wants to needle you, get you irritated. A good analyst does not get irritated; it is part of your analytic function to see that this person, for some reason or another, is being immensely provocative today. Instead of being provoked – he can find umpteen people among his family and friends who will get stirred up – you have to hold that, feel it for what it is and formulate something about it.'

One wonders how often such cool interpretations have further stoked a patient's rage? How infuriating to have one's angriest outbursts met by the calm distillation of another person's intellect. The patient wants to get under the skin of analyst, but nothing said or done has any impact. The analyst, it seems, is wafting on the clouds above. Is it not far better for analysts to show that they are touched? To declare that although, like a 'good enough' parent, they can tolerate the fury vented upon them, there is a place beyond which they cannot go, at which they will say 'Stop!'

'There is a point,' says Sidney, 'where, as human beings, we have to say, "That's enough."' He tells me about an analyst whose patient would spend the session banging his forehead with his fist. Finally, after a number of sessions had gone on this way, the analyst yelled 'Stop that!' The patient asked 'Why?' The answer was, 'Because I can't stand it.' Sidney also told me the story of a patient who, when told to stop what he was doing, sat up and said, 'At last! At last somebody is telling me what I am doing wrong.'

George considers that those analysts who will not let their reaction to anger show through are denying their own humanity out of a need to present themselves as all-good analysts. 'At times,' he says, 'I have got angry with patients. They are able to cope with that. I might say, "Bullshit, I don't believe that at all." When you do that, you have to be sure that the patient knows you basically care for him. That the anger comes out of a basic connectedness. I have to be careful when I get angry. I ask myself, "Did I eat well? Am I angry with someone else?" People have to confront each other in strengthening ways. You must not, however, hurt someone's feelings or damage their sense of self-worth.'

Patients who drive analysts towards a confrontational stance seek to make up for a lack in their past, as do those who call out for physical affection. The growing child needs discipline as it needs care; in a way one is the paternal and the other the maternal version of love. Those analysts who respond to their patients' outbursts must carefully measure the degree to which they respond with aggression as with physical comfort. Just as analysts must not suggest that they are going to satisfy all the patient's demands for affection, so, when it comes to confrontation, they must wait long enough to provide a guarantee that they are not hitting back out of hate and helplessness. The patients must feel that the anger is for real, but experience the difference between it and what they experienced in the past.

Andrea has a patient, the daughter of a psychoanalyst, who is very confrontational. Her opening gambit ran something like this:

'I know you are a Lacanian. Lacanian theory is rubbish.'

'So why are you here?' Andrea replied.

'Because all the other things are no better. But this won't work for me either.'

Andrea calmly pointed out to the patient that she had put herself in a contradictory position by asking for help from someone she believed could not provide it. The patient went on trying to irritate her, using her attacks on Lacan as a way of avoiding the need to confront her own material. However angry this made her, for a long while Andrea did not express her irritation. To have done so would probably have recapitulated the patient's experience of her mother. She contradicted her lightly, responded with humour to her attacks and made a few other minor interventions. But the point came when it seemed right to confront the patient with her self-destructive behaviour.

'I could do that,' Andrea says, 'simply because I had waited so long. It was almost a relief for us. Had I done it earlier, it would have been a disaster. So I let her attack. I waited until she had shown that I could survive her attempts to destroy me and that I was not the same as the parent she had taken me for. She had the certainty that when I confronted her, I was not going to attempt to destroy her.'

Charles, a follower of Hyman Spotnitz's school of 'modern' psychoanalysis, believes that an important part of the analyst's function is to explore and resolve the resistances to expressing the aggression which patients have stored up from the period of their infancy, before they had the words and symbols to understand their feelings. His technique facilitates the patient's access to primitive experiences of anger and aggression. Through this approach, the patient can ultimately begin to relax his defences against libidinal expression and intimacy.

He illustrates his method by describing the case of a patient who appears determined not to stay in analysis. He comes five times a week, at his own request, but always complains about the difficulty of getting to the consulting room, how much of his time is taken up with the analysis, and the cost involved. Sometimes he will announce that he wants to stop.

Charles judges that the patient, by trying to repudiate him, is repeating a pattern of rejecting people that runs through his life. In an attempt to make the patient aware of this he might say, 'How come I have not been consulted on this decision?'

The patient, Charles argues, would be made aware by this response about his own rejecting anger towards the therapist. Since he did not really want to leave, he might say:

'Just because I bring up that I want to leave, you are getting angry and hostile at me. I don't think that is helpful.'

Charles would then seek to make his insight register more deeply. 'Why shouldn't I be angry? I am not consulted. I am pushed around. I have no say in the matter.'

Charles believes that occasionally the overt articulation by a therapist of feelings stirred up in the therapeutic encounter helps patients to resolve their resistance to expressing what they feel.[8] As he talks, I gain the impression that during his years as a corporate man the game-playing of business life stirred increasing resentment. Having found an outlet for his repressed anger in therapy, in a context which took the cork out of his own bottle, he wants to offer the same release to others.[9]

His approach comes close to non-analytic therapies which encourage patients to 'express' their anger, and it is subject to the same charge that it can be brutal and sadistic, throttling the autonomy of patients by directing their feelings in a single direction. I heard a possibly apocryphal tale of a Spotnitzian who turned on the air-conditioner full blast shortly before the arrival of a patient who was sensitive to cold temperatures. It was the only way she could see to elicit his emotions.

But at the heart of Charles's technique is the insight that some patients will simply clam up if they are confronted by a silent and unresponsive therapist. If the therapist does not respond to their expressions of love or hate, that may leave them not relieved but confused. They do not want to launch themselves at a paper cut-out. Considering that they are in a real relationship, not just reliving infantile emotions, they consider that their feelings have something to do with the person they are with. They want that person to respond.

Different patients need different levels of responsiveness from their analysts. One would like to believe that everyone finds the analyst whose individual style best suits their personality and their pathology, someone with whom they can feel comfortable. What probably happens is that they either have a totally frustrating and very painful experience which brings no significant benefits, or they simply become accustomed to whatever is offered. They know what to expect and adapt accordingly. If a classical analyst, under the impact of an attack of dyspepsia, were to scream out, 'I just can't stand it any more,' the effect on the analytic relationship might well be devastating. But if the pattern had been confrontational from the beginning, the reaction would be, 'There he goes again.' In analysis there are, perhaps, few ultimate taboos. Each analyst must define his or her own set of rules.

6

Tricks of Fantasy

A way into the unconscious

DURING many of the hours they spend in their consulting rooms therapists do not have a clue what is going on. 'It takes a long time,' says Harold, 'to know what motivates someone unconsciously, and what causes him or her to behave the way they do with you.' He describes without any evident embarrassment two occasions when he blundered on for an age in almost total ignorance. In one case, a patient came to see him four times a week, but would not reveal his name. In another a woman visited him three times a week for six months without ever uttering a word. 'She would get red in the face,' he recalls, 'and that was about it.' These are extreme examples, but 'a certain amount of ignorance is always present', he admits.

Unlike Harold many therapists find it hard to accept that they must grope so long before getting a handle on their patients' reality. 'We cannot go out in the streets and admit that we are terribly ignorant,' says Max, who sometimes wonders whether analysts will not look back in 50 years and remark that their predecessors were blithering idiots, unable to see the obvious before their eyes. Because this uncertainty is so difficult to tolerate, some are driven to declare their convictions with more dogmatic certainty than the evidence justifies and to claim that they have access to a body of knowledge which can be directly applied to all the phenomena brought before them.

Any claims to knowledge on the part of the therapist are precarious. Those who forget this can be drawn into asserting their own authority and that of their theoretical system against patients, cajoling and bullying when they should more properly seek to persuade. The good therapist, however, must accept that he or she starts from a position of knowing nothing, and go on to work out theory anew in each specific case. How therapists build on this acceptance of ignorance is the main subject of this chapter. It concludes by examining the interest in inner fantasy that too often leads therapists to ignore patients' accounts of their own experiences, and the difficulty of sorting out reality from fantasy when talking to adult patients about the possibility that they were abused as children.

A willingness to accept that one does not know has been described by one British analyst as 'an accomplishment' and a 'necessary condition for the analytic endeavour'.[1] It contains an acknowledgement that every individual is unique and that it is the analyst's job to be curious about difference, not obsessed with similarity. There is no map into which each person can be fitted and from which can be deduced cause, effect and cure. Wilfred Bion described analysis as an encounter between 'two rather frightened people'. If they are not both frightened, he wrote, 'one wonders why they are bothering to find out what everybody knows'. The uncertainty that patients have about the cause of their psychological ills should be mirrored by their analysts. They should assume that coming to know the person in front of them will be a difficult and uncertain task. This is an idea that is reflected in many of the remarks made by the classical analysts quoted in the previous chapter, and echoed by the British analyst Nina Coltart when she wrote that 'in all of us there are some things which will never be within our reach; there is always a mystery at the heart of every person, and therefore in our job as analysts'.[2]

What analysts have to offer, then, is not a diagnostic manual, but a technique for exploring the complexity within each individual. They know a way to get at the history underlying the symptoms that drive people into their consulting rooms. Although that knowledge is rooted in the study of numerous other case histories, the classificatory schemes evolved by psychoanalysis are no more than aids to understanding. Attaching labels like 'narcissist' or 'schizoid' to patients provides only the loosest hints as to what lies behind their unique stories.

Analysts invite their patients to offer up memories, dreams, fantasies and any other sort of information which they may consider of possible help in their joint enterprise. They listen to what is offered, measure the material against their past experience and their understanding of theory, and proceed from there to offer interpretations, which are hopefully more than guesswork, but are nevertheless far from definitive. Most analysts put forward such interpretations tentatively, knowing that they may be wrong, that they may have to withdraw and start again. 'I fall down many times,' says Michael. 'I often do not understand what the patient is saying or trying to say. My interpretations are often clumsy, wide of the mark. I just hope that more often than not they are appropriate and accurate, and that the patient learns something from them.' Not all analysts were as disarmingly honest as Michael, and I had to hope that, to themselves at least, they could acknowledge their limitations.

Patients do not present themselves like books, waiting to be opened and read. They display a range of attitudes and behaviours, metamorphosing before the therapist's eyes as treatment progresses and the relationship deepens. Each shift represents another facet of their personality that the analyst must take in and assess. Just how unnerving a process this can be was illustrated for me when I attended a seminar given by Arthur Robbins, a sculptor and analyst in New York. He talked about a particular case to demonstrate how he takes his bearings on a patient by reading the visual clues that he or she gives off and the feelings stirred inside him. The summary below reveals how, over the course of a long treatment, patients can turn different faces towards their analysts. This multi-dimensional aspect to human character helps explain why analysts must regard their patients' material as essentially mysterious.

From his second-floor office, Arthur saw a woman drive up in an open-top sports car with the radio blaring. Her manner, as she slammed the door and walked up to the building, exuded the self-confidence of the *femme fatale* in a 1950s' movie. For most of the first session she spoke to him in hushed tones about her husband, a policeman, who was beating her up. The atmosphere suggested a conspiracy that might very well evolve along the lines of *The Postman Always Rings Twice*. 'I was going to help plan a murder,' he recalled. 'I was very interested. We arranged to meet three times a week.'

Arthur could have anticipated from her *femme fatale* manner that the air of confidence and trust would not endure. Their understanding quickly fell apart and, for a while, every interpretation he offered was aggressively shot down. 'That is not it. What a stupid thing to say,' she would snap back at him. Although he longed to help her, for three months he spoke hardly a word. She was in control and he would go through sessions with the sensation that a cat was clawing at his face.

Then one day the mood changed. Instead of snapping at him, she ranted, reproaching him for the long silences. 'Why am I here?' she wailed. 'You do nothing but sit and stare at me.' With tears in her eyes, she started to tell him about the enormous changes that had taken place in her life since therapy began. She had left her husband but her children were screwing up at school, and she was worried about them. Arthur was struck by her helplessness. He felt like Dr Higgins – responsible for the lost waif he had found on the streets.

The patient now took him deeper into her story. Her mother had been frequently depressed and her father used to molest her. To escape his sexual intrusions, she had joined up with a gang of toughs. Arthur learned from this that the patient needed to be offered an alternative model of fatherhood, one from which she could learn both how to defend herself and that men were not always aggressive and abusing.

For a year the patient talked about her children and, through them, the losses she had endured in her life. Meanwhile, she started to pick up men for one-night stands. One day she seductively alluded to the fact that she and Arthur had been seeing each other for three and a half years. 'Do you have an ulterior motive?' she asked. This time the charged sexuality of their encounter was very different from that of the first session. He felt 'warm' towards her, happy that 'good things' had happened between them. But in the back of his mind he kept hearing the Nazi war song, 'Lili Marlene'. Among the many things he still needed to find out was why on earth he should feel like a Nazi.

After three and a half years of treatment, some of the mystery in this patient had been resolved. She had begun to trust her therapist and to understand the way in which she had projected on to him an image derived from all the other brutal men in her life. She had started to hear the questions he asked, to reflect upon the material that came up in the sessions and to take an interest in the interpretations he put forward. Arthur was finally beginning to feel that he knew what was going on, but his understanding still remained very partial.

Whether the therapy proceeds through long stretches of silence or outpourings of words, endless tears or violent recriminations, the analyst's task is often simply to endure. 'If I can stick with uncertainty long enough,' says Gavin, 'I trust that something will give.' Andrea had a patient who for session after session simply lay on the couch and cried. For a long time she allowed the tears to continue, but then her own impatience, mixed with anxiety that the analytic process had become stuck, compelled her to intervene and order the patient to stop. 'It was disastrous,' she recalls in the resonant tones that characterize the more interesting moments of our interview. 'I had become the mother who would not let her cry. For a long time she would turn against me, whatever I said or did. I only had to cough. My presence had become unbearable to her. I became docile. I did not speak any more. I was cornered.'

As Andrea's example shows, therapists who act upon their need to know what is going on, or a strong desire to impose themselves upon the treatment situation, are likely to receive a response that leaves them feeling even more perplexed and battered than they were before. During the many hours that must pass before they know enough to justify offering an interpretation, analysts must simply listen to patients' material, trying to hear within it the voice of the unconscious. They must be responsive not only to the overt messages which are being given out – I am crying, please console me – but to what lies behind those messages, possible clues to the history that drives this patient.

Analysis is in essence the art of listening. It calls for an attitude which was described by Freud as 'evenly hovering attention', where the therapist's mind roams between various levels, never focusing on one to the exclusion of any other. Analysts must try not only to make sense of patients' speech, but also to attend to their gestures, their eye movements and the feelings that might lie behind the words. As they search for what lies below the immediate surface, they bring to bear on their understanding of the patients' present material the ideas, images and memories that have been gathered in past sessions. And the analyst should listen to the emotions stirred in them by the patients, discovering in their own reactions some clues to their past and present relationships with others. The aim of spreading the analyst's attention in this way is to lift the analytic dialogue from the level of polite discourse to that of intense communication between two people.

'It is sort of like an altered state of consciousness,' says Robert of evenly hovering attention, 'like the material is washing over you and you are not particularly paying attention to any of it. Not that your mind is wandering; it is just that your mind is not especially focused. Then, all of a sudden, something will grab you. Like, for example, someone will tell you a story four times, and at the fourth telling they will mention something differently. They will revise the story somewhat. All of a sudden, click, your attention snaps.'

Evenly hovering attention is a state that has been compared to meditation. However, analysts do not receive any special training in meditative techniques – unless, that is, you count their many years in analysis – and one can reasonably be sceptical about the amount of time that most analysts spend with their minds in the evenly hovering mode. Several admitted to me that they had dozed off during sessions. Others that their minds, once let loose, wandered to many places that had nothing to do with the patient's material. 'I cannot be fully engaged the whole time,' remarks Sophie. 'Other thoughts do come into my mind. How could it be otherwise?'

'It is more an ideal concept than one that is always in play,' says Robert. It is impossible, he admits, to leave all one's personal cares at the door of the consulting room. They will often intrude. 'If you have a stomach ache, if you have had an argument, if you are about to leave on a trip, if your dog has developed a tumour and you are supposed to pick him up from the vet today, these are all things that might interfere.' But he insists that it is possible to put such thoughts to one side most of the time. The ideal state of attention is, he says, 'more in play than the average person might imagine'.

For Jo, the idea of evenly hovering attention expresses the therapist's aim of keeping his or her own personality and theoretical convictions from seriously disfiguring the patient's material. The concept that the patient must lead the process is an ideal one, and he has doubts about anyone's capacity to achieve it. 'We try,' he says, still using that wretched plural pronoun, 'to have a balanced form of listening, with no areas given too much or too little weight. In fact, we all have our hobby-horses, so that we are a little bit more interested in certain kinds of material than in others. For one analyst it may be memories, for another dreams, for another certain kinds of fantasies.'

I have already said that psychoanalysis is a profession full of paradoxes, where goals are set whose achievement would lead to disaster, and where therapists sometimes find themselves pursuing contradictory aims. Bion implied such a paradox when he argued, in an oft-quoted phrase, that analysts should approach each session 'without memory or desire'. By this he meant that they should not allow their listening to be distorted by thinking directly about the material that had emerged in past sessions, nor should they be looking for anything specific in a way that might tempt them to bend the patient's words to fit with their own theories.

Edward suggests that the ideal can be something of a cop-out. 'Sometimes,' he says, 'you might actually be quite interested in what happened to the patient after the last session.' He seems to miss the force of Bion's paradox. Bion was aware that clearing intention out of the analytic exercise was neither possible nor desirable, but the aim to do so would counter any tendency the analyst might have to concentrate exclusively on a single aspect of the patient's material. The therapist must sometimes direct the patient, but not at the cost of missing out on other things that are happening concurrently. 'The need,' Edward acknowledges, 'is to tune into the patient's feeling state at a particular time. But you do not want to lose touch with curiosity, and sometimes you need to remember.' So it was necessary for Arthur Robbins in the case presented earlier both to let the patient pass from *femme fatale* to desperate mother without his questions confining her to one mode, and for him always to bear in mind the whole history of the case, so that he could start to piece together her history.

One of the most important differences between analytic listening (evenly hovering attention) and most ordinary listening is that the analyst must listen not only to the patients' words but also to the way in which their communications – verbal, gestural, aural and emotive – register in their own psyche. Understanding how responses provide clues concerning the patients' early lives has been one of the most significant developments in analytic technique over the past half century. 'The analyst's emotional response to his patient within the analytic situation represents one of the most important tools for his work,' wrote Paula Heimann, a lapsed British Kleinian, in a paper of 1950 which, with several others appearing roughly at the same time, marked a breakthrough in analytic technique.[3]

Whereas contemporary analysts see this so-called 'counter-transference' as a valuable therapeutic tool for insight into the patient, Freud saw it as a disturbing indication that analysts had not been sufficiently analyzed, and that too many of their own conflicts were influencing their perspective on the patient's own material. Frederick substantially accepts Freud's position. However, he also recognizes that there is some value in seeing how a patient forces the analyst into a certain role, like that of a key parental figure. 'You feel a pressure to act in a certain way,' he says, 'and to say certain things to them. It is what you pick up from the transference expectations they have of you.'

Frederick's disagreements are with analysts who argue that everything untoward they feel in a session could have some relevance to the patient's inner life. 'The idea that actual feelings like anxiety, sexual excitement, boredom are put into you is just spooky,' he says. 'There are analysts who, whenever they feel puzzled, bored, sleepy, angry or anxious, think this is a wonderful, unconscious message from the patient. I tend to think that I had better get a cup of coffee.' Frederick may present a conservative trend in thinking on counter-transference, but his gentle sarcasm usefully counters the view that a classical analyst cannot have a sense of humour.

In his scepticism about the possibility of intense, unconscious communication between patient and analyst, Frederick is in a minority.

Most therapists described to me a process of monitoring their reactions during sessions to see whether they were picking up messages from their patients' unconscious. Having tried to work out whether there was any alternative reason for particular feelings, and having decided that these emanated from the couch, they will feed this information back to the patients as a way of deepening the analytic process.

The lay person receives messages from others in much the same way as therapists, but for the most part these messages remain unread, lodged in the unconscious and drowned out by internal chatter. It takes a measure of inner calm to pick up the emotional vibrations from another and decipher their meaning. Nora speaks from long experience of analytic practice when she says, 'I know that certain feelings are alien to me. I do not get anxious at all now, and I am not normally angry. So if I feel anxious or angry with a patient, it is very unlikely to be coming from me.' She recalls having a patient who seemed to be in a cheerful mood. Things were apparently going along nicely. Nora, however, began to feel more and more unhappy, until her eyes were full of tears. She made a guess and said, 'Underneath what you are saying today, I think there is a flow of something very different. It is very sad. Do you think we can tune in?' It was a glancing insight that took her to the heart of what the patient was feeling, and enabled the patient to focus in upon deep concerns that he had been evading. Until that point, patient and therapist had been skating over the surface.

Robert had an equally forceful insight when he was waiting for a patient who was late. His office was at the back of a dark building. It was after 9.30 at night and the place was otherwise empty. Suddenly he imagined his patient kicking in the door and blowing him away with a shotgun. 'There was blood and guts all over the walls,' he recalls. 'I said to myself, "Gee, what did I do to deserve that?" All of a sudden, I had an insight about this patient, that she wanted me to feel as guilty as she felt her reprehensible mother should have felt for what she did to her. I only thought the patient was angry. I did not previously understand that the patient was making me feel that I should feel guilty.' The revelation contained in the fantasy was based on information that Robert already had, but it had not fully registered on his intellect. He could have hit upon the same understanding by pure deduction, but he had not.

Working at such a level can also be like tuning into a far-distant radio station. The analyst works from faint signals and is often surprised by what emerges in the patient's response. Charles once had a daydream during a session and decided to test it out on the patient. He had imagined Moses crossing the Red Sea. The people of Israel had all crossed over, apart from one man who remained on the other side. 'Why would I have a dream like this?' Charles asked his patient. The patient thought a little and made a reply that was obviously of great significance for the treatment. 'I guess,' he said, 'that is because I recently started to go with my wife for marriage counselling. Maybe I should have told you about that.' In Charles's case, a whole variety of small indications that the patient had somehow absented himself from the therapy crystallized into a fantasy. Only questioning the patient could reveal what it meant.

Sometimes the feelings that patients stir in their analyst can be so deep, so covert, that they manifest themselves in actions long before they become conscious. Rosamund was preparing to go out when a patient arrived for her second session. She had completely forgotten to put her in the diary. 'When she told me her history, it turned out that I had actually put her out of my mind in exactly the same way as her mother used to do. I was acting out her inner conflict about being abandoned by her mother. It was really shocking to think that I had only seen her once, did not know her story and already I was involved.'

John was less lucky than Rosamund. He had already made it to the park near his home when the patient arrived. A few days later he had to deal with the rage his error had provoked and help the patient to face the fact, which he himself found difficult to bear, that this had happened just because she was the last person in his caseload to whom such a thing should have happened. 'She had an absolute minimum of self-esteem. She was very lonely and unhappy. I had put another nail in her coffin by saying that she mattered so little that I had forgotten her. What I learned from that is that for two or three years I had been persuading myself that I had the empathy and insight to see something good in her. What I was denying was the bit of me that made me forget her, that did not have that much regard for her. I had to face her with the fact that she did not matter that much to me.' John's honesty with himself and his patient suggests that good analysts may require not only an acute sensitivity to their own motivations and weaknesses, but also a willingness to accept self-chastisement. A Catholic background or a Jewish one, like John's, obviously assists in developing the latter faculty.

In fact, all therapists will fail at some point to live up to their professional ideals. Under pressure from the patient's unconscious, they will be induced into behaviour that is improper and unprofessional. If analysts defensively refuse to acknowledge that they have been idiots, the therapy may grind to a halt. But the mistake can also be the making of the therapy. Analysts who acknowledge their blunders give their patients an opportunity to experience them as fallible. By admitting that they are as caught up in the emotional interchange as the patient, they cut through any idealization that may have built up. The resulting breakthrough can lead to a new level of mutuality. John feels that his big blunder finally put that therapy on an honest basis, and gave it a new impetus. What had been ignored and concealed by both patient and therapist, in a mutually self-protecting conspiracy, was finally out in the open and could be explored.

Since such mistakes are responses to something in the patient's inner world, they can bring to light crucial facts which had been ignored up to that point. The momentary raising of the emotional temperature carries information to the surface in a particularly clear and defined way. Robert, whose case examples are never less than colourful, had a patient who constantly responded to his interpretations with expletives. (This case has already been alluded to in Chapter 4.) 'Fuck you!' he would exclaim, or 'You dumb arsehole!' This constant provocation needled Robert to a point almost beyond enduring. Finally, he did something to show he was irritated. The patient had a field day.

'That proves you are a piss-poor analyst. I always knew you were no fucking good. Analysts are not supposed to respond to their patients.'

At this point Robert remembered how the patient had once described regularly provoking his father to a point where he would beat the hell out of him. That gave him a clue to the clarification required. 'It seems like you have been on a campaign of provocation against me,' he said, 'and that you would not give up until you had got me irritated. You are like a kid waving his fingers in another kid's face, who will not stop until the other kid explodes.'

'No, no. It is just that you are a piss-poor analyst.'

'That kind of response is just an attempt to try and re-escalate the situation.'

'I bet you did want to tell me off on a few occasions.'

At this point, Robert reminded the patient of how he used to behave with his father. The experience helped him to understand that the patient was not just a sadist, taking out his anger on everyone around him, but a masochist, trying to induce others to turn on him. 'It was a conflict of mine that had made me vulnerable to his provocation,' he says, 'just as another conflict of mine made me blind to the masochistic features of his behaviour. The eruption from me was unfortunate, but it then got used in a constructive way. It was a transformational kind of experience.'

Being a classical Freudian, Robert reproaches himself for his blindness. Most analysts are happy to admit that mistakes, sometimes quite serious ones, do happen and that they can be the making of the therapy. However, since their cause is something in the patient's material that had escaped their notice, they have to regret them. It would be better, they feel, if everything could be made articulate in consciousness before it was acted out. Since they do not see any possible benefit to the patient in experiencing the analyst as capable of error, they create yet another paradox of psychoanalysis – that mistakes, although possibly beneficial, are absolutely not desirable.

Psychoanalysts sometimes aim for the unachievable; here they try to avoid the inevitable. In both cases they need to accept that they will fail. They have entered into a relationship which, being human, must be flawed. Surprising things will happen if patients are allowed to explore wherever they want to go, and if analysts are not afraid to rely upon imagination or instinct. In an endeavour that often seems difficult and dangerous, acknowledging the likelihood of error is an essential to preserving, or enhancing, the sanity of both therapist and patient.

At that point in the dialogue when therapists move from not knowing to formulating insights that they believe can help patients to disentangle elements of their personal history, their assessment of the probability that they are wrong will help determine the way in which those interpretations are offered. An interpretation can, after all, be presented in many ways – as a tentative presentation wrapped in conditionals, or a vigorous statement handed down as a piece of unassailable wisdom.

Some analysts believe that it is right to articulate interpretations as soon as they have achieved clarity in their own minds. When that moment arrives for Jack, he does not ask himself whether the patient is ready to absorb the material, he simply presents it. 'I deal with things as they come up,' he says. 'If someone is not ready, that does not mean they are going to be hurt. It means that they just will not hear it, or tell me to shut up. I try to create an atmosphere where people talk very directly to me and tell me to back off or shut up. I do not think that people are fragile. Raising questions or issues is not likely to do harm if it is not done with any real intent of doing harm.'

Seeing psychoanalysis as an adult-to-adult interchange, Jack would consider it patronizing to withhold an interpretation from patients because of his judgement that they are not ready for it. It may be that they are ready, despite his assessment to the contrary, and that his procrastination would unnecessarily withhold enlightenment from them.

Most analysts, however, view the giving of interpretations as a more delicate and subtle process. Some patients, they would argue, are too sensitive to receive any but the mildest of interpretations. Anything else they would experience as a vicious attack. Also, there is not only a right time for an interpretation, there is a right part of an interpretation for each significant moment in the analysis. One should offer up to patients only such insight as they are ready to hear at a particular time, rather than forcing them to digest the whole thing in one go. An interpretation is something that patients, for the most part, do not want to hear. It is only with the steady growth of understanding that they become ready to take in different perspectives on their past.

Stephen believes that analysts should only gradually reveal to their patients the insights that they have formulated. One of his female patients has never felt comfortable in the presence of young men. At one session she recalled an occasion when her father reprimanded her for putting on a pair of culottes to go to work. He thought them much too revealing. She compared the way he made her feel on that occasion to the sensation of wearing a leotard among men at her gym. 'I wonder,' Stephen put it to her, 'whether you do not feel that when your father criticized your clothing, he was not also drawing attention to something sexual which was humiliating.' What Stephen did not voice, because he did not think the patient ready to hear it, was his own conviction, rooted in Freudian theory, that sexual desire for her father, and guilt about that desire, were mixed up in her feelings.

Robert argues that giving interpretations tentatively ensures that patients do not have the impression that he is trying to fit them into his own theoretical scheme. Nor does he run the risk of disturbing patients unnecessarily by trying to pull down the defences they have erected in order not to acknowledge painful aspects of their past. 'To just say I know what is going on and this is it when they are not ready to hear it could be harmful,' he argues. Interpretations are tried out on patients to see whether they make any impact. If they lead to some sort of response, then Robert might deepen the effect by offering them more of that interpretation. If he was not to do it that way, then it is possible they would feel overwhelmed and put up a brick wall against everything he subsequently said. 'What you do,' he says, 'is to test out the patient's readiness to use the information constructively. Just being right is irrelevant. You have to be right in a way that the patient can make use of.'

Robert presents his views to me with such passion and conviction that I find it hard to imagine him holding back his insights from patients, and yet it is clear that this is a crucial part of his approach to analysis. He gives me a very simple example to illustrate his point. He had a patient who always experienced the last session of the week as an abandonment by the therapist. As a child, her mother could not deal with her and always threatened to leave her with the 'Indians'. One day, when she was eight years old, the family staged an abandonment in downtown Minneapolis. Throughout her life subsequently she expected others to leave her behind, the analyst being no exception. While she was reliving her experience of being abandoned, it would have been inappropriate to have analyzed the roots of that feeling. That could only be done at the beginning of the following week, when she had confirmed that the analyst was still there for her.

'One of the hardest things,' says Robert, 'is waiting. Being able to keep quiet and know that, as much as you want to help someone with an interpretation, you cannot overload them. It is one of the most common mistakes and it happens because the analyst is anxious. It is wanting to help the patient and to prove that you are effective.' Faced with an 'incredible' interpretation, patients may overtly accept it as valid, but it will not have registered in their deeper levels and it will not lead to change. For this reason Patrick Casement has warned about the 'self-deception of premature understanding, which achieves nothing except to defend the therapist from the discomfort of knowing that he does not know'.[4]

For Robert, the process of analysis should be a smooth one in which there are no raised voices and no attempts to strong-arm patients into accepting insight. Interpretations should be offered in the right proportion and at the right time, so that they are absorbed by the patient with the ease of an oyster passing down the gullet. For him, confrontation is a bogey word: 'It is the worst thing you can do with a patient, no matter how much you want them to know something. It would seem to me that usually the reason people have to confront patients with things is that they want them to know. I do not want patients to know things. If they do not know it and they do not want to know it, then I am curious about why they do not want to know it rather than wanting them to know it. Confrontation helps the therapist sometimes, when they feel frustrated. I do not think it helps the patients.'

He gives the hypothetical example of a patient who comes to see him five times a week and never mentions his mother. 'A confrontation would be to say to the patient, "You really have some problem with your mother if you can come here for five or six years and never mention her. Just the law of averages would suggest that you ought to mention her." I would be more interested in how it came to be such a conspicuous omission than in confronting the patient with the fact that it *is* a conspicuous omission, and that he ought to start talking about his mother. I do not care whether he talks about his mother.'

It would be fanciful to imagine that many analysts attain the ideal which Robert describes. An interpretation is too sharp a weapon, touching the patient at a point of extreme sensitivity, for many to be able to handle their despatch without mess and pain. 'Interpretations,' says Michael, 'contain the implication that the patient has got it wrong. Why don't you listen to me? Why don't you take another view of what you are saying?' Given that just repeating such an interpretation could be seen as hectoring, it is difficult to see how a certain amount of friction can be avoided when dealing with sensitive clients. Cynthia takes what seems to me an idealistic view that every interpretation should be presented to the patient as a hypothesis, capable of being immediately withdrawn and shuffled away if repudiated. But I believe her testimony when she reports that therapists often tussle with their patients. They will put forward an interpretation, then challenge the patient's reluctance to accept it. 'It does not sound like an argument, but what is going on is a bit of a battle. The person responsible for it is the therapist, who tells people what they should be thinking and feeling.'

The argument for putting forward interpretations tentatively is based partly in a desire not to trample on the patients' sensitivities, and also in the possibility that the analyst's supposed insight might be wrong. There is a problem here for the analyst. At what point should repudiation of an interpretation be taken as indicating that it is mistaken, rather than something which the patient does not want to know at that particular moment? Since the patient's rejection can mean both that the interpretation is right, and that it is wrong, how on earth does the analyst decide?

We have seen that some analysts do have a capacity to accept that they are wrong. But many have sufficient self-esteem to ensure that they will tend to blame resistance to an interpretation on unacceptability rather than inaccuracy. And this attitude – that the analyst is right, he or she only has to help the patient to see that – presents a temptation to bully patients into submission. To every declaration from patients that they are not being understood, analysts can riposte with the unanswerable reply that the patient is simply unconscious of the truth being revealed by the analyst. The angrier the patient becomes at the analyst's idiocy, the more the analyst can become convinced that he or she is homing in on a sensitive area with pinpoint accuracy. This is one of the deepest traps that analysis lays for the incompetent therapist.

The ideal may be for patients to formulate their own understanding of their past. In reality, the analyst must often subtly direct them along the right path. In Jo's account of how he would make a patient understand the role of his past upon his present condition, one can hear elements of coaxing pressure. 'I say to a patient, "Did you notice how upset you were when I announced that we would not be able to meet on such and such a day? You were quite irritated with me. That irritation followed my announcement that there would be a cancellation. And much the same thing happened when, after your father died, you became much closer to your friend. And when he was away, you became very upset. In all these situations you can see how dependent you have become on parent surrogates. Any time you feel that the 'parent' is not there for you, you become very anxious, very frightened." In that way it is all put together for him.'

Put in such a way, the case sounds unanswerable. But how would he respond if the patient dismissed the whole thing as Freudian claptrap? 'Sometimes,' he replied, 'that is because the analyst has been clumsy. Other times the patient is refusing to believe it even when you show them the evidence for it. They gradually come around when they see that the evidence is incontrovertible. They see it in their relationship with you, or with a friend. They realize they have become so dependent on a friend that they could not go one day without five telephone calls. Then, when the phone rings in your office, or you have to cancel a session, they go bananas. We have to persist through resistance because a lot of people fight against feelings of dependency, and it may be difficult.'

Persisting through resistance and avoiding confrontation are concepts that seem to be at odds with each other, but the analyst must try somehow to do both. Those who never put their finger anywhere near the patient's wound, who value 'empathy' above everything else, run the risk of never helping the patient to understand his or her situation. Analysts who are too mild, too tentative, will never lead their patients towards a position where they can face painful truths about themselves. But equally there should be a way of helping patients to confront their inner reality without putting a finger in the wound and causing excruciating pain. All therapists will regularly fall to one side or other of the ideal, depending upon their personality. Some will be too mummsyish and indulgent, others will be always confronting, challenging and provoking. Each must struggle to find a way towards a middle course.

Psychotherapy is inherently hierarchical. However much both sides may wish it, patient and therapist cannot simply have a civilized person-to-person conversation about the ailments of one and the solutions proposed by the other. There may be long stretches during the treatment when therapists acknowledge that they do not know, but at some point they come to offer themselves as guides to another's internal workings. However much they wrap up this fact in talk about helping the patient to reach self-understanding, that is essentially what they are doing.

The problem for those who want to put analyst and patient on to a basis of full equality is that the process is not concerned with the sort of reality that one can easily discuss with one's neighbours in the kitchen or sitting room. The therapy relationship may become more equal as it proceeds, when the patient has fully grasped what it is that is being opened up for exploration, but it cannot start out that way. There is too much that distinguishes analytic relating from ordinary relating. The process is designed to shift the focus away from worrying about the latest news on the home front to what is happening in the patient's inner world, and the numerous events in the patient's past which have left their traces in the patient's psyche. Therapists aim to help their patients to see things that they cannot easily uncover without help. To do so involves directing their attention away from the obvious.

'When I am in my consulting room,' says Rafael, 'what I am preoccupied with is what is happening between my patient and me.' He recalls one session where the patient spent the entire time talking about his fantasies regarding the books on the consulting-room shelves. 'I thought afterwards that if I told someone off the street that I had just spent an hour with a patient talking about his fantasies about the books in my bookcase, they would think that I was mad and he was even madder. As far as I was concerned, it was an extremely important session in terms of understanding something of the patient's views about our relationship.'[5]

For those who are unused to tracing the roots for their actions back into their unconscious, which is most people who have not been in analysis, the therapist's attempt to relate external happenings to inner reality can seem like a hard-hearted disinterest in what is really happening in their lives. They look for 'natural' sympathy and are confronted instead by intellectual curiosity. Adam had a patient whom he had been seeing for over a year. Halfway through a session she reported that she had seen a dog being run over. Although he did express some concern about how this made her feel, Adam went on from that to analyze what this experience might mean to her. The unhappy event was used as material to find out more about the patient's inner world.[6]

'What I asked myself,' he recalls, 'is, "Why am I being told this at this particular moment rather than something else? Why has the patient waited 30 minutes to tell me this when it seemed to be an important thing for her?" It is not that the dog being run over is not important or significant, but it is much more to do with what the event outside is being used to represent in the patient's unconscious. My assumption would be that the thing the patient is telling me about has both a conscious meaning and an unconscious meaning. One has to try to give the patient the experience of there being other levels of meaning to what is being said that will hopefully in the end be to do with connecting the patient up with lost or inaccessible feelings.'

In the effort to foster the patient's autonomy, the therapist may have to adopt a position that seems harsh. A woman who is being beaten up by her husband might look for sympathy, and hope to be told that men should not be allowed to get away with mistreating their women. That is not Mary's approach. In order to empower such a patient, she tries to make her accept that she may have played a role in bringing on the attack, and that she can do something about it, if only she can break out of the role of passive victim. 'I would want to know how it came about,' she says. 'Was there provocation and, if she was badly beaten, why has she not done something about it? Does she want to be beaten? Does she see herself as only deserving that kind of treatment? What is she thinking of doing about it?'

For a woman whose acceptance of abuse started in her earliest childhood, when there really was nothing she could do about her uncle's or her father's intrusions, the idea that her fate is now in her own hands may be difficult to accept. Mary would ask her why she was allowing herself to be abused now, when her position was so different from what it had been before. 'She may have been helpless as a child,' says Mary, 'but that does not apply now. She can do something about it. She has more resources. She is being listened to by the therapist, for a start.' If the patient accuses her of being cold and inattentive, Mary will take up that issue. 'You told your mother that daddy had interfered with you. She did not believe it. So you feel that by telling me now I will not believe you now many years later.' The analyst is not here suggesting that the report of sexual abuse has been made up, but it can be seen how her remarks could be taken as having that implication.

At such points in the therapy, a patient's anger with the analyst who challenges her habitual responses to things can become confused with her fury at both the parent who abused her and all those who would not believe her account of what had happened. As therapy proceeds, the feelings of patients towards their therapist become increasingly confused with the way they felt about other significant people in their life. Patients become more and more preoccupied with what is going on between themselves and the analyst, bringing to bear on that relationship many of their past emotional experiences. 'Gradually,' says Frederick, 'the relation to the analyst becomes a much more prominent focus than their own problems. Their problem shifts to worrying about what the analyst thinks of them. What did he mean by saying this or that? Why was he a minute late? Who is this other person knocking at the door? The analytic sitation becomes the new focus.'

Frequently, patients in analysis become totally absorbed in their inner world. To outsiders it seems that they have become withdrawn, and that their malaise is deepening. Analysts, however, will feel that they are making real progress. They have plumbed the area of their psyche where the threads of the past that lead to present pain can be picked up and examined. This process brings with it no short-term benefits; indeed, the pain of discovery may bring on a deeper gloom. The only force carrying the analytic process forward is the analyst's conviction that real benefits will flow from this exploration.

Clearly, someone who has begun to confuse therapist and parent, while reliving some of the most painful experiences of his or her early life, is in an extremely sensitive position, where the possibilities for abuse are considerable. I discussed in Chapter 4 the enormous value that 'transference' interpretations – for example, 'You think I am going to abandon you because that is what your father did' – have in enabling the therapist to piece together a patient's life. But they also present many pitfalls for the unwary therapist.

Transference interpretations are easy to make and seem clever, even though, when used promiscuously, they are often lazy, predictable and hackneyed. They can lure therapists into narcissistically exaggerating their importance to the patient and making absurd 'me too' interpretations that, even if they have some grounds in reality, make no impact on the patient and seem to ignore what is going on in the patient's outside life. The therapist says, 'You are talking about this, but really you are talking about what is happening in the therapy.' In this way therapists can appear totally insensitive to the turbulence that brought their patient into therapy. When Cathy, for example, was in analysis during the break-up of her first marriage, she recalls the analyst responding to her reports of battles on the home front by saying, 'Come along, why are you telling me all this rubbish? What is going on between you and me?'

'The danger,' says Peter, 'is that therapists want to demonstrate their potency. It reduces their anxiety. They feel more comfortable clutching the levers of power. One of the things that makes you feel more comfortable is that you have knowledge and the other person does not. If you say, "I feel you are treating me as if I was your mother or father," it reduces your anxiety.' Therapists are notorious for using transference interpretations in this way to disclaim responsibility for anything of which the patient accuses them. Told that they were irritable, had fallen asleep, or were not listening, they deflect the patients' words by turning the patients' suspicions back on them. They do not accept that there may be an element of reality to the charge.

As an analyst who emphasizes his own participation in the analytic relationship, Jack feels that it is important to give the impression that the patient's remarks could be plausible. 'The patient tells me I feel angry with him,' he says. 'Let us say I do not know what the hell he is talking about. I do not feel any anger. I would look for it in myself to see what the patient might be seeing that I myself am not seeing. My attitude would be that their perception is plausible, and that they should go with it.' Samuel sums up the difference between a Freudian and a so-called 'interpersonal' analyst like Jack with this joke: 'If a Freudian analyst is told by the patient, "Oh, you are ugly," he would say this is transference. If you are an interpersonal analyst, however, you go to a mirror and take a peep.' Caricature though this is, it conveys an essential truth about the difference between the two positions.

Frederick, however, for all his Freudian convictions, holds to a position very close to Jack's. He considers it outrageous for an analyst to say that the patient's statement does not mean what it says, but what the analyst thinks it means. 'I would think,' he says, 'that no sensible patient would put up with this. Some of them do. I think you have to be careful to give the impression that you are accepting their communication as partly what they say it means. You may be able to add something to it, but to undermine it completely and say it really means you are thinking about me, that is outrageous.' Frederick, who adheres to Freud's advice only to interpret the patient's feelings towards the therapist when they are blocking the analytic process, is often sent patients who have become 'phobic' about such interpretations.

Robert, a Freudian who shares many of Frederick's beliefs as well as a similar sense of humour, also accepts that the therapeutic relationship is both fantasy and reality. He has one patient who is profoundly paranoid. One day she came into the office and started to rant and rave at him, to say that behind his affable manner what he really felt about her was that she was a 'fucking cunt, a piece of shit'. Eventually, she asked him to explain why she should have such thoughts. He told her that she had probably picked up that he had been feeling rather ill in the previous session. 'I do not think your thoughts started from thin air,' he said. 'They started when you saw something different about me and did not know how to make sense of it.'

Sidney emphasizes that, although it is important to acknowledge the reality component in the patients' characterization of the therapist, it is also crucial to alert them to the role that their inner world played in determining the nature of their response to the analyst's inadvertent action. He gives the example of a patient who became angry with him for dozing off momentarily during the session. 'Yes,' he said. 'I am very tired. If you are angry, I do not blame you.' But he would then go on to explore the reason why the patient considered what had happened to be a big issue. Why did he feel the way he did about the analyst falling asleep?

While inadequate therapists may be all too eager to use a transference interpretation as a way of extricating themselves from any charge patients launch against them, they may also, rather paradoxically, attempt to involve themselves in every statement patients make about their external life. Roderick Peters has supervised many therapists who, when told by a patient about a row with a spouse or with the boss at work, turned that into a 'communication and expression of the patient's infantile relation to the therapist'. The patients responded to such interpretations by drying up and starting to ask themselves whether there was any point in going on with the treatment.

A friend came to me in some distress from her therapy session. She had asked her therapist whether, for the following session, she could come 30 minutes early and sit in the waiting room. She suffers, as the therapist knew, from an illness which leaves her physically drained after any exertion, and she had an appointment in the vicinity an hour before her next therapy session. The therapist could have said no on the grounds that this would make her other patients anxious, or have given some other such excuse. Instead, she asked my friend why she felt the need to bid for extra time in her therapist's house. She may have been hoping that she could work from this point to persuade my friend to start coming more frequently, as she had often urged her before.

'It is not that,' my friend replied, 'it is just that I need somewhere to wait.'

'There are plenty of cafés in the area.'

'But I have told you, I will get very tired if I sit in a noisy, smoky café.'

'I do not think that's why you want to come and sit in my waiting room.'

The therapist, in my view, handled the session badly. She had triggered my friend's anxiety that the therapist, like the rest of the world, considered her illness to be psychosomatic. And by making what the patient perceived to be a narcissistic, aggressive transference interpretation, the therapist made sure that she could never be perceived as the nurturing and supportive person that she clearly thought herself already to be in the patient's inner world. Given that my friend had been in therapy with her for only a couple of months on a once-a-week basis, the therapist's behaviour seemed absurd. 'It is mumbo-jumbo,' says Peter, to whom I outlined the case, 'to talk like that about someone you are only seeing once a week. You are really crazy. You would lose the patient.' During the subsequent Christmas break, my friend wrote to say she would not be going back to therapy.

Owen, who abandoned his ambitions to become a psychoanalyst for a career in television, had a Kleinian analyst at a time when he was intensely preoccupied with a programme about sex which involved him in flaming rows with everyone on the team. His work situation was extraordinarily complicated. The programme's presenter had various complex sexual inhibitions, the producer was gay and Owen himself had strong views of his own that he wanted to put across in the programmes. Of this reality, his analyst took not the slightest notice. 'I would come in,' Owen recalls, 'and tell my analyst about a dream which was evidently to do with a phenomenal row on the set and he would tell me it was all about my anger towards him. Throughout all these incredible shenanigans, as I was thundering my way through the thickets of the television business, this bloody man was telling me that everything was to do with my relationship to him.'

I put it to Nancy that such an approach was giving Kleinian analysis a bad name. She replied that one should not ignore the realities of what was going on in the patient's life and make an 'enclave' of the analysis. Treating someone's psychological problems should not involve an exclusive focus on the relationship between patient and analyst. The pressing, fascinating, stormy external reality must be closely listened to and acknowledged.

'What he has come for,' she said, 'are not his life problems but the psychological problems in his life. It could be that something was going wrong in the therapy and he was not being listened to. It could also be that the same kind of psychological problems that were arising in his television work were arising with the analyst. The only place, however, that analysts can work with them is not out there but in here.'

It may be true that there were parallels between Owen's work experience and his analytic experience, but what mattered most to him at the time was his work, and not the relationship to his analyst. Producing interpretations that related to what interested Owen least seemed like narcissism on the part of the therapist rather than sensitivity. And Owen did not accept the interpretations that were rammed at him. Possibly, the analyst did not make an error of fact, but he certainly failed in tact.

Analysts who interpret everything that patients tell them about their day-to-day life, their memories and their dreams in terms of what is or is not happening between patient and analyst step down a slippery path, the end result of which is a refusal to investigate real traumatic events in an individual's life. This is a failing which is most often laid against Kleinians. 'I am very disturbed,' says Birgit, 'that the classical, Kleinian analyst, in my experience, takes up all reality as projections of some fantasy system, so that whatever actual malpractice one may speak of at the hands of parents or others, it is pushed to one side and utterly disregarded.'

The possibility that analysts will push aside reality in favour of fantasy has inspired many attacks on the profession, and it is the issue at the heart of the controversy over whether Freud neglected the abused child and the battered adult in the patients who presented themselves for treatment. Alice Miller's attacks on the theory of infantile sexuality (which suggests that children have a complex sexual life),[7] and Jeffrey Masson's condemnation of Freud for cowardly abandoning the seduction theory (the shocking idea that all women have been abused by their fathers)[8] have persuaded many that there is something fundamentally unsound about psychoanalysis. But in reality they have only pointed up the difficulty of the course that therapists must always steer, dividing fantasy from reality when their patients have no way to tell the difference.

Some commentators have argued that, far from abandoning the seduction theory, Freud simply appended to it the theory of infantile sexuality.[9] This seems somewhat facile. Once Freud became convinced that much of what his patients were describing was unconscious fantasy, he put a

wholly different slant on the way in which he listened to his patients'
stories. Previously, he had assumed that his patients were telling the
truth about what had happened to them. Now he worked from the
belief that they could well be making it up. It was an epochal shift.
The strength of the analytic approach subsequently was that analysts
no longer fell, as someone put it to me, for the 'cheap truths of reality'.
They would probe deeper. Excited by his discovery about the workings
of the unconscious mind, Freud looked for fantasy in every corner. And
Melanie Klein took his argument a stage further by constructing a theory
that some interpret as largely ignoring the impact of external events on
an individual's primitive mental organization.

But what Freud had discovered was not, of course, that there was no
such thing as infantile trauma. It was that one could no longer draw a
firm line between inner and outer reality, and that, in the human mind,
there is a continuous interplay between fact and fantasy, reality and
illusion, the images and feelings taken in from the real world, and the
ideas mediated by imagination and memory. The model he evolved was
far more complex, rich and subtle than that which he had abandoned.
'The critics of his theory of infantile sexuality,' writes Stephen Mitchell,
'often fail to note that the development of this theory brought with it the
shift from the overly simplistic and shallow contaminant model of infantile
seduction to the view of the mind as intricate, variegated, inevitably torn
by passionate conflicts, and actively generating personal meanings – the
view that has inspired subsequent decades of psychoanalytic theorizing
and clinical psychoanalysis.'[10]

By trying to make the question of fantasy and reality into one of
either/or – either children sometimes fantasize about sleeping with their
parent of the opposite sex, or children who talk about having sexual
desires towards their parents have been abused – Masson and Miller
seek to drag us back to a pre-Freudian age, where we believe again in
the child's essential innocence. 'I do not believe,' Masson writes, 'that
children have Oedipal fantasies about their parents, if by that you mean
that girls want to sleep with their fathers. On the contrary, I think parents
act upon their children quite literally by hurting them, and in the case of
fathers, sexually abusing them.'[11] The dogmatism behind that statement
is shocking, and the implied denial that mothers can also abuse their
children seems as blind as anything of which Freud stands accused.

In his fixation upon the Viennese master, Masson seems unaware of
the extent to which post-Freudian theory has focused on the impact of real
events on the child's formation of reality. Nor does he see that balancing
inner against outer is a juggling act which all therapists have to engage

as best they can. 'It is quite difficult,' says Samantha, 'for psychotherapy, which is about the individual's inner world, to give its rightful place to external factors. But also, of course, external factors do get internalized. One has to have a continual dialogue about the relationship between the internal and the external world.'

People have argued, much to Masson's disgust, that there is no clear dividing line between being abused and imagining that you have been abused; that fantasy can have an effect quite as devastating as the reality, given certain attendant circumstances. There is, however, a difference in the problem that each case presents for the therapist. Where patients only imagine that their father molested them, without any significant basis in reality, the job of the therapist is to persuade them that what really happened was much less horrible than what they fantasized. Where real trauma was involved, by contrast, the therapist is confronted with the much more daunting task of persuading patients to forgive.

Relegating certain experiences to the dustbin of fantasy can be a great relief for the therapist. A world in which people imagine horrible things is much less awful than one in which horrible things really do happen. Therapists will have their own range of tolerance and an area where they find it difficult to accept the believability of the material that the patient is presenting. 'Every analyst,' says Eve, 'has areas where they are not comfortable probing. It is a fact of life, although it does a disservice to the patient. And they give off messages about what they can understand, what they are interested in and what they can tolerate.'

The aim of a training analysis is to give therapists-to-be a grasp of their own potential for evil. They must learn that they too could hate, kill and abuse people, could slip into darkness and madness. But everyone emerges from the process with blind spots and no-go areas, with part of themselves still ready to share in the very human tendency to block out horror and believe that everything is for the best. Why do so many juries fail to convict in rape cases? Because they cannot believe that men can be such beasts. Sexual abuse of infants is another area that the human mind finds it hard to contemplate.

'Sexual abuse,' says Nicholas, a child psychiatrist, 'is dreadful. It is impossible. You would do anything to avoid hearing what actually happened. I have to struggle and force myself to ask for the details – "Who did what to whom?" For every new case I have to put myself through the same learning process. You want to talk about anything else. You do not want to know. Or one terribly much does want to know, which is just as much of a problem.'

Michael recalls attending a case presentation given by a general practitioner and a psychotherapist. It occurred to him that the patient they
were talking about had suffered from sexual abuse. When the time came
for questions from the floor, he put his idea forward. 'I asked whether
they thought this was a possibility,' he recalls. 'There was a polite
acknowledgement of what I was saying. Then the group carried on as
if I had not spoken. So I put my point of view forward more strongly.
The whole group rejected it as a possibility. It later turned out that the
person had been abused.'

And therapists may be protecting not only themselves but also, perhaps
unconsciously, their patients. Gloria had a patient whose life had been
truly wretched. As she looked over the poems and pictures that this patient
presented each week, Gloria slowly began to realize the true horror of the
story they depicted. 'It was in the third year of the therapy. I said to her,
"I think that you are talking about real events, not fabrications. These
are things that have happened to you." That was a turning point in her
life. But how was she going to live, knowing that such appalling things
were real? It still troubles me. What have I done by translating these
pieces into a story of nightmarish reality? I would often think I do not
have the right to do this. She has had fantasies of flinging herself out of
the top of a high building, doing something violent to smash it all away.
She still sometimes says, "I wish you had left me as I was."'

When Masson accuses analysts of ignoring the reality of their patients'
trauma, he underestimates the enormous difficulty of the task before them,
as they seek to disentangle fantasy from reality. Sexual abuse has become
a fashionable complaint, and most therapists now have their antennae
sensitized to pick up the slightest hint that it may have taken place. It is
difficult not to wonder whether it is now frequently found where it never
happened.

Masson charges analysts with not listening, and the charge seems
weighty. But what is involved is not just a refusal to hear what the
patient says and acknowledge its possible truth, but a failure in many
cases to pick up the slightest possibility that something might be the case
and then devote a considerable amount of time and energy to eliciting the
truth. 'You have to make a decision,' says Nora, 'as to whether there is
juice to be extracted from hanging around their second year, trying to
figure out whether they were abused or not. It may matter, it may not. If
you get there, then it probably matters. If you do not and they are better
for what they came for, then I think that is what matters.' Nora is not
here denying the possible significance of child abuse, but saying that, in
specific cases, there may be much more important determinants to later

psychological distress. There is no absolute significance to be attached to the molesting father or intrusive mother, just as there is no absolute definition of where love ends and abuse begins.

For analysts trying to grapple with the inner lives of their sometimes very disturbed patients, the line between fantasy and reality can seem like a very fuzzy area indeed. Rosamund, for example, had a patient who vaguely felt that she might have been abused as a child. After five years away from therapy, she came back because she was afraid that she might abuse her daughter. What the patient then discovered was that it was probably not she who had been abused, but her brother, who had later developed schizophrenia. 'She felt she could have prevented her brother from becoming schizophrenic because she knew that he was being sexually abused. Coming from a nice upper-class family, she had blocked it out and all the guilt associated with it.'

Another of Rosamund's patients left her constantly confused about reality. Her mother had thought she was bright; her father that she was stupid and a legitimate object for abuse. Rosamund found herself tossed between these two extremes, between thinking the patient was mentally retarded and thinking she was clever. 'She does not know what her reality is, and she complains that I cannot help her. It is because the characters in her inner world and her exterior world do change places. They were all a bit mad and so you cannot get a hold. They keep changing very quickly and there are psychotic bits in all of them. I just think I have got it figured out, and then everything changes again. It makes you crazy too.'

Psychoanalysts are often accused of giving interpretations that fly in the face of common sense. Many undoubtedly do. But analysis has as its aim the appreciation of the human psyche in all its complexity. Once you accept that the mind truly is complex, that there are no maps to reveal its workings in any individual case, that there is no easy way to determine how much fantasy and reality contribute to any individual's mental structure, then the mistakes that otherwise good analysts do make become understandable. Analysts have to acknowledge how little they know, and to absorb that insight into a technique that is never unnecessarily confrontational, bullying or cruel. There is no other way to do the job properly.

7

Outsiders

Questions of class, race and gender

○□
○○

I ARRIVE 15 minutes early for my appointment at a London psychiatric hospital. A weary receptionist directs me to the raised area set apart for psychotherapy patients. There, apparently as a mark of their higher status, they wait in comfortable chairs, place their feet on carpet rather than tiles and look at walls that carry paintings rather than information about Aids and the latest health service price rises.

Downstairs a woman is screaming. She stomps around the floor, waving a cigarette in one hand, a styrofoam cup in the other. 'Where is my doctor?' she shouts. 'I rang to say I would be late. I am pissed off with waiting. I am not paid whatever she gets a year. I don't have time to wait.' Her voice falls off as two women approach to attend to her demands. 'I was better before I started coming to this place,' she declares in a final gesture of defiance.

None of the patients on the psychotherapy floor takes any notice of the hubbub downstairs. Perhaps they are used to raucous displays from the less privileged patients on the lower level. Here the tone is hushed. The loudest noise comes from two women discussing the mental distress endured by a friend following her hysterectomy. 'You know,' the younger one says, 'she actually paid for that man who pulled her to pieces. I don't think you're ever well after having it out. I am going to try and talk to her and get it out of her what really is the trouble.'

This woman and her older friend carry on with an intensity that seems to silence everyone else. A bearded man in a brown leather jacket reads a photocopied article. A young couple whisper between themselves. They seem anxious and occasionally turn away from each other in tired irritation. A man with large, protruding ears and a wide smile that reveals a paucity of teeth gazes at a copy of the *Sun*, occasionally looking up to see who has come, who is going. I have a good idea what most of these people are here for, but the two

140

women mystify me. Are they cleaners? Has one of them wandered off a ward? Or are they locals who have come for a chat to get out of their respective houses?

The door at the corner opens. A fresh-faced youth – he cannot be older than 25 – summons the man in a leather jacket with a loud 'Good afternoon' and holds out a hand in greeting. The older woman starts to recount a recent shopping expedition to Safeways. Now, however, she has competition. A tall, long-haired man with stooped shoulders has come in, and addresses a black man who has been sitting quietly in a corner. 'It ain't good, man,' he says. 'I've got bad problems, man.'

The couple, meanwhile, have reached an impasse. 'It's a joke,' he says, but their relationship has gone a long way beyond the point where a hurtful remark can be so easily passed off. He turns away from her and nods his head, evidently bemused by the ways of women. She seems deflated. He folds his arms to further indicate that he has had enough of highly charged emotional exchanges. Relief comes in the shape of a smiling, oriental woman, their therapist. Short, wearing a yellow jacket and skirt, she reminds me of the American sexologist Dr Ruth Westheimer. One of the women announces that it is time to leave. 'Let's stay another 10 minutes,' the other one replies.

This hospital atmosphere was quite unlike that of any private therapy practice I had visited. Located either in residential streets among the more affluent sector of the population, or within office blocks in the centre of a city, most therapy waiting rooms exude an air of monastic calm, even when two or three are gathered to await their therapists. And for the most part one could imagine that patient and therapist, meeting in such a setting, would find that they shared common experiences, values and attitudes. They can set out on an exploration of the patient's inner world without having to worry about aspects of his or her social background which the therapist might not understand, or the way in which reality impinges on the patient's capacity for change. When patient and therapist meet in a public hospital, there can be no such guarantee.

Is there an unbridgeable chasm between these two worlds, the public hospital and the private waiting room? This chapter looks at the provision of psychotherapy to those outside the ranks of the affluent white middle classes, and at the problems which arise when members of one culture, class, sex or religious group confront members of another across a consulting room. I argue that, while therapists in such situations need to pay special attention to the social and economic realities of their patients' lives, they must not be distracted from exploration of internal fantasy. Targeted therapy services are in danger of providing an enclave, where oppression and disadvantage are taken to be sufficient explanation for much more complex realities.

The idea has grown up that psychotherapists are interested only in the well-off, the articulate and the highly educated – those whose immediate concerns do not distract attention from the exploration of inner reality – and that they do not want to have their perspective on the psyche muddied by talk of poverty and unemployment, racism and sexism. There are certainly therapists for whom this is true. They claim to find the successful, privileged and prosperous with whom they deal to be more interesting and more satisfying than others, although one doubts whether most of them have ever ventured very far in order to test out their convictions. More financially rewarding such patients certainly are, and their analysts may well subscribe to the myth that those who cannot pay, or cannot pay very much, will not benefit.

The social profile of psychotherapy patients has broadened considerably in recent decades. Nevertheless, in the absence of a large, publicly funded psychotherapy sector, economic reality ensures that the majority of patients in Britain and America who receive psychoanalytic psychotherapy still come from the middle classes. But there are many therapists who find that the drive which originally took them into social work, medicine or any other occupation that put them in touch with many classes of society, still motivates them, and that they have an interest in the way that people far outside their social circle construct reality. To them, the idea that therapy is exclusively for the well-off is unacceptable. They may work on the Robin Hood principle of charging high fees to some and low fees to others, or run a private practice alongside work in the public sector.

William, for example, is an experienced analyst, with an apparently prosperous practice. He has a patient whom he sees twice a week for no fee, sometimes for two or three hours at a stretch. Once high functioning, this tall, lugubrious man who passes through the waiting room while I am there, had a breakdown and lost his job. William does not think that non-payment changes the nature of his analysis. 'The patient recognizes the value of having the relationship with me,' he says with a sigh that is meant to indicate this is one of his most trying cases. 'He feels that, without this link, he would disintegrate altogether. I do not think he is altogether deluded about that.'

I did meet several therapists who clung to the theoretical nostrum that 'people have to pay because otherwise they feel they are getting something for nothing, and that makes them feel guilty.' And I began to see their point when I met up with Barbara, who dispenses free therapy to some of her patients. As she described the patients she takes on for no fee as 'the most reliable, the most concerned for me', telling me proudly that they never come late and never miss appointments, I began to wonder whether they had not been cheated out of their right to rebellion and anger. For them, therapy would not happen if a significant charge was involved, but not paying may put them under pressure. Perhaps it would be better if she charged them something.

In reality, this is one of the many complex areas in psychoanalysis where it is impossible to make absolute rules. Each case is different because everybody has a different attitude to money. For some people, the amount they pay is an important measure of their self-worth, and one British analyst has written convincingly about a case where he felt that charging too little sustained his patient's low self-esteem.[1] But others have an attitude towards money that leads to their feeling punished and persecuted by paying a high fee. And doubts about whether they deserve to spend so much on themselves can have just as much of an impact on the therapy as guilt about getting something for nothing. Analysts must understand their own motivation for setting a high fee, a low fee or no fee at all; then they can use the patient's response to the fee as material for the analysis. The question of money certainly provides no justification for depriving the less well-off of analytic treatment.

In Britain most patients who receive free psychotherapy are protected from the problem of excessive gratitude by receiving treatment as a health service provision. They have grown up thinking that free services are a right and not a gift. But money is not the only problem that providing treatment to less prosperous, less well-educated members of society may present to middle-class psychotherapists.

Those who have not been brought up with the idea that a talking cure can do them good may resist therapy. They do not have the information necessary to facilitate the sort of trust that is a necessary precondition of the therapeutic relationship. Since what people ask for is a crucial determinant of what they get, patients who resist therapy may end up receiving inappropriate physical or medical treatments. One psychiatrist told me about a depressed woman who had been sexually abused since the age of 17. She was so adamant that she would not submit to the talking cure that she was given electric-shock treatment instead. 'A lot of people,' the psychiatrist commented, 'would prefer to see their problems in terms of biochemical derangements. It distances the problem. They would rather see this as an illness being visited upon them than acknowledge that it is an internal problem.'

That is not to say that everybody outside the articulate middle classes looks upon therapists with suspicion. I heard from several people of working-class patients who had a gift for thinking psychologically about themselves, and an instinctive understanding of the way the process worked. Edwina described a housewife coming to see her, after taking pills for years, who had heard on the radio that depression could be treated by psychotherapy. 'Nobody has ever talked to her about her problems. She comes to therapy and she is a natural. She goes to her doctor and says, "No more Valium!" '

Therapists once believed that all patients should be thrown in the deep end, being received in 'analytic' silence from the moment they enter the door. Such an approach may not be appropriate for many patients: it is certainly not right for those who, when sent for therapy, have little prior understanding of its peculiar techniques. They will need to have the process explained to them. 'If someone has no experience of psychotherapy,' says Molly, 'then it is worthwhile starting off by talking about what kind of difficulties they are likely to encounter. It is important to let someone know how odd the situation is.' And modifications in technique may also be required, including a more natural and spontaneous approach, with less emphasis on distance and long silences, more advice and reassurance.

When therapists talk about working with patients from different social groups, they often appear to feel they are bestowing the fruits of a higher culture on the deprived. This can sound paternalistic. 'It is like giving to a child who has never had toys, enabling them to experience something they have never experienced before,' says one. Felix describes the need to encourage his patients to be playful, to fantasize. 'They did not hear fairy-tales as children,' he says. 'They did not have the same opportunity to be creative. Once they learn how, they catch on.' What seems to become lost is the search for a position of equality, of two people involved in a journey of exploration into the psyche of one of them. In the gap between the cultures there is a possible loss of balance.

The greater the divergence between the patient's cultural background and that of the therapist, the more likely it is that problems of understanding will emerge. George, whose affability throughout our interview makes it easy for me to understand why he would be frustrated by any failure to communicate with a patient, feels that there are certain 'cultural nuances' that he misses when patients who grew up in England attend his New York practice. And he recalls with evident remorse the occasion when he tried to analyze a black woman who had grown up on a farm in the Deep South. 'I just could not understand her,' he says. 'Half the language I could not catch, and her frame of reference was so different. We could not find a common discourse. So the help I gave her was minimal.'

Good analysts will take nothing for granted with any of their patients. Wherever they come from, they will find out something in advance about their background, the source of their attitudes and values. But many discover, like George, that there is a point when difference becomes insurmountable. Nora once tried to treat an Orthodox Jew. It was not, she acknowledges, a great success. Having been brought up in a Christian culture, she could not grasp her patient's inner world. 'There was too much that she actually believed in and I did not know what to analyze as being neurotic and needy and better done without, and what was at the core of her being, as a religious faith is to somebody who has got it. Although I helped her through a difficult time, I do not think I was the right person for her and I probably should not have done it.'

In theory it should not be hard for a white man to analyze a black woman, a Christian to analyze a Muslim, or an American WASP to analyze a Mexican-American from the ghetto. Each, after all, has the same basic human needs – to be nurtured, loved and understood. The differences between cultures simply add another layer to the enormous variations in the way people are brought up and experience life, even within the same culture. Every analysis is a research project. If the patient is a Puerto Rican in his late twenties who is still living with his mother, the good analyst would not simply label that behaviour pathological; after all, it is not so difficult to discover that it is normal in some Hispanic cultures for children to stay at home until they are married.

Therapists who regularly deal with patients from different ethnic backgrounds must take an interest in the difference between cultures. They must continuously ask, 'What is normal? What is appropriate?' And instead of measuring the patient's behaviour only against their own values, they have to form a scale that represents the attitudes picked up by the patient in his or her earliest years.

Arnold is known as one of the few analysts in New York with some understanding of patients from Asian cultures. We meet at a café in Greenwich Village, where we both order a bowl of oatmeal and a cup of tea. The contrasting behaviour of our two waiters – one a reserved oriental, the other a tall, outgoing guy with his long hair tied back in a ponytail – seems relevant to our discussion. In his mid-fifties, Arnold wears a black beret over his balding head. From his tweed jacket and green tie, one might judge him an academic from an English university.

Arnold's interest in Asian culture started at college, when he became fascinated by Japanese art and Indian philosophy. These enthusiasms were in abeyance during his professional trainings, first as a psychologist and then as an analyst. They were stirred up again by a visit to India in the 1960s, and then by an Indian approaching him for therapy in the early 1970s. The son of a civil servant, the patient had learned while growing up under the British to denigrate everything Indian. But when his father committed suicide, he turned to Hinduism as an expression of his disillusion with the European way. The rest of his life had been a struggle to marry the two cultures within himself.

Arnold says that an analyst who is not aware of the way in which Asians define themselves in relation to others can easily misunderstand their patients' behaviour. Asians will usually become much more dependent on their therapist than the average American, with Indians expecting their analysts to assume some responsibility for them, and the Japanese coming to look upon them as mentors. Such attitudes are determined by their upbringing, and the cultural significance allocated to respect for superiors.

Arnold tells me the story of a Japanese man who met his therapist at the airport some time after their analysis was over. His immediate impulse was to grab the analyst's suitcases and carry them for him, to the analyst's deep dismay. At home he kept a picture of the analyst in a sacred niche. 'Some people would say,' Arnold comments, 'that the Japanese patient had not completed his analysis, that he was still trapped in an idealized relationship. I think it is just part of the in-built reality of the relationship.'

Asian patients who have this attitude of deference towards their therapists find it difficult to express negative feelings about the therapy. Arnold has had patients who were in intensive treatment for over a year before they could voice the slightest criticism of him. Having stepped over that line, the fear that they have put the relationship in jeopardy makes them extremely anxious. 'They can get angry over other superiors who have let them down,' he says, 'but they cannot express that directly to a superior.' Given this attitude towards authority, it is no use therapists suggesting to Asian patients that they become more assertive and talk back to their over-demanding and restrictive parents. It is a solution to their problems that they cannot accept, and nor would their parents.

Psychoanalysis is so strongly associated with individualism that many Indian psychiatrists have rejected it as an appropriate treatment in their culture. Arnold challenges this view. 'I have found,' he says, 'that it is not an intrinsic goal of psychoanalysis to be on your own. That is where Western cultural patterns have entered into the theory.' Therapists, by enabling patients to settle their interior conflicts, make it possible for them to function better within the group. As long as they understand the importance of their patients' various enmeshments, therapists can make patients feel more comfortable in their world, without suggesting solutions that go against the cultural grain.

Patients from particular ethnic backgrounds can have a hard time making themselves understood to people who do not have an insider's perspective on their culture. However, there is a universality to human experience that makes it possible to cross that gap, given patience and care on the part of the therapist. But the difficulty of understanding may be further compounded when patients present problems that relate to the reality of their position within the shared culture – such problems as the way they are viewed by others on account of their colour, accent or race.

Mrinal was a teacher when he became interested in therapy. At the time he was suffering from chronic problems with his low self-esteem – of which one can still detect slight traces in his quiet, careful and slightly self-deprecatory manner – and had consequently spent 10 years on the bottom rung of the career ladder. During all that time he had never had the confidence to speak in a staff meeting, nor to apply for a post that would give his career a lift. 'It was like being in an unhappy marriage for years and not being able to do anything about it,' he says. He traces his low view of himself at the time partly to his relationship to his father, but also to a sense of being an alien in British society.

What worried him about his therapy training was that it addressed only the first part of his problem. He was being told that if only he could resolve the problems he had with his father, then all doors would be open to him. But he did not feel that an individual's internal inhibitions were the only factor that might keep him or her at the bottom of the social pile. 'I remember thinking,' he says, ' "What are you going to say to a beggar in Calcutta who is the son of a beggar?" There are other things that affect where you are. It is not all you.'

His own therapist, he feels, addressed the issues relating to his parents, but evaded questions of race or class. What was not being acknowledged during their sessions together was that even after he had shaken off his father's baleful influence and accepted his own relative autonomy, he would still have to struggle more than an equivalent white person to climb up the school hierarchy. His situation was not simply something that he had brought upon himself. He acknowledges that he had a part to play in keeping questions of race off the agenda. 'It was to protect him and to protect myself. Bringing up that issue would make a profound difference between us. I needed him as a good father figure.'

I asked Mrinal how he would now bring in the social dimension if a patient resisted dealing with it. There might, he replied, be a patient who had been brought up in India under the British, and who talked about how he thought he was not good-looking. 'I might suggest that he was at a school which was full of Europeans. Did that have something to do with it? There was this other dimension. It was not just your mother saying you were a shit, but being in a situation where the people who were appreciated were the white ones.'

One of Mrinal's patients is an Asian who had picked up from his father the message that he and his like were doomed to remain third-class citizens. The man started his career in a low-paid job and for a while accepted that this was his rightful place. But he was too clever to stay put, and having grasped a little of his potential, he started to rise up the hierarchy very fast. In doing so he triggered a lot of jealousy in the white people working alongside him. 'People,' says Mrinal, 'are out to trip him up. It is not just him thinking that. That does not mean I sit back and say to him, "Isn't it awful? It's so hard for you." But it is important to have that in my mind when I work with him.'

Mrinal works part of his week at NAFSIYAT, a centre in north London which provides therapy for ethnic minorities. Jafar Kareem, the centre's founder, believes with Mrinal that therapists must give a different weight to external realities when dealing with patients who have experienced racism. 'We openly say that we will take up various issues which are not in the domain of the inner world,' he says. 'We know that the people we see will have suffered some kind of discrimination. We say that we expect them to tell us about that. We also know that most of them will be very poor. We expect them to bring that into the clinical context. While we are ready to explore what is happening internally, the external bit is having an effect on the internal, and you cannot leave that out.

'Patients who are poor, unemployed and homeless cannot be

expected to give the same weight to exploring the psyche as to solving their problems. We have to adapt. The patient will say to us, "You can keep exploring what happened with my mummy and daddy. I want to walk out of here better equipped to start finding a job." But the same man who says one week that he needs a job might start talking the next week about some internal trauma. We have to respond on several levels at the same time. It is not all fantasy, it is not all reality. If a patient says, "Somebody looked at me in a racist manner," my interpretation would be that that could be a fact, but it could also be your imagination. We can explore both. I am not denying that it has happened, but I also want you to know that there are other things which could equally well have happened.'

Kareem's model of intercultural therapy is not, he emphasizes, about providing patients with therapists of the same background as themselves, but about educating all therapists to be attuned to the differences in people's upbringing, the experience of racism, and the way both these realities impact on their internal world. 'We do not match therapists and patients by race,' he insists, 'we do not believe in that.'

Before visiting NAFSIYAT, I had been concerned about how my presence would be viewed in a setting where the ills of racism are being addressed. But I was made welcome. That experience eased the anxieties I felt about my likely reception at the Women's Therapy Centre (WTC), also in north London. I was taken aback, therefore, when, on the morning of the day scheduled for our appointment, Rosa rang to change its location. She had not been thinking straight. As a man, I could not possibly darken the doors of the centre. Could we meet later, at her home? I had wanted to enter the centre and learn what I could from being there. I felt irritated at being excluded because of my sex.

Many of NAFSIYAT's therapists themselves come from the ethnic minorities, but the organization does not claim that only such people can help their clientele. By contrast, a central tenet of women's therapy is that women need a place unsullied by the male presence. NAFSIYAT has been known to take into therapy white Anglo-Saxons who turn up at what they take to be the local therapy centre. It is difficult to imagine the WTC doing the same for men from the neighbourhood. Women's therapy is a women-only preserve. 'The assumption of women's therapy,' says Joan Woodward, who *did* welcome me into the Women's Therapy and Counselling Centre in Birmingham which she founded, 'is that patients are not going to be told by men what is wrong and what they can do about it. Which means that, at some level, there is a hope that a woman knows what it is like to be a woman in our society. She may not be the same colour as them, she may not be the same class as them, but she is a woman.'

I find it difficult to accept, however, that it is necessarily easier for a woman to understand another woman. Superficially, when two women meet, this is true. But it should not be so at the level where analytic therapists work. The problems that men have in understanding women are not really of a different order from the problems that women have in understanding each other. And the appearance of shared experience can, in fact, be a barrier to analytic understanding. Someone who says, I am a woman and therefore I understand you, another woman, is in danger of ignoring the differences between herself and her patient, and drawing unjustifiable assumptions from their common sex.

Individual therapists, of course, will find it more or less easy to deal with patients of the other sex, depending on how they experienced the men and women in their past. Birgit, who takes me aback when she expresses the view that 'women have gone ahead of men in integrating the helpless, vulnerable part of themselves with the powerful and creative part', will not take men into therapy. Similarly, Jack confesses to a lower success rate with women. 'I tend to feel more comfortable, freer with men. I do not form close relationships as easily with women as I do with men. It is an extension of my personal life.' But Hilda, who grew up with strong and interesting men around her, prefers taking male patients.

The difference in attitude between NAFSIYAT and the women's therapy movement is partly historical. Whereas intercultural approaches to therapy were developed from the mainstream of the therapeutic profession and seek to be re-assimilated there, women's therapy is rooted in feminism. Deriving from a philosophy which asserts that women must look to each other for protection in a male world, it embraces separatism. It argues that, where many women are abused, raped and battered by men, some of them by male therapists, women's therapy centres are needed to offer some assurance of safety. Those who have been damaged almost beyond repair by their encounters with men may need that extra reassurance which a women's therapy centre can offer. There they can expect to be protected from the sort of hectoring, questioning approach that might remind them of the abusive men in their life.

Women's therapists have also argued that their male counterparts, as well as the enormous number of women working within the 'male' system, have not been sufficiently attuned to women's experience. 'It was to say to the whole world,' says Susie Orbach of the Women's Therapy Centre in London, which she helped found in 1976, 'that you have not been able to hear because you have not had particular ears to hear with.'

At one level this makes perfect sense. The different pressures on women, and the obstacles they confront, do have to be taken into account during therapy. 'There is a reality,' Peter says, 'that women are not as well paid and do not have as much flexibility in their lives.' He gives the example of one of his patients. A relatively successful lawyer, she was concerned that her career had stagnated and that less competent people were being promoted above her. This mirrored a situation in her family life where the brothers were the preferred ones, and she had to struggle to get on. Her response to the family reality had been an attitude to male competition which tended to mess things up. 'Nevertheless, it is true that generally speaking men do get promotion, and things are tougher for women. You have to take cognizance of that.'

The traditional view of the relative significance of fantasy and reality did tend to put too much emphasis on the former, so that women's oppression was simply written out of the picture. And women were right to find in the traditional Freudian concept of 'penis envy' the offensive and wrong suggestion that all women are coded by their lack of external genitalia to a position of social inferiority. But that should not lead to the wholesale dismissal of Freudian theory, nor even of the penis envy concept. 'Every now and then,' says Nora, who had to fight hard against her own analyst's attempts to explain her condition through this concept, 'you do come across it. There are women who distinctly do have penis envy.'

The concept of penis envy, like much else in psychoanalytic theory, *can* be deployed to take account of the way in which social and psychological issues are intertwined. When Robert, a classical Freudian, defends his continuing belief in the idea as an important constituent in the development of some girls, he explicitly acknowledges the importance of social issues. 'She came in,' he said of one patient, 'and talked about how she was the only girl in a family of boys. All the boys were prized, but her mother and she were depreciated for being female. She was a real tomboy when she grew up. When she has sex with a man, she likes to be on top and cannot have an orgasm unless she is. She describes how, when she gets angry, she "puts on her bat and balls" and goes elsewhere. This ineluctably leads you to a concept like penis envy. You can talk about social issues if you like, but it is not so much to do with social issues as with infantile fantasy. You would talk to the patient about how she began to take on the same depreciation of herself and over-estimation of the boys in the family that everybody else did.' Robert's twist to the penis envy theory shows that one can approach the same patient's experience from different angles – focusing on social aspects or questions of inner fantasy – and come up with much the same result.

There comes a point when women's therapy, in some of its manifestations, seems set to unravel the whole analytic project, to reject that approach to therapy as too hard and too challenging. Linda is a devotee of the arguments for a feminist line in therapy. Her patients complain that male therapists do not accept that their traumas were real, or that they found themselves helpless when they were battered or abused. 'Could you not have told somebody?' they are said to ask, or 'Did you never think of running out of the room while this was happening?' Linda does not acknowledge the possibility that these patients misinterpreted their therapists' attempt to make them see the difference between their desperate situation then and their relative freedom now, challenging their acceptance of their own helplessness in the way that Mary described in the previous chapter.

Some feminist therapists would argue that Mary's approach is too aggressive and that it fails to address the problems of growing up as a woman in contemporary Western society. Every mother, they say, hands on to her child some grievance at the fact that women are second-class citizens, who cannot expect to have their needs met. They grow up trapped at the stage of childhood – frightened, nervous and angry, unsure of where they belong in relation to others and terrified that the adult carapace they built around themselves will quickly be ripped away.

Therapists, the argument goes, need to respond to this reality by offering their female patients a different sort of treatment relationship. 'The task of feminist therapy is to address the original not-getting and to provide an experience of consistent caring,' write Luise Eichenbaum and Susie Orbach. 'This does not imply that the therapist can "make up" for the loss that woman carries with her. However, the present contact can carry the sorrow, rage, upset and confusion surrounding past unmet needs while meeting the need for relating that occurs in the present.'[2]

Feminists, therefore, have embraced the idea of therapy as a 'corrective emotional experience'. The therapist, they argue, should offer a real, nurturing relationship to the patient, within which she can feel accepted, understood and loved as she has never been before in her life. Therapy, according to this argument, can only help women to be more independent by first fulfilling their dependency needs within the therapy relationship. Linda is one of those who feel that many more traditional therapists try to hector their patients into autonomy. Their approach, she says, goes along these lines: 'Don't let these women become too dependent. Not for a single second. Just crash it out of them. This is women's problem.'

Linda keeps a large teddy bear on the couch where women sit for their therapy sessions. It is her way of showing women that they can expose their needs, that they do not need to hide anything. One woman walked straight into the room at her first session, picked up the teddy and started to rock. Linda did not even have the time to welcome her. The patient said nothing, just sat there and wept. Finally she said, 'I have needed a teddy bear for so long.' At the following session she seemed ashamed at having revealed her need so overtly.

The 're-mothering' paradigm has been embraced by women's therapists as an alternative to 'male' orthodoxy, but the view of that orthodoxy against which they have defined themselves is an outdated stereotype of the psychoanalytic therapist as a cold, aloof, domineering figure. It produces in its turn an over-simplified view of the needs that women have, and does them the disservice of suggesting that women are necessarily too damaged to benefit from a more analytic approach. Some feminist therapists have acknowledged this. Henrietta, whom Rosa caustically referred to as a 'Freudian', considers the concept of re-mothering to be a 'load of nonsense'. 'You cannot re-mother,' she says. 'I am working with adults, not children. By the time you are an adult, your relationship with your childhood has changed many times over.'

By working with a stereotypical image of psychoanalytic therapy, women's therapy tends to build itself as a mirror image of that negative stereotype. Believing that Freudians necessarily attribute penis envy to their female patients, they hunt for an equally generalized and unsatisfactory account of women's development. Believing that all therapists fail to appreciate the value of the therapeutic relationship, they create a model of therapy that is all about nurturing, never at all about analyzing. Thinking that psychoanalysis is all about upholding the status quo, they present a programme for psychotherapy as a fomenter of change. And believing that therapists undervalue social reality, they emphasize that to the possible exclusion of internal factors.

By adopting such an approach, feminist theorists can too easily give
their followers the impression that they have discovered new answers,
when all they have done is declared their allegiance to one side of an
ongoing argument. This was brought home to me when I spoke to
a therapist at the WTC about one of her patients, a first-generation
immigrant. 'I can almost see through the schizophrenia to what is
actually causing it,' she said. 'It is the separation and the losses she
has experienced. She left her extended family and came to England
where she is not accepted because she is black. She is completely
isolated. That is the core of the schizophrenia.' Such an approach
is overly simplistic. Just because a woman is an immigrant does not
mean that her internal reality can be ignored as a factor explaining
her symptoms. Similarly, belonging to the female sex does not really
indicate that one necessarily needs nurture rather than analysis.

Women's therapy has made a valuable contribution to discussion
of the role of social reality in the formation of the individual's inner
world. Today, women's therapy centres both provide a refuge for
frightened women and carry out vital research into eating problems,
sexual abuse and other 'women's' issues. But feminist therapy can
lead to easy assumptions about what it means to be a woman in
contemporary society, turning therapy into an occasion for mutual
condolence rather than a journey of discovery. Instead of exploring
the complex question of who they really are, women are encouraged
to borrow an identity from the organization offering help. Therapists
should encourage change and growth in their patients. To assert that a
man cannot understand a woman, or a white person cannot understand
someone who is black, is to deny that change is possible.

In all areas of psychotherapy patients need to have their prejudices
questioned and explored, and in no area does this require more
sensitivity from the therapist than in the area of religious belief.
'It can be an enormous problem,' says John, 'if a patient has a
sense of having discovered religion. They will experience therapy as
a rival scheme that will damage or undermine the credibility of their
religious beliefs. That can be very sticky. They do not want to explore.
The religion functions as a sort of inner resistance.' Although not an
adherent to the Freudian view of religion as something infantile that
has to be cleared away, John does believe that it can be used to fortify
people's reluctance to change.

The therapists' problem is to find a way of challenging the beliefs that
are at the root of patients' psychological distress, without denying their
freedom of religious belief. It is a complex disentangling operation,

sorting out the pathological from the healthy. Like many analysts in New York City, Dan is Jewish. One of his patients grew up in a strict Catholic household, an experience that scarred her deeply but which she cannot throw off. Whatever brings pleasure, she labels indulgence. Whether she wears a short skirt, eats chocolate or has sexual thoughts, she expects her therapist to disapprove of her, just as her father, mother and schoolteachers all did.

Sometimes she accuses Dan of not liking her because she is Catholic. She also suggests that he does not understand her and that it is time for her to find a Catholic therapist. 'What she wants,' he says, 'is confirmation that she is guilty of all those things and for someone to say that she has sinned, as they would in the confessional. I have to say that what Catholicism tells her is the opposite of psychoanalysis.' Such a declaration comes close to associating the Catholic creed with pathology. It would be truer to say, perhaps, that the way Dan's patient understood her Catholicism, and the mismatch between her belief system and her deeper desires, were at the roots of her suffering.

In the struggle to free an individual from his or her past, psycho-therapy must put everything into question. There is no safe ideological platform on which it can rest. While it is important for therapists to recognize that growing up a woman, or a coloured person in white society, can have a devastating impact on the inner life, it should not be argued in response that there is a universal pattern to the experience of femininity or ethnicity. Specialized therapy centres run the risk of denying people an opportunity to confront themselves truly. In choosing a therapist, there is always the danger that one will go for somebody who will strengthen the problem rather than provide help in understanding it and going beyond it. When people look for a way to make therapy less painful, they are likely to destroy its potential for transforming lives.

8

Perfect Partners

Matching patient to therapist

○□
○○

Bᴜᴛ does psychotherapy work? Do people get better? Certainly they often benefit considerably. And where they do not, the reasons may lie not in the therapist's theory or orientation, but in the workings of the relationship between patient and therapist. Good work can be done, it is true, when patient and therapist do not much like each other, even perhaps feel quite a strong degree of antipathy. But the way that the therapist makes the patient feel will influence what material comes up and how it is explored during the session. When the two parties are not well suited – failing to spark off each other the sort of emotional reactions that feed the analytic process – the treatment may grind to a halt or turn out badly. And yet there is no sure guide to what it is that makes for a good alliance between patient and therapist.

There are analysts who, like the proponents of arranged marriages, argue that personality match is much less important than the attitude of the betrothed. If patient and therapist, it is said, both apply themselves conscientiously to the business of getting to know each other, then love and healing will come in time. 'If one works classically,' argues Stephen, 'personality factors should not be that important. In my personal experience I do not think there are very many patients that I would even consider might have done better or worse with someone else. Some people are more sensitive to certain issues than others and could get there quicker, but I have a sense that the work I do does eventually get to the core of what the person has come to treatment for.'

Such is the view of most classical analysts. They argue that the 'repetition compulsion', which determines what material emerges in treatment, ensures that patients re-enact with their analysts their relationships to parents and others in their early life. The analyst's own manner and personality have little to do with what emerges. As will already be clear from Chapter 4, I find untenable the claim that analysts can, in a significant sense, absent themselves from the relationship. And most of the therapists I spoke to seemed prepared to give some, often limited, acknowledgement to the role that personality match can play in determining the success or failure of analytic treatments.

The problem for those of a romantic disposition, who argue that there is a right therapist for every patient, is that they have no idea what makes for a good match. If the analyst has character traits which bring back memories of a patient's past, is that a good sign or a bad one? Is difference more important than similarity? Should they get on or distrust each other on sight? If difference is important, when does the gap become too wide? 'The match of patient and analyst pairs seems extremely relevant to outcome in some analyses and not so crucial in others,' the writers of one survey have concluded, 'but we have not determined a way of knowing in advance when pairing will or will not be an important variable.'[1]

Patients looking for such a match may be distressed at the confusion that analysts reveal when questioned on this point. William, for example, asserts that ensuring a good match is vital. He says he is willing to refer people on if he does not feel that the match is right. But when I ask him to give me an example of such a case, he cannot think of one. 'Perhaps my range of tolerance is a very broad one,' he says, 'or my optimism is excessive, or I am not a good judge of what it takes to ensure a good match. Or perhaps, although I claim to believe that a good match is important, I do not really believe that it is. While I tend to believe that it is important, I also believe that something useful can probably be accomplished notwithstanding a less than good match.' Decades of practice have given William the wisdom to acknowledge that there is little of which he can be certain.

Without guidelines, patients and therapists circle the analytic dance floor on the lookout for partners. Therapists in the business of brokering patients to others in the business talk vaguely of their 'hunch', their 'intuition' or their 'gut feeling' to explain the allocations that they make. And patients who have the luxury of choosing their therapist from among several whose manner and method they have sampled can never know whether the grounds for their choice were sound or dangerous. Have they chosen a therapist who reminds them of a cruel parent out of a masochistic desire to relive the agonies of childhood, and without the hope of a happy outcome at the other end? Or have they opted for an easy ride with someone who will skirt around their more sensitive and difficult issues?

Whatever therapists themselves may argue, patients usually feel that it is necessary to look for the therapist who is right for them. But how should they assess someone into whose care they may be about to entrust themselves? What requirements should they make when asking for a therapist? Given that one cannot ask the really important questions – whether the therapist is kind, empathic, sensitive, intelligent – what is it relevant to ask?

I assumed that the first thing many people would want to know was their prospective therapist's theoretical orientation. The answer might not indicate much of any significance, but it seemed the obvious place to start. I was surprised to learn that this does not often come up. That may be, as some argued, because patients themselves thought such a question irrelevant. Or they may have learned in advance that this is a query which therapists traditionally do not answer.

In fact, many therapists said to me that they would answer such an enquiry. Perhaps that is because not to do so now invites too much flak from psychotherapy's critics. What good reason, they ask, could anyone have for not being upfront about their theoretical beliefs? There is, however, a genuine dilemma here for the therapist. It is all very well attaching labels to one's orientation, but these may have no relation at all to the fantasies that the patients have about Kleinians, Freudians, Lacanians or whatever. At their crudest, the labels suggest that Freudians are interested only in sex, or Jungians only in dreams. As such, they are grossly misleading. On the other hand, for the therapist to reply with a detailed account of his or her convictions is not only to befuddle the patient with science, but also to show up the irrelevance of the question to whatever it is that really concerns the patient. An innocent question produces an over-complex reply which leaves the questioner confused and uncertain.

One good reason, then, for asking the question would be to see how the therapist deals with the answer. The therapist who simply gives a straight reply to a question that always has a deep subtext shows as little respect for the patient's genuine anxiety as someone who evades it entirely. 'If a patient asks me what I am,' says Vanessa, 'I do not answer directly. I know that is very frustrating for them. They want an answer. Sometimes you have to give them an answer before you can go on to think about what it means. I prefer to try and get to what it means. Then it may turn out that it is not important, that what they are really concerned about is what you are going to do to them.' That seems to me a reasonably flexible approach, which takes into account the anxieties behind the question and attempts to give a straight enough reply.

Many patients looking for a therapist will know, or think they know, what it is that they want. They will ask for a woman, say that they do not want a Jungian, or insist upon someone who is young. They do so in the belief that someone in that particular category will be more likely to have the qualities they seek. Little is to be gained by challenging such prejudices. Before they have settled with a therapist, patients often feel at their most sensitive and exposed, and they may need to have the sense that their wishes will be taken into account. Most therapists are happy to go along with these choices, believing that there is no particular reason to counter them. Do they want a Jungian rather than a Kleinian or a Freudian? Then let them have one. 'If somebody expresses a preference,' says Michael, 'that is what I go by. I would not stand in the way.'

The referral process is so nebulous in any case that therapists are sometimes grateful when people do express a preference – for a man, say, rather than a woman, or vice versa. The sex of the analyst, most argue, does not make any difference to the ultimate outcome of the process. But if the patient's history predisposes them to find working with a member of one sex rather than the other more comfortable, then that is something the assessor can respond to. 'There are some very maternal male therapists,' says Rachael. 'But if you have a fantasy about wanting a woman, then you have to go through with that. There is so much else against you when you are looking for a therapist without settling for something that frightens you.'

But when patients do exercise choice, on grounds that seem reasonable to them, they may end up with someone who reinforces a self-destructive pattern rather than helping them to deal with it. Charles saw a rabbi for an assessment session. As they talked, Charles formed the conviction that this was someone whom he could understand and help. The prospective patient, however, felt differently. He felt uncomfortable about having poured out his deepest emotions so shamelessly. In choosing to go to someone else, Charles feels, the rabbi opted to avoid unearthing his sensitive issues. 'Often,' he says, 'the fact that someone seems wrong is the very crux of the person's problem. This guy was so needy. I am not the most giving guy in the world. He will go to somebody who talks a lot, is warm and sensitive. He will feel like he is in a crib being taken care of. He will love it. But I would *explore* it. I think I am the perfect person for him, but he does not.' It is unnerving to think that the more people have the right to choose, the more likely it is that they will make the wrong choice. They choose someone who will support them rather than challenge their assumptions.

Patients reach therapists from many different places. They may come through a friend who had a good experience with a particular therapist. They may call up the clinical services operated by most of the training institutions and be referred on to one of their therapists. They may have responded to an advertisement in the Yellow Pages, or have seen a card in a shop window. Some come from their doctors, others from the psychiatric departments of hospitals.

Prospective patients may find themselves in the presence of someone who does not have many patients, is desperate for any additional cases, and would barely consider the possibility of not taking them on. Alternatively, they may have the good fortune to come across an experienced therapist who, having made a genuine assessment of their needs and character, will hand them on to someone he or she considers suitable. It is obviously far better to be seen by someone with a full caseload, who will allocate the patient to someone within a wide network of therapists.

The first question that therapists must answer is whether prospective patients are suited to analytic therapy. Do they have enough internal strength to support them through analysis? Do they have a realistic sense of what therapy can achieve? Do they really want to change? Only then can therapists consider who might be the right therapist for a particular person. To do so, they try to get a feel for the way prospective patients interact with others, and how their treatment might evolve. A single assessment session throws up a lot of information; indeed, there is a maxim that the whole of an analysis is contained in the first session. Everything that will emerge later is latently there, although its full significance has yet to be revealed. The problem is how to analyze that information. It has also been said that the whole of psychotherapy is 'merely one long continuous assessment'.[2]

The nature of the patient's pathology may suggest a particular therapist. For example, there are practitioners who are known for being good with anorectics, young depressives and psychotics. Gloria once saw a patient whose difficulties seriously limited the range of possible therapists. She was nervous and anxious, could say nothing about her family and did not want to talk about any other aspect of her past. She was also very thin and came across as someone who had been terribly injured. 'She was very disturbed, very depressed and absolutely unable to recover significant memories,' Gloria recalls. 'She had to go on for-getting because it was too awful to remember.' The character profile of the appropriate therapist was immediately clear.' She needed someone firm and kind and clear, who could make a good joining to her.'

In most cases, however, the choice of therapist is made on the basis of temperament, and those who do assessments must work from their emotional intuition. How, for instance, does the patient make the therapist feel? Does this patient come across as angry, depressed, or as someone who needs much nurturing? 'One uses one's affective response to the patient for understanding more about them,' says Vanessa. 'You have to think carefully about what it means if particularly strong feelings are evoked in you. If you feel frightened or dislike the patient, then you have to ask yourself about that. Most of the time the feelings are much more subtle than that.'

Given that it is difficult at any stage to formulate deep insights into the patient's difficulties, there is clearly a limit to how much can be found out in an hour or two. Nancy emphasizes how little she can learn about a patient at a preliminary interview. 'One will get an initial impression, but people are not an open book really. And thank goodness for that! You can see some things, but you do not know what they are about. Somebody may be very excited. Somebody may be very touchy. Somebody may be very depressed. You can see things like this. But how? why? when? where? That you cannot tell.'

The ability of therapists to make a suitable match will depend partly on how perceptive they are about the patient, but also on how many therapists they know well. Therapists often make referrals to people they have taught, supervised or worked with, but it may be to someone of whom they have only heard through friends or colleagues. 'Generally,' says Vanessa, 'you take some care in referring people. Usually I would want to refer a patient to someone whom I know. Sometimes that is not possible if all the people you know have no vacancies. You are then asking them whether they know anybody. If the patient lives in an area where there are less people, I may end up referring to somebody I do not know directly. That is more difficult. There you may easily make a wrong judgement.'

Since it is impossible to learn much about how any particular therapist works behind the closed doors of the consulting room, and patients can conceal a lot about themselves during an assessment session, the process of referral is necessarily somewhat hit and miss. Nora, who has a formidable reputation as a 'broker' between patients and therapists, and was frequently described to me as an 'excellent diagnostician', readily admitted to making some mistakes in her assessments. 'To this day,' she says, 'I can get it badly wrong. At the end of an intensive consultation, I can still say to someone, "This is a nice patient. You take him. He won't be too much trouble." Ten years later someone will say to me, "That was a real stinker you sent me." '3 Many therapists will be left wondering why on earth a particular patient was referred to them.

But despite this acknowledgement of the fallibility of the assessment process, most therapists feel that they should go along with the judgement of the assessor. They will not inspect a patient to see whether he or she should be wrapped up and returned to sender. They just get on with the work. Now the onus is on the patient to decide whether this is someone to whom they can entrust their psyche for as many months or years as treatment will last.

There are cases when the feelings a patient stirs in the therapist are so strong that there is no option but to refer him or her on. Charles talked about one such that stumbled at the first hurdle because of his sensitivities and inner conflicts. A man came for a session and recounted how he had been persecuted by his family because of a harelip. Charles warmed to him and began to see the way ahead to a successful treatment which would help this talented person, then working as a messenger boy, to attain his potential. 'But,' he recalls, 'I could not wait for the session to be over. I did not want to be in the same room as him. He reminded me too much of the pain I had endured from my mother's disapproval. He aroused uncomfortable feelings which I could scarcely tolerate and it would not have been helpful for him or me to continue.'4

But very few therapists see their first meetings as part of a mutual process by which therapist and patient size each other up and determine whether they really want to work together. Benjamin, for one, is convinced that this is the best way to work. He ignores my opening question to declare his belief in an extended checking-out period for patient and therapist. He sets out a series of intervals at which the relationship should be put in question. Can we work together? he asks after the first session, four sessions later and then again after three months. 'On an unconscious level,' he says, 'that provides the client and me with security. Commitment frightens all of us.' Benjamin evidently believes that understanding this facet of his style is the key to understanding his approach to therapy.

Most therapists simply do not feel that it is their responsibility to judge at the beginning whether patients are well matched with them. Barring the emergence of violent negative or positive emotions, they leave the choice to the patients. It is, after all, their fantasies about the therapist that form the centre of the process, and their reactions that will determine whether the therapy will fail or succeed. 'I am not thinking, "Will I take this person? Won't I take this person?"' says Nancy. 'The assessment must be from the patient's side. "Can I talk to this therapist? Could this therapist understand me?" People choose to go to someone or not go to someone for conscious reasons and reasons of which they are quite unconscious. It is a difficult decision for the prospective patient.'

Such an approach puts considerable responsibility on the patients' shoulders. They may know next to nothing about what to expect from a therapist and have no views upon what might be a good prognosis for the treatment's success. Having been referred by somebody, they will often believe that this therapist has been wisely chosen to match their temperament and their needs, even though the selection may have had more to do with geography or availability. The road to therapy can be a difficult one – all the more reason why people who have finally found their way into a consulting room may want to get the process under way and not ask too many questions about the future. Also, the time at which people seek help is likely to be when they are least able to make a sensible decision. It does, after all, take a certain amount of self-esteem to challenge a therapist and say, 'I want someone else.' I put these objections to Nancy. 'You say people may be so desperate,' she says, 'and you are right. They may clutch at whatever is being offered. That is true – sometimes. But I think people are entitled to make a choice.'

While it may be true that analysts are in little better a position than patients to assess whether any particular therapy will have a happy outcome, they do have the advantage of relative emotional detachment. It would seem to be quite proper to ask of therapists that they read between the lines of their patients' responses and make a guess as to whether specific patients will work out well with them.

In theory, patients can leave their therapists whenever they want, but most find that therapy, like marriage, brings out their needs for dependency. They would rather have the pain of being with someone unsuitable than take the risk of being on their own. They begin to feel like helpless children trapped with a parent. 'One of the problems about therapy,' one therapist said to me, 'is that you do depend on another person, and all your problems and experiences with past dependent relationships come up. You feel trapped, manipulated and misunderstood.' Patients may think that the therapist is talking nonsense, but then they will go on to wonder whether the fault lies in them for failing to understand, rather than with the therapist who cannot make himself or herself understood. They feel unable to judge.

Therapists' self-esteem may be dependent upon believing that they can help anybody. This can have the unfortunate result that many patients find themselves trapped in an unsatisfactory therapy, unable to move for fear of damaging or hurting the person who is supposed to be helping them. Therapists cling on to the unhappy patient, resulting in a battle which is unsatisfactory for both sides.

'I just hope,' says Mark, who works with deeply disturbed patients, 'that the person will leave me and find someone else. It is so hard to make that judgement. I have been working with difficult people for such lengths of time. I would not want to short-change someone from having this experience of going through this shitty thing with me and having a good outcome. I would not want to make the judgement that this is someone who would go through this shitty thing and have a bad outcome.'

Mary had an experience which suggested the correctness of Mark's attitude. A woman in her early fifties came to see her and started to recount a truly horrendous history. Mary decided that she could not cope and tried to get herself off the hook by offering the woman some times which she was reasonably certain she would not be able to manage. The woman made all the necessary arrangements to attend therapy at those times. 'I did not have the heart,' Mary recalls, 'to say "I am not the therapist for you". So I took her on. It took many years of bloody hard work, but now I would say she is one of my best cases. She is now happy and enjoying her life more than ever. It was an example to me. Don't prejudge people.'

When is it more responsible to ask the patient to leave than to urge him or her to stay? It is a question to which there is no easy answer, but therapists are too ready to prefer the latter option to the former. Sarah, who belongs to a network of like-minded women therapists, feels that patients should stick with the analyst to whom they have been referred. I ask her about patients who are in such distress that they cling to a therapist even though things do not run smoothly. Is there sometimes a responsibility on the therapist to refer a patient who does not seem to be experiencing them as sympathetic?

Sarah replies by pointing out how difficult it is to know that anyone will have a good experience of therapy with you. 'It can be a long time,' she says, 'before someone feels they want to be in therapy, or that it is "doing them good". It can be years.'

But what about the people who, having been assessed by you, decide that they have been referred to the wrong person? Can they come back to you and ask to try someone else?

'I would listen to what had happened,' says Sarah. 'Possibly I would consider referring them on, but I would hear what the therapist had to say about how things had gone.'

There is a suggestion here that the patient's judgement is not to be trusted, that they should be goaded back into the pen to work on their ambivalences. Their complaints are seen as relating to therapy rather than to the therapist.

Sarah's belief that this is the right way to do things is rooted in her confidence in the therapists within her network. 'They know one another well, and they know each other's work. They are well trained and professional in the way they work. They think very carefully about how they work. They are very conscientious and do not mess people up through carelessness.'

She takes lightly my own scepticism as to how much anyone can really know about the performance of a therapist in the consulting room. She is also confident in her own instincts about a patient. 'I quickly develop a sense of who a particular patient would fit with,' she says. 'When you are sitting with somebody, a certain therapist comes into your mind.'

What, I ask, if patients come back and complain that a therapist is too unfeeling for them. Would she urge them back to that person's consulting room?

'I might. I would not refer someone who could not cope with a cold, distant therapist to that sort of person. Remember, I have sat with that patient for an hour. I have got some idea about that person. Things are always difficult in therapy. And it is not easy to make someone feel held who feels all over the place, and feels threatened by other people.'

Sarah's answers illustrate how entangling the therapeutic encounter can be, and how difficult it can be to escape its adhesive power. But she is right to acknowledge that a certain amount of discontent is built into the therapy process. Indeed, it can be an indicator that the therapy is working. Fearing change, distrusting other people and worried about dependency, the patient may kick up an almighty fuss, complaining about every aspect of the therapy. And yet they are still securing some benefit. 'You just don't know,' says Michael. 'Patients go away spitting at you, saying the whole thing is rubbish, and yet changes are taking place. There are other patients who are compliant, say everything is wonderful. And yet you know they are not taking in a thing. Getting angry with the therapist can mean any number of things other than that the therapy is not working.'

From the patients' point of view too, it can be very difficult to work out whether they are being short-changed. Mrinal went into therapy with someone he found rude and aggressive. For a while he thought that the man, who reminded him of his father, might well be 'gold', and that he was at the beginning of a 'brilliant experience'. The therapist would walk around in the middle of the sessions and respond to accounts of Mrinal's feelings with bald statements along the lines of, 'I am not doing that.' When questioned about his technique, he would say 'I am the expert. When you take your car into a garage, you do not tell the mechanic what to do.' Mrinal used to go home from his sessions very upset, unable to determine whether or not the process was helping him. Eventually he did stop going. 'I decided the guy was an arsehole.'

As many of them are happy to confess, therapists have a tendency to narcissism. Perhaps that is why it is so difficult for them to acknowledge the fact that a patient may be getting little or nothing from the therapy. And when a case is going badly, they have all the more incentive to push it through to what they hope will be a satisfactory outcome. The prospect of winning against the odds is what enables many of them to get up in the morning. Psychoanalytic theory, after all, gives them a licence to persist through bitter complaints by suggesting that the patient who complains and kicks against the treatment is 'resisting'. Many feel, with some justification, that they have a responsibility to hang on for the patient, to show that they can stand all the abuse and reproaches and come out the other end undamaged.

Another argument for resisting is that breaking up a therapy partnership can be just as disruptive as ending a marriage. 'Every patient who is passed on,' writes Patrick Casement, 'will take this rejection as the latest of many, and (often) as evidence of some dreadful truth about themselves that is assumed to be hidden behind whatever reasons are given for the treatment decision.'[5] Nini Herman confirmed that judgement when she wrote about the sense of inner devastation that ensued when her therapist appeared willing to give her up: 'He seemed defeated suddenly, ready to leave the battlefield; while far from feeling some relief, I was simply terror-stricken to see this gentle warrior lay his empty rifle down. For with this gesture he now confirmed my very worst anxieties, that I had drained and emptied him, so he was now about to die.'[6]

Confronted by a problematic phase in the relationship, the therapist seeks to find a way around it. What am I not seeing? What does the patient really want? Where should I push a little harder, linger a little longer, interpret more intensively? 'If it gets stuck,' says Irene, 'that is something you work at.' She recalls a sketch by the mime artist, Marcel Marceau, in which his white gloves register the walls of a cell gathering closer and closer around him. 'You have to feel all the walls all the way around to see if there is a chink of light. You explore together.'

Sometimes holding on turns out to be just the right thing to do. Eve had a patient who was desperate to find herself a husband. After several years the therapy had become bogged down in an endless litany of talk about dating and the qualities of the various men in the woman's life. It had become repetitive and was clearly not very useful. The patient was becoming resentful. 'What gradually emerged,' Eve recalls, 'was that she had the fantasy that if she only came to her sessions regularly, never missed a session and was never late, then I would find her a husband. We explored her disappointment at great length and eventually she was able to take on the responsibility for herself. That moved the treatment along.'

Despite this experience, Eve feels that therapists should be more willing to concede defeat. 'I think there are bad fits. Sometimes something that was good for some years no longer works. The patient finds it hard to leave. I don't often hear of analysts helping patients to leave and find a different analyst. Maybe if that was more common, it would feel like less of a big move. I would feel very guilty saying that. Maybe that is not fair to the patient, or to the analyst.'

It helps when the problem is relatively clear cut, as in one case described to me. Peter had knocked around and tried many jobs before becoming a therapist, but he had never been to university. He was worldly but no savant. One of his patients was an Oxbridge graduate whose father had been a high-flying academic, and he found it difficult to accept his therapist's lack of intellectual credentials. 'He would read the journals,' Peter recalls, 'and ask, "Why aren't you on the editorial board?" I was a total disappointment to him. I also represented his mother, who was very bright but had no formal education. It was an interesting non-marriage. I am not a writer, not an academic. He made me feel inadequate because I was not the academic father he wanted me to be. It became too much of an issue in the therapy. He decided that he wanted to be with an internationally renowned analyst.'

But many less obvious cases lead into a protracted stalemate where patients who no longer feel they are changing have become too dependent on the analyst to move on, and where analysts fight on in the hope that one day they will hit a breakthrough. Patient and therapist become locked into a process that is extremely painful to both of them, stuck behind the closed doors of the analytic encounter. For

Paul one such treatment went on for eight difficult years. 'The patient did not want to change. He would not take any responsibility for what he did. His behaviour was too difficult to stomach. He recognized my vulnerability. I do not think I was the right therapist for him.' And Gavin saw a patient for six years, always hoping he could resolve her difficulties, but never quite getting there. 'If I had been able to recognize how destructive she was,' he says, 'then I might have got somewhere. It would have been incredibly painful for both of us, but it would have been better than the endless chuntering that we went through. She would tell you that I helped her a lot, but I do not know how she justified the therapy to herself.'

Perhaps what therapists need to ask themselves more often is whether everyone might not benefit, at some stage, from a fresh perspective on their problems. Retelling the story of one's life for a second time can be painful, even tedious, and the bond that comes from having exposed so much to another person can be very strong. I know someone who, when her therapist died, declared in some distress, 'Nobody else knew more about me, not even my husband.' But it can be stimulating, nevertheless, to abandon the cosy and familiar for a new terrain. Antonia has had several patients for whom she was the second therapist. 'Almost without exception,' she says, 'they have been amazed at the newness of the second therapy. They say things like, "I never talked about that. That never came up in my first therapy." I do not think that is because I am so brilliant and intuitive. It is because there are certain things that interest me which do not interest other people. Patients pick that up very quickly.'

Marriage is meant to be for life, therapy not necessarily so. But the fear that therapy offers no escape in divorce leads many people to hesitate before entering treatment. Do therapists sometimes keep patients in treatment for too long? Since so many refuse to judge when the therapy process has ceased to do any good, the answer must be yes. But a good therapist will know when the sessions have become tired, when patients are no longer bringing up interesting fantasies about them or profound material about themselves. They will look in the patients' words for some hint that they are ready to leave, and then gently bring up the idea.

Cathy surprised herself by suddenly asking one woman patient whether she had begun to think about leaving therapy. The patient was silent for some time and then said, 'I am absolutely terrified of that.' She went on to say, 'It is funny, though, I was thinking as I was coming here that this next year was going to be my last in therapy.' Cathy traces her perception to the fact that the patient had not been reluctant, as she usually was, to leave the room at the end of the previous session. From being someone who expected everyone to send her away, a consequence of having been banished to boarding school for four years when very young, she now accepted that the therapist would always be there. 'That session,' says Cathy, 'she could imagine that I would be there next time, that it would not be such a terrible loss.'

The analyst may cling to the patient in the hope of engineering new developments, and the patient may cling to the analyst out of a belief that there are new avenues to be explored, but both will eventually have to come to terms with the fact that the conclusion of analysis can never be totally satisfactory for either party. Vanessa recalls the process of ending with someone after a seven-year analysis. 'The magical hopes that he had at the beginning became a big issue. Some hopes which had been somewhat secret burst on to the scene with fury. "Why hasn't this been changed?" he asked. It is part of the ending to reconsider what you have done, what has not been done and why it has not been done. People hope that the past can be redone, but it can't.'

9

Playing with Fire
Under pressure from the deeply disturbed

OO
OO

IT IS sometimes argued that only those therapists who work with really tough patients – psychotics, psychopaths, sexual offenders and those suffering from narcissistic disorders – are any good. Dorothy Rowe, for example, expostulates against those who turn away patients because, she asserts, of their 'wish to avoid those people whose lives have been filled with tragedies beyond repair and recompense and whose education has not fitted them to speak of their experiences in a way typical of the white, middle-class English'.[1]

This could be called the 'macho doctrine' of psychotherapy. It prevails especially within psychiatric hospitals, where for any therapist to admit that some patients make them feel uncomfortable or ill at ease would be to put their professional competence into serious question. It is also common among analysts who view themselves as doctors dispensing a cure for every illness. 'I look on myself as a general practitioner,' says Nancy. 'When somebody comes I do not know whether they have a knee complaint, a neck complaint or a gastric ulcer. I am a GP and it is only when we get working that I know where the area of complaint is. I feel ready to try and work with whatever comes.' Macho therapists take pride in their ability to cope with all patients.

Taking the full measure of a patient's problems at the beginning of treatment is, of course, difficult, but the macho attitude ignores some of the dangers of therapy, the difficulties that therapists find in establishing a rapport with some sorts of patients, and the necessity of such a rapport for a successful outcome. Therapists should exercise a right to choose. Those who feel threatened by the anorectic, the psychotic or others from very disturbed backgrounds would be much better off working with people who do not challenge their ability to cope, rather than endlessly trying to overcome their inhibitions and sharpen up their skills on luckless patients. Far better to acknowledge one's limitations than to go into the consulting room without hope or confidence. Psychotherapy is hard enough for both patient and therapist without making it even harder.

Jim realized early on that he felt happier working with more integrated high-functioning patients. 'I treat a lot of lawyers,' he says. 'They are articulate. They can pay your fee.' He turns away very disturbed, borderline patients, or people who act out and are uncooperative. He also avoids patients who require medication. It could be said that he has a cushy life. One could accuse him of being greedy, élitist and socially useless. (In fact he claims that political radicalism drove him into the profession, and remarks that the financial rewards are not so great.) One could accuse him of all those things, but if that is where he wants to make his contribution, so be it.

There are many in the ranks of the 'worried well' whose lives are constrained and limited by their distress. Their problems might seem trivial to those who work with florid psychotics, and Dan's patients often express feelings of guilt about requiring treatment despite their relative normality. 'I don't have the problems other people have,' they say. 'My parents didn't beat me. I was well brought up. What am I doing here?' But what is bothering them, Dan remarks, bothers them intensely. 'What matters is the feeling attached to their experience. They may be doing great things, but if they feel that everyone is looking for them to slip up, and they have to use all their energy so that they are not exposed as frauds, then they are suffering.'

Yet many therapists, as the discussion in Chapter 1 showed, are drawn into the profession because of an interest in their own potential madness. They want to plunge into the world of deeply disturbed patients, in order to get in touch with the crazier parts of themselves. Paul, for example, was working in a mental hospital when he first became interested in psychotic patients. 'There was something,' he says, 'about the primitiveness of the psychotic patients that for me represented a whole area of the human psyche that I had not thought about in myself. I found it interesting to discover that I could actually bear being in touch with the most primitive aspects of myself. It is very hard work, and most people understandably decide they are not going to work in that area.'[2] He now divides his work between the relatively normal patients he sees in private practice and clinic work with criminals and the deeply disturbed.

For all psychotherapists, their work is partly a voyage of self-discovery. Adam traces his interest in psychopaths to growing up isolated as a child. 'It made me feel something of an outsider, and interested in other outsiders,' he says. After working as a social worker with delinquent adolescents and then in psychiatric day-care with adults, he set up a practice which brought him a caseload with a large number of criminals. He 'enjoys' working with such people, partly because of the insight they provide into the effects of childhood deprivation and into the 'primitive, ruthless, shameless, psychopathic' elements in all of us.

Such patients can be extremely demanding, and many therapists do not feel able to put themselves out to the extent that they require. Their interest in the disturbed parts of themselves only goes so far. Robert was approached by someone who wanted him to be available all day, every day, and to drop everything in response to his calls. 'He really thought that is what an analyst does. He did not understand that there is no one who does that unless you are in a hospital or specialize in taking patients home with you. I would find it too stressful, too demanding, and it is not the kind of problem that interests me. But I do know somebody who has an interest in profoundly disturbed people who need a lot of attentive support.'

I was continually told by therapists that they knew 'someone' who dealt with very seriously disturbed patients. When I met Mark, I wondered if they had all been referring to him. He describes himself as a therapist 'of last resort', the person to whom patients come when everybody else has failed them. There are not, he says, 'a lot of virgin people' in his practice. Many will have seen 15 or 16 therapists before coming to him. He works out of a consulting room on the ground floor of a large apartment block. It is a narrow, untidy room. Papers are scattered over the desk by the window. Two non-matching chairs jostle for space with the bed that serves as a couch. Most analysts' rooms suggest order, restraint and control; Mark's emanates chaos and disorder. He is in his early fifties, but he offers a smile of perpetual youthfulness.

When I ask him why he became a psychotherapist, he quotes Jung, who once said that a good psychologist is someone who has no choice but to spend his life in a hospital, whether as a doctor or a patient. He speaks of psychoanalysis as an experience of 'undergoing pain with another person'.

From his first session with his very first patient he felt excited by the opportunity to immerse himself in another's psychic reality. 'I loved the chaos,' he recalls. 'I was away from having to shape up and be a certain way. I could just sit there and let the whole business impact on me, just let the emotions and the images come.'

It is perhaps his openness to his patients' most extreme experiences, his willingness to go wherever they go, that enables Mark to work with those whom others have judged untreatable. 'Maybe I too am one of those incurable types,' he suggests. Probing the more disturbed levels of the human mind is, for him, an adventure. 'You have this feeling,' he says, 'that you are going to unlock the secrets of the universe when you work with the stuck parts of people.'

He tries to adapt his 'way of being' with a patient in the hope of finding 'a place where one can be at home with a patient, and have a real interweave in such a way that they can say, Yes, I can talk to this person. This person is going to help me.'

He also likes to be at the cutting edge of psychoanalysis, constantly evolving new ways of reaching out to help deeply disturbed patients. 'But,' he says with regret, 'there are certain people whom we have not evolved the capacities to work with. They come in, knock everything, are super-critical, terrifically destructive and negative. What you do is the wrong thing. If you do not do it, you were wrong not to do it. It is awful knowing that 40 years from now someone will be able to connect with this person, but that you cannot do it now.'

Very disturbed patients will expose their therapists to experiences which can be deeply unsettling, unnerving and even psychically dangerous. Mary worked with someone who often had panic attacks and fainted. At one session, shortly after the death of her mother, Mary felt the room go into a spin. 'I was sitting in my chair,' she recalls. 'The patient was telling me something quite innocuous and the room just whizzed round. I sat there, saying to myself, "Just hold on to your chair." I knew it was not something I was feeling. There were these psychotic feelings that she had projected into me. I was just about able to hold it.' One has to be very sure of one's ground before exposing oneself to these sort of experiences.

The roots of serious psychological disturbance lie in the relationships that people had with their parents and others who were around when they were growing up. Having only had chronically deficient relationships in their pasts, they find it extremely difficult to bond to their therapists. They cannot form the sort of relationship that normally evolves in the therapeutic encounter, and oscillate between cold fury and stormy rage as the therapist proves unwilling to play along with their inflated view of themselves.

'It is hard work,' says Edwina, who is one of many therapists who made me feel that, despite my own acquaintance with schizophrenics and depressives, I had never met the sort of people she described.

Perhaps it was only that I had never looked so deeply into their pain and distress. 'You can feel emotionally devastated at the level of their anguish, negativity and despair,' she remarked. 'These are people who cannot spend a night in a bed with anyone because of the feelings of disgust and horror that come up. They cannot achieve any form of sexual love, never mind decent friendship. They are tragic figures. The relationship with you has to be absolutely solid. It is based on reliability, consistency and sheer hard slog. It is only when they feel secure that some people can let themselves slip into the despair and anguish of early childhood.' Edwina gives the impression of stretching herself all the time to reach out to her patients.

The strain involved in working with such people means that most therapists will have only one or two such patients in their practice at any one time. 'They are the sort of patients who function reasonably well outside,' says Adam, 'but when one is with them in therapy, they can be very disturbed. Often at the end of the session, they can put their coat on, go out and do an important job. They are all right outside but not inside.' They have, he says, a particular way of monitoring the state of mind of the people they are with, and locating all the weak spots in the therapist. They are totally unpredictable. 'It is a bit like being a bomb disposal expert,' he says, 'where the enemy continually invents a new bomb for which you have not got a manual.' The anxiety felt by the patient is projected into the analyst, who then has to contain it. Such a level of tension is impossible to sustain through the working day and week.

I went to interview a psychoanalyst who had worked with murderers as part of a special research project, but when I raised the subject, I felt as if I had asked him to talk about an experience which was still very raw – something he could not bring himself to talk about.

'I haven't got time to go into that really,' he said.

'We have the rest of the interview,' was the gist of my reply.

'Going back to something more innocuous, I started out doing army psychiatry. I found it very interesting. When I came back . . .'

'Why do you want to talk about something more innocuous?'

'I don't want to talk about my main interest at the moment.'

'But why not?'

'Why are you writing this book? Is it to make money? Is it to make fame? What is the aim?'

Eventually he did reveal that his work with murderers had been 'fascinating, disturbing and by no means hopeless', before going on to talk about his interest in natural history and his work as a nature warden. I took his reluctance to talk about his patients as indicating just how disturbing the therapist's experience of such patients can be.

All therapists have areas of the psyche where they are less able to cope. It took Birgit some time to discover that she had severe problems with manic-depressive psychotics. She learned that lesson the hard way – by taking on such a patient and failing to pick up the crucial fact that the patient's husband was carrying on a love affair with her sister under their roof. 'It never seemed manifest in the material,' she says, 'and was enough reason for her to remain ill.' The patient became irreducibly psychotic and shortly afterwards died in a mental hospital. Birgit had to cut off another case abruptly because the patient threatened to murder her youngest child, and there were reasons to think these threats should not be taken lightly.

Birgit traces her difficulties with patients like these to her own childhood, growing up with a severely disturbed mother. She admits that she could go back into analysis to try and work through problems relating to psychotic patients, or she could soldier on with them until she felt more competent, but neither course seems worthwhile. 'If,' she says, 'one functions as a container for a great deal of psychic pain, either in one's current relationships or past formative relationships, then I think one may be asking too much of oneself at times and stretching one's capacities too far.' It was the psychosis Birgit witnessed in her childhood that drove her to become a therapist, but those early experiences remain too raw to allow her to deal with such behaviour in others.

And even at much less disturbed, neurotic levels, therapists may have particular areas of sensitivity, where they find it difficult to cope. Robert revealed that he was ambitious to go beyond the small-time when he requested information about a career in psychoanalysis from no less a person than Freud's daughter, Anna. In reply, she told him that psychoanalysis was a profession where therapists put their personality at serious risk. It is an assessment with which he concurs. 'You may not be clinically neurotic,' he says, 'but that does not mean you do not have a lot of conflicts. If you really permit what is going on in other people to resonate within you, rather than just being an intellectual computer cooking up analytic theory in your head, then it is going to kick off problems for you that would not be kicked off in other ways. There are some patients who get to areas where I have to spend more energy trying to cope with it than is valuable or useful for either of us. Their narcissism might be too much for me to tolerate – or their sadism, or their sexual overstimulation. If I have a problem in any of these areas, and I know it, then I will pick that up and recognize that this is not someone I should be working with.'

'You get a strong feeling,' says Nora, 'not only for what you like and dislike, but what you can do better and what you are not going to do so well because you get fed up, irritable and battered.' Therapists have to find out, from what they know about their past and from their work with patients, what sort of experiences they can tolerate. Will they, in any particular case, allow patients to say whatever they want and to plumb their deepest depths, or will they constantly be striving to shift the discussion on to another track? 'I will try to assess whether I can form a relationship with this person that can become alive and meaningful,' Nora states. 'It can be difficult, miserable and angry. That does not matter. But is it going to be alive, or do I have to work terribly hard to get some life into it?'

Many other therapists spoke to me of their raw patches. Adam finds acutely depressed patients will remind him of his difficult relationship with his mother, making him feel hopeless and angry. 'I think I would find it hard to see too many like that,' he says. 'It would be a bit too close to home.' And Samantha suspects that her own unresolved feelings about death lie behind her difficulties with patients who communicate a sense of emptiness. 'I find it very difficult to concentrate with patients to whom everything seems empty,' she says. 'What I find happening is that either I stop thinking or I fill the nothingness with all kinds of irrelevant thoughts – the colour of the walls or something like that.'

What all therapists hope is that the self-analysis going on throughout their work will eventually enable them to overcome such problem areas. At the beginning of her practice, Edwina too had a no-go area. For six sessions she saw a woman who was 'incredibly negative about everything. Nothing would be adequate. Everything and everybody was against her. She was like my mother, only 50 times worse. I could not stand it in my mother, and this lady made me want to crawl out of my skin. Now, 15 years later, I might be able to handle it. Then I certainly could not.

For similar reasons, Felix used to steer clear of hysterics. They reminded him of his mother and brought back a complex array of childhood memories. But as he became more experienced, he began to take on one or two until he felt as comfortable with them as with the rest of his caseload. And it was only after Nick had a series of talks with his mother, who had endured two severe bouts of depression in his childhood, that he conquered his fear of depressive patients. Whether out of a delayed desire to make her better, or a sense of inner guilt about his own imagined responsibility for her condition, or a need to conquer his own fear of becoming like her, he now always has a number of severely depressed patients in his practice.

Once therapists have conquered their sensitivity to a particular pathology, they often find that the former problem area becomes a central interest. What they have conquered in themselves they want to help others to deal with. Antonia, for example, finds herself drawn to women who are 'quite high-powered, dominant and clever, but who suddenly feel that all their success has turned to ashes in their mouth, that their inner world is barren, bleak and despairing'. In working with these patients, she continues to explore the questions about her mother that formed her initial interest in therapy, and the parallels in her own experience of bleak times when she wondered, 'What is the point of it all?' Many therapists find it especially satisfying to work in the area of their own pathology. 'I love hysterics,' Nora said rather disarmingly, 'because I am one.'

There are limits to the capacity therapists have for shaping their caseload in accordance with their interests and sensitivities. Patients are not predictable and the contours of their pathology may only become visible well on in the therapy. They also tend to stay a long time, with the consequence that there is no space to fit in an interesting case when it comes up. And when therapists do have a vacancy, they do not want to keep it open indefinitely while they wait for a 'good' patient to be offered. But therapists will feed into their referral sources information about areas of pathology where they feel a particular sensitivity, or where they have a block, and expect to receive appropriate cases. For Rosamund the process works mysteriously well. Whenever she is interested in something – self-destructive women, gay men, pregnant women – she suddenly gets a cluster of appropriate patients. 'They seem to find you in some magical way when you are ready to talk to them.' I found no one else who could testify to such felicitous experiences, but then Rosamund gave me the impression of someone who had always attracted good luck.

Despite the problems some have in acknowledging the need for a 'match' between patient and therapist, many therapists do declare that they need to 'like' their patients. I found this initially disarming. 'Liking', says Peter, 'is terribly important. You have to put up with so much rubbish over the years that your gut reaction has to be taken into account. Do you like them as human beings, despite all their problems? Do you feel okay with this person being in the room with you?' Harold put the emphasis more on the absence of strong negative feelings: 'If the therapist starts out with a feeling of dislike, that is unfortunate, regrettable and probably not a good prognostic sign.'

'Liking' has a different meaning in the consulting room than it would in the therapists' social world outside. They are not asking themselves, 'Can I get on with this person?', but whether there is a person behind the pathology that they could like. Being unlikeable is seen as the result of the patient's difficult life, and what the process of therapy is there to do away with. 'If you understand someone's impoverishment,' says Paul, 'then you can actually put their behaviour in a context and it becomes more understandable.'

For those who deal with the 'worried well', it is easy enough to talk about liking. But there are other sorts of patients who bring out hate in everyone they deal with. 'How do you work with a paedophile who is abusing children and wants to be hated?' asks Paul. 'You become the abuser and they become the abused patient.' He finds that he can work with sexual offenders, but an attempt to treat a murderer was abortive. 'It was difficult because he made me feel so murderous. He could not accept any responsibility for the person who had died.' A similar sense of being pushed up against a brick wall overcame Mitch when a patient who came to see him with sexual problems revealed that killing was his profession and that he felt no conflicts about that at all. He said to Mitch, 'A job's a job. You try to understand people. I kill them.'

Therapists working with patients who provoke hatred in them have to acknowledge that feeling rather than trying to pretend that everything is sweetness and love. Their job is to endure the emotions that are being hurled at them in the hope that they can move the patient on to a different place. Samantha compares the experience to being with children in the middle of a tantrum. 'You do not actually like them, you probably hate them, but in a way that is irrelevant. You have to have the capacity to tolerate it when the patient is trying to do terrible things to you.' In a famous paper Donald Winnicott reported the case of a patient who had been 'loathsome' to him for some years. 'I felt bad about this,' he wrote, 'until the analysis turned a corner and the patient became lovable, and then I realized that his unlikeableness had been an active symptom, unconsciously determined. It was indeed a wonderful day for me (much later on) when I could actually tell the patient that I and his friends had felt repelled by him, but that he had been too ill for us to let him know.'[3]

Therapists have to open themselves to all the emotions that their patients fling at them – to accept, to understand and not to prejudge.

How tough that might be was illustrated for me by Nicholas's speculation on how he might respond to Hitler – a rather obscene example by his own admission. 'Suppose he says, "I am having this terrible problem. I want to gas all the Jews." "What is this about?" I would ask him. Eventually he says that he wants his fatherland to be a great country. That may not be something that I can admire, but I can see there is something noble about that. I do not end up liking him, but I can accept his goal. The patients who irritate one are the greatest challenge, but you try to get through their brutal, vicious fantasies to what the patient is trying to do that could be good.'

'I listen to them in a different way than I would to someone I met on the street,' says Alexa. 'They may be trying to put me down, talk about people in a way I don't like, or manifest cruelty. I don't think, "Naughty, naughty." I try to understand what they are telling me about something in themselves. You have to hold on with your mind to the idea that once this is understood, once this is worked through, it is going to be different.'

Whether therapists have the desire and the inner strength, to deal with psychotherapy's hard cases – sexual offenders, criminals and borderlines – or expose themselves only to the psychotic and psychopathic elements in relatively undisturbed patients, they work in a profession which requires them to put their psychic health on the line for every session. Those who do the work well, who do not cut themselves off from their patients' pain and misery but rather leave themselves open to the full impact of the material, expose themselves to enormous strains. Inevitably, some therapists crack under the pressure.

10

Going Astray

Malpractice and breakdown

□□
□□

M ASUD KHAN was a prominent member of the British psychoanalytic community, who impressed all who knew him by his height and bearing. He was an Indian prince, and the model for a sculpture by Giacometti, who, in his youth, had charmed paintings out of Matisse and Braque. He had been analyzed by Donald Winnicott, whose complete works he went on to edit. He was also editor of an important series of books about psychoanalysis and an incisive writer on the analytic process. Yet there hung around his career a whiff of scandal. Did he sleep with his patients? Many said that he did.

The whiff became a stink in 1988 when, shortly before his death from cancer, Khan published a book called *When Spring Comes* (*The Long Wait* in the US). It constituted the final confessions of an analyst with no respect for the traditional boundaries between patient and therapist, who had been drawn into multiple 'acts of transgression' in his attempts to satisfy 'needs, desires and demands'. He describes involving himself in the family life of one patient, lending money to another and delivering a now-celebrated diatribe against 'self-made Jews, who pretend to be artists, atheists, writers or dancers', and 'gilded, ageing' homosexuals, who filled him with 'instant disgust and disdain'.[1]

'I succeeded,' he claims of the seven cases he describes in the book, 'in helping these patients to find their own way, as none of their previous analysts had been able to do. I do not believe it was because I was wiser, or better, than my colleagues, but humbler, and prepared to enter into a relationship of mutual sharing in which analyst and patient gradually established a rapport whereupon they could begin to learn from each other and thrive. Those who can take this risk will earn the same benefits, both clinically and personally, that I have done.'[2]

The innocent reader might take Khan's book as a provocative contribution to that perpetual debate, How far should a therapist stray from the path of 'correct' technique in reaching out to really needy patients? What 'risks' are justifiable? And are there any rules to guide their actions when confronted by people whose disturbance calls out for special help? To the British analyst Christopher Bollas, however, the tome was a 'sordid joke book', and many to whom I spoke of it would nod their heads and mutter about how sad it was that terminal illness should have so affected the mind of a once-distinguished analyst. Most of them had not read the book, but they had heard about its anti-Semitic and homophobic revelations.

It is too easy to write off *When Spring Comes* as the final rantings of a man about to die. Such evidence of chronology as its pages provide indicates that some of what Khan describes took place before the first onset of his cancer, and he never acknowledges that he is describing a radical shift in his practice. The testament of someone no longer afraid of what his colleagues think or will say, Khan's book forces one to wonder what else happens in consulting rooms that is never spoken about, when therapists have finished their training and no longer feel that anyone is looking over their shoulder, when they are alone week after week with nobody but the innocent patient to tell them what they are doing wrong.

Many therapists spoke to me of the joy and sense of relief that came with that first taste of freedom. After the agony of being compelled to 'do it right' comes the pleasure of feeling those shackles fall away, of being able to follow one's own educated instincts with each patient. 'I think,' says William, 'I have become increasingly free, increasingly spontaneous, increasingly willing to take chances, to take risks, to dare to act in a way that seemed right. To take risks in the belief that I was being conscientious and responsible and thoughtful rather than rash and foolish.' There is no way of judging such a confession, of knowing whether what William describes is an indication of sensitivity or some gross act of impropriety.

When you talk to analysts and therapists about malpractice, they will argue that it is other people who are doing it. It is those who have not had proper trainings, who have not been properly analyzed, who have not learned either to manage themselves within boundaries or that it is wiser to refer the seriously disturbed to somebody else than to labour on in well-meaning kindness.

There is some truth in these claims. Many of the more scandalous cases of patient abuse involves counsellors, social workers and psychologists who tried to operate far beyond the capacity for which their trainings qualified them. The highly trained become tarred with the same brush as the totally inadequate. There is nothing to stop anyone putting out a sign and laying claim to the title of psychotherapist, then accepting all comers. Some US states require accreditation for psychologists, social workers or medical practitioners as a precondition of eligibility for third-party payments. A consultant psychotherapist in the UK must have been a psychiatrist first. But in the private sector it is an open ballpark.

I met someone whose sole qualification for seeing patients five times a week had been that he had read 'everything' and knew many distinguished analysts. He gave up his 'practice' when one of those he was seeing committed suicide. I also went to a seminar at which members of the audience were invited to describe situations that were causing them concern. A woman spoke of a couple she had in therapy. Their marriage was on the rocks, and she had heard the 'death rattle' in their relationship. Instead of maintaining a professional distance, she had set out to save the marriage. 'I can identify with this woman,' she said. 'I was in her shoes.' I never discovered what training this speaker had been through, but she clearly had no conceptual tools to analyze what was going on in the relationship she was supposed to be treating.

But malpractice is not confined to the under-qualified. It affects everybody. Some men who sleep with their patients are well trained, thoroughly analyzed and hold prominent positions in their associations. Many stray in other ways from the path of good analysis, forgetting the reasons behind the principles they once mastered and justifying their infractions by tendentious claims that they get 'results'. A series of small defeats and frustrations may have soured their confidence in the psychoanalytic process. 'All of us,' says Paul, 'make mistakes from time to time and do things to our patients which are wrong. I am sure that is true.'

There will also be those, like the therapist Elinor whose approach I described in the introduction, who buckle under sufficiently to get through a 'kosher' training, but then abandon all the principles they have learned. Psychoanalytic therapy is a demanding occupation, and many prefer to take shortcuts that will make things easier on themselves and possibly on their patients. 'It may be,' writes Joel Kovel, 'that the task is too great, or the demand too enormous, or the training too inadequate. But whatever the reason, the low level of therapeutic competence is a painful reality to be faced.'[3]

Therapists normally start out their careers with a certain amount of therapeutic zeal. They want to get patients better quickly, and the ways in which change is resisted challenge their ability to rein in their enthusiasm. Gradually the best of them learn to stop worrying about whether the patient is getting better, and just trust to the process. 'I have learned not to burden myself with worry about where each therapy is going,' says John. 'It is not that I am a heartless or uncaring therapist, but I just think that there is an ongoing process of the patient finding their true self. In the process, other problems iron themselves out.' Therapists have to learn to treat the stubbornness of the patient's character formation with a certain amount of reverence. 'What we deal with,' says Gavin, 'is extremely serious and pervasive. People's personalities do not change very quickly.'

Therapy is a fantastically slow business. It can be quite shocking when you read accounts of analytic cases to realize that a revelation on page five was separated by almost 300 hour-long sessions from that on the previous page. There are long periods of time when almost nothing happens, when therapists may well begin to wonder whether they are doing anything useful at all. Week after week, as the patient prods at the same tangled web without ever seeming to come close to breaking through, the pressure steadily builds. 'Sometimes,' says Paul, 'it is a plod and really boring. You are screaming sometimes. There is a bit of you that would really like to do something else.'

It is the ability to find fascination in the slow unravelling of the patient's story that leads someone to become a psychoanalytic therapist, rather than practising a more active, problem-solving approach. Some find that even the most apparently ordinary encounters bring revelations. 'Every session is breathtaking,' says Cathy. 'You do not know what somebody is going to say. Sometimes the next session refers to the last one. Sometimes it is quite different. The dreams often link up so that you can see the themes. And although change comes ever so gradually, it does come. After weeks of someone saying how cruel and horrid you are, and how you really do not understand anything about them, they might suddenly say something that makes a connection with you. The following session they may be back to where they were, but gradually they seem to be more able to relate to you as a person.'

But confronted by a steady flow of patients who seemingly all exhibit similar problems, it can be difficult for therapists to retain the curiosity needed to penetrate to the deeper levels of the patients' personalities, to avoid the feeling of 'Not this again!' And when treatments become stuck and nothing seems to move, they have to believe that, over time, they will eventually come to understand, and that their understanding will bring repair. There may be patients who keep coming back just as ill as they ever were, who commit suicide during treatment, or relapse into a psychotic state and end up in hospital. Therapists who work with the more disturbed patients must harden themselves to disappointment and hold on to the belief that they have a method which will help others to recover. Otherwise the hold-ups and the setbacks will drive them mad.

Therapists are at constant risk of burn-out, of losing the sense of lively curiosity that should sustain them. I spoke to one therapist who had wisely moved into an administrative job because she had found that she was beginning to experience her patients as repetitive: 'I realized that I was becoming bored by the stories which patients were giving me. I was losing the energy to attend to the particular individuality of that person.'

Some therapists start to feel that all patients are the same, that individual stories lack interest, and that the challenge of unravelling meanings no longer excites them. They resort to stock answers and bully patients with interpretations. They can no longer establish a rapport with the people who come to see them, and they do not really care that much. These are the practitioners, one American analyst has written, who conduct analysis in an atmosphere of 'sarcasm, denigration of the patient, devaluation and lack of appreciation', and who 'intrude into the patient's life, give guidance and advice, are grossly directive and paternalistic, and attempt to maintain the patient in childlike devotion'.[4]

Psychoanalytic work puts therapists under considerable pressures. They may sit alone in a room hearing hour after hour about suicidal desires, sexual fantasies and desperate longings. They become involved in the patient's unconscious world, taking on some of their despair, anger and anxiety. It is difficult in such circumstances to remain neutral and sympathetic, and to concentrate closely for every minute of the working day. 'There is real psychic work,' says Paul, 'just to stay with the patient every step of the way.' For those of an active disposition, just sitting all day is tough – not being able to get up, walk around and stretch. One therapist described it to me as an 'unnatural burden', another as 'physical torture'.

Many analysts add to the challenge of the job by working too hard, trying to secure a good living for their families or to prove their worth to themselves. I found no evidence to confirm the common assumption that it is easy to get filthy rich, either in England or on the West Coast of the US, from psychoanalytic practice, although many to whom I spoke were certainly well-off. But there was something disturbingly entrepreneurial about the American habit of running three or four 45-minute sessions back-to-back. To do anything else, they said to me, did not make economic sense. To British analysts, accustomed to a 10-minute break between 50-minute sessions, the US practice seems an outrage.

'I would not dream of taking a break,' says Jack. 'It would be 10 minutes of dead time. I could not do anything in those 10 minutes. I cannot read anything, I cannot write, I cannot take care of any meaningful business. The best I can do is to return phone calls and then sit there staring at the wall. It is totally lost time. Added up at the end of the day, that means you are going home an hour later.' But what, one might ask, do patients feel as they pass each other in the corridor, knowing that their therapist must try to tune into their deepest thoughts only minutes after attending to those of another? They may wonder how a therapist can switch so easily between patients. When do they have time to take in and process all the material from their sessions?

To be fair, most American analysts do have a period in the middle of the day when they can read, think and give interviews to visiting journalists. But British analysts, almost without exception, cherish that space between patients in which to think about what they have heard, drink a cup of coffee and prepare for the next person to come through the door. Linda, who has worked both in the UK and the US, considers that the American system makes 'absolutely no human sense'. Fine, she says, to be the first patient in the day, but 'I would not want to be the fourth one, paying 100 dollars a shot for a shrink who has seen three people and never gotten out of his chair and who, while I was rabbiting on, was thinking he needed a drink or an aspirin or any of the other things that people ordinarily need.'

The macho spirit takes hold of analysts in other ways too. Instead of giving themselves space to reflect upon their patients, they try to jam in as many as 10 people in a day, five days a week, driving themselves on in heroic effort. They will also soldier on through illness and other afflictions of life. Birgit is not alone in feeling that Freud's achievement in working through pain and distress has provided a bad example to follow. Her analyst once had shingles of the eyes: 'He was in appalling pain and really should have taken months off. He resumed work within three days wearing dark glasses.' Gavin, who has recently started a family, says, 'I tend to work through illness. It is partly because of the mortgage, but also because I know from past experiences that cancelling is much more hassle than not cancelling. You might as well get in, grit your teeth and then go back to bed.'

Some people make therapy their whole life. When they are not in their consulting rooms, they are writing, teaching, or sitting on committees. Others, perhaps more wisely, believe that they need other activities to refresh them for their patients. Whenever Gloria has a chance, she will put her dog on a lead and stomp around the park that adjoins her home. She feels that the 'next person has the right to have you there properly'. And Rosamund takes a day off in the middle of the week to ensure that she does not become overwhelmed by her patients' material. 'I paint, I write, I garden,' she says. 'I argue with my husband. I cry about my children. I make a real point of looking after myself and enriching myself, trying to put in as much beauty and good material as the really painful, awful stuff that I hear.'

One wonders how therapists who do not give themselves space between patients, who work and work until it is time to go home to the kids, can hope to keep themselves attuned to their patients' deeper material. If they let them, patients will intrude into therapists' dreams and personal life. 'There are patients,' says Robert, 'who will give you a pain in the neck or make you pee blood or make you impotent. You have to ask yourself, "Why is this happening? Why am I still involved with this patient? Why am I not equally involved with the others?"' Such disturbing material can be of enormous assistance to understanding a patient, and although one can appreciate why therapists might not want to make themselves so exposed, those who do surely become better therapists.

The frustrations of the therapy process, combined with the emotional exposure that treatment demands, make for a dangerous brew. The analyst's situation has been compared to that of Odysseus and his men when their boat sailed past the Sirens. Therapists cannot, like the returning Greek sailors, plug their ears with wax. Instead, like Odysseus strapped to the mast, they have to listen to the Sirens' song – to the emotions of neglect, anger, abuse, despair, or whatever else it is that the patient is trying to make them feel. Some put themselves apart from their patients behind barriers of distance and coldness; others struggle to keep themselves from being overwhelmed. 'You get terribly involved,' says Rosamund. 'Your unconscious and their unconscious, your inner world and their inner world, they all become scrambled up. You let that happen, but you also have to stand above, watching all the time. That takes a degree of self-awareness and of being able to empty yourself of your own complexes. The average person cannot do that.'

Therapists will often become the butt of a sustained torrent of anger and abuse from patients who seem determined to destroy them. The fury may be stirred by the therapists' coldness and insensitivity, or it may be a reliving of past feelings towards others. In either case, it can be extremely powerful. 'The more disturbed patients,' says Stephen, 'want to confirm for themselves the fact that nobody will ever be able to give them what they want.'

When under attack, Gloria finds it useful to draw on her previous experience as a child psychotherapist. It was not so hard to tolerate disturbed children who would kick her in the shins and bite her hand. 'If the patient hates you,' she says, 'you have got to be able to see it for what it is. You do not tell a patient to bugger off because they have shouted at you. You have got to be able to bear it and to keep on thinking. It is bearable as long as you have some sense that there's an alliance that will get you through.'

Therapists have to hold on to the insight central to psychoanalysis that patients' attacks most probably have nothing to do with them, that what they are venting is the anger that others have made them feel. Insofar as they are expurgating the experience that brought them into therapy, they are producing useful material for analysis. Sidney, for example, has a patient whose intense onslaughts render him speechless for fear of provoking further attacks. The patient follows him home via the telephone answering machine, leaving messages that tell him how ineffective he is and attempt to humiliate him in other ways. 'How I cope,' he says, 'is to say to myself that this is probably the way she grew up. All she had to do as a girl was to open her mouth once to her mother, and whatever she said would provoke an onslaught. If I can withstand the onslaught without getting defensive, it will relieve her rage.'

Therapists confronted by such a bombardment must constantly ask themselves, 'How long should I endure this attack? How long can I stand it without cracking and retain the capacity to think?' 'With some damaged patients,' says Patrick Casement, 'we take on a terrible responsibility. We could make things worse for them if we fail to survive at the point when they most need to test our capacity for survival.'[5] How to respond? Reassurance can be as harmful as reciprocal anger. 'Hatred needs understanding,' says Alexa. 'If you soften the edges of it, it is tremendously frustrating because the patient needs to see you as someone really bad.' But how long can the patient endure such negative feelings without being carried straight out of therapy? 'How are they going to hear what you say,' remarks Sophie, 'until you can light on something that is an element of trust, just a thread here or there of positive feeling?' To such questions there are no simple answers.

Under such pressure, therapists can become destabilized, losing their sense of balance and their ability to take a dispassionate view. They may hit back with savage interpretations of their own. 'Suppose something happens which prompts you to abandon your analytic stance,' says Sophie. 'Something gets to you which you find you cannot process. You respond aggressively, angrily or punitively rather than firmly.' Such slips, she says, will not be disastrous if they are caught in time. 'If one were to yield to the temptation to make a punitive remark to a patient in response to some aggression of theirs, then I have got to find out why you did that and whether there is a way of retrieving your failure.'

Nina Coltart has written about a case in which the crescendo of hate became unendurable. It was in the sixth year of a classical analysis, and she experienced a build-up of 'angry, contemptuous and horrible feelings' in response to the patient's constant expressions of disdain. One day, she writes, 'the volcanic rumblings erupted into a white-hot row between us, when we were both screaming at each other out of all our pent-up rage and frustration'.[6] She recognizes that such behaviour was 'inelegant', but claims that she was always aware of 'precisely where we were'. Less experienced analysts might not be so sure-footed under such an onslaught. Having so far abandoned the analytic stance, they might lose their footing and their control of themselves, drawing down from their own stock of unresolved anger and letting loose a destructive tide of unruly emotion on to the patient.

Even more unsettling than a torrent of hate can be declarations of loving admiration, perhaps because of the confused emotions these provoke in the therapist. Therapists who are feeling a little insecure and uncertain may ask themselves, 'Am I really as wise as this patient makes out?' They may find themselves taking too seriously those patients who put them on a pedestal and regard them as magicians who can cure all psychic ills with their words. 'We all have to be careful not to become gurus,' said one therapist. 'Patients will idealize you if you let them. Then you miss out on the interesting part of the work, which is two human beings trying to work together.'

And when events in the therapists' lives leave them feeling friendless or loveless, so that they start to mistake the therapeutic relationship for the real thing, the situation becomes yet more dangerous. Is there something about me that my patient loves, the therapist may ask, or is it really just my therapeutic persona? We are getting along so swimmingly, why don't we go out to the theatre together some time?

'There are some patients,' Robert says, 'who will treat you like you are really wonderful because they have a need to idealize you. You are not entitled to take that seriously. There are patients who might be just the kind of people you would like to be friends with, but you are not entitled to transform the nature of the relationship so that you are satisfying what you want out of it. That deprives the patient of analysis. There are people who have a hard time not being important to other people. It is true that you are important, but only as an analyst.'

This is a hard, self-denying ordinance. There are many analysts who refuse to accept it and who do not necessarily inflict harm on their patients. Ian introduced me to one of his ex-patients, and I gained no hint from talking to her that the transmutation of their healing relationship into friendship had done any harm. I have a friend whose therapist gives her presents, talks to her about his homosexual love affairs and puts freelance work her way. She testifies to the enormous changes for the good he has wrought in her. She knows that he does not treat his other patients in the same way. That makes her feel special. She likes that and it does not yet appear to have brought dire consequences.

But there will be other patients for whom their therapist's signs of caring and affection will set in motion an accelerating demand for love. They start to want more sessions, longer sessions, some indication that the therapist really cares. Therapists who are a little too kindly and cosy with their patients can get into terrible trouble this way. Their warmth becomes misinterpreted. The patients' love rapidly turns into hate.

When Paul started out in practice he was, he admits, very keen for patients to think of him as a 'friendly chap'. One of his younger female patients built from these signals the conviction that he was in love with her. 'She made me feel that I was the answer to all her prayers,' he recalls. 'Due to my inexperience I had allowed the fantasy that I was indispensable to her to develop in her mind. What I did not pick up was the anger that she felt against me for failing to be her saviour. My affability invaded her, leaving no space in which she could explore herself. She ended up attacking me for this. It was unbearable.'

Nowhere is the danger of the therapy process becoming two-way greater than when a middle-aged man takes a young, attractive woman into treatment. 'When I am working with a helpless young woman,' says Stephen, 'I will watch myself more. The work is more of a strain. I have a tendency to want to do more, to step out of my role. I am not

189

beyond stepping out of my role. I will be more sympathetic. That is not going to help the patient.'

Sidney is a strong, well-built man. I can imagine women being attracted by his stockiness and masterful manner, and it does not surprise me to learn that many request physical contact. 'If I am going away for a vacation, or it is the summer break,' he says, 'they will ask if they can hug me before they go away.' How should he respond? And what if their behaviour becomes much more seductive? 'It creates an inclination not to have the seduction stopped,' he says. 'If she is telling you how attractive you are and how much she wants you, you have to get past the gratification at your end and deal with it from her point of view. She might be using the seduction to avoid her anxiety about dependency.'

Therapists who offer love and affection may start off by doing so out of neutral concern for the patient's emotional health. But there may come a time when they look for a return. The American analyst Michael Eigen has written of a therapist who treated a patient as a needy infant. 'Then he turned on her. He became impatient and angry and put her down. He told her about difficulties in his life. He wanted her to give him something too.' That therapist, he goes on to say, 'believed in working with the baby soul like a parent, if need be. But he was a big baby himself and expected the parent-baby business to go two ways.'

As patients talk about their primitive longings for love and affection from their father, their uncles and from other men in their lives, about their dreams of romance and sexual fantasies, they draw their therapists into their own inner world. 'Her fantasies, hopes and dreams may touch him,' writes Peter Rutter, 'infuriate him, puzzle him, fascinate him and stimulate his own fantasy life.'[7] In response to the patient's belief that all her problems would be solved if only this man would make love to her, the therapist begins to wonder whether it might not really be helpful to gratify such a strongly-expressed need. He is on the route to chronic self-delusion.

Patients may come to feel that having sex with their therapist will relieve their distress, but such relief can only be momentary. It is the therapist's job to point out that carnal relations cannot achieve the desired cure. When Lionel Schwartz, an assistant professor at Harvard Medical School and a man in his mid-sixties, was expelled from the Boston Analytic Association for having sexual relations with his patients, he declared: 'While it is a wrong thing to do, women patients are not helpless, vulnerable individuals. These things went on for a long time. There had to be cooperation.'8 Cooperation perhaps, but in an act that could be satisfying and healing for neither party, and where one was exploiting the dependency his professional status had created.

During Jane's 13 years of analysis there was a long period when she was convinced that going to bed with her analyst would be the solution to all her problems. Having grown up with an image of men as bogies, with no father on whom to model her internal male ideal, and with paranoid anxieties about sexual relationships, she looked upon her therapist as someone who could break the spell. 'I thought that if I went to bed with this man, that would fix things.' Her feelings were also, she feels, a repudiation of the idea of therapy as an exploration, a call for something simpler and more concrete. 'It was as if I was saying,' she says, 'I can only feel you know me and care about me if we have physical contact.'

Patients like Jane reach out to their therapists in desperate need. In her case, it was the loss of her father and her feeling that she was somehow responsible for his death, even though it took place before she was born, which fed that need. Female patients who long for the male therapist to caress them bring up their frustration at not having had a father who could love, care for and touch them. They feel a sense of loss, of not being able to contact a man with whom they could feel happy and equal. 'When people get over-attached to the analyst,' said one analyst, 'it is because they are empty inside.' The therapists' first response to such desperate need may be a sense of total helplessness. 'How on earth can I respond to this woman's call?' Gradually the idea will grow inside some of them that there is an answer, something simple they can provide. The British psychotherapist Jeremy Holmes has spoken of how the therapist may come to feel 'that the patient has had a terrible time, that the patient has been abused in childhood, that what they really need is a loving relationship, something that they, the therapist, can offer. The therapist may in good faith offer sex to the patient.'9

Therapists who sleep with their patients are not necessarily sinister people who entered the profession with malevolence in their hearts. Everyone, it is true, is taught that sleeping with patients is wrong, but it is an ever-present danger in a process that involves two people being drawn into a relationship where being open to the emotional impact of the other is a primary requirement. The drive that leads the therapist to sleep with his patient on the couch comes from the same place as the decision to depart from the model of distance and aloofness. And yet kindness can turn into ugly abuse.

'I certainly would not say that therapists who sleep with their patients are necessarily bad people,' says Antonia. 'I would say that they need to go back into analysis and find out what is going on. We have all been attracted to our patients, and in a way we say, "There but for the grace of God go I." Hopefully the setting and one's own life are not conducive to that sort of behaviour. But we all fail, as parents and therapists. It is only by learning about those failures that we grow and learn.' Antonia's openness about her own feelings was refreshing, given the tendency of other therapists to depict such temptations as happening only to other people.

Jeremy Holmes has described the sort of case which can lead to therapeutic abuse. A woman in her early thirties came to see him. Both her parents had been concentration camp survivors. Her mother had been a depressive and her father may have abused her as a little girl. 'The feeling that she evoked in me,' he said, 'is best described as like being in a small boat becalmed at sea, with someone in intense distress, whose distress one wanted to alleviate, but for whom one could not do anything that would be helpful. I was experiencing that feeling of helplessness and trappedness which she may have felt when left with her father while her depressed mother was away in hospital. It seemed to me that this was the kind of situation in which sexual abuse could happen, where the outside world was abolished and the therapist felt cast adrift with the patient, so that normal rules did not apply.'[10]

But normal rules do apply. The patient may seem to want sex, but in nearly all cases it is the last thing that will be helpful. 'I would probably have panicked,' says Jane of the possibility that her therapist might have taken her requests seriously. 'I would not have understood very much, and I would have lost my analyst as someone who was prepared to help me think about my urgent impulses and convictions.' The therapist's intrusion may bring back memories of being abused as a child or raped as an adult. The line between the therapist as a real person and as the container for the patient's fantasies concerning other men or women in their life becomes hopelessly confused. The delicate balance of the therapeutic process is shattered. The therapist has betrayed a duty to facilitate insight and understanding.

'They fly too close to the sun,' says Holmes. 'There is a search for a loving father and a nurturing mother. But the result is in fact confusion. How could this person whom they trusted and felt was going to do something that would make them feel positive and good in fact do something that makes them feel dirty or horrible? They hoped for a magical rescue rather than the painful transcendence of difficulty.'[11]

Few therapists have seriously argued with the proposition that it is wrong to gratify patients' apparent wish for sex with their healer. But ever since the beginning of psychoanalysis, reliable reports have trickled out of such malpractice. These have to be acknowledged and confronted, not swept under the carpet, for there is an antidote that lies in all therapists' maintenance of curiosity about their own feelings and those of the patient – their desire to explore deeper rather than to seek the gratification of simple solutions. 'I do not think it is ultimately to do with ethics,' says Adam. 'In the end, ethics will not protect the patient or the therapist. Saying to oneself, "It is wrong to sleep with a patient" is of little use if one has an unresolved, unconscious need to act on one's impulses. The need is for something that says there is an analytic boundary here. It is legitimate to feel something. You can feel what you like about a patient. What is not legitimate is to act on that feeling. You have to think about why you are feeling this.'

Therapists can never rest on their laurels. They may have undergone a thorough analysis, proved to a training institute that they were relatively stable with a strong and supportive circle of friends, and completed their training with flying colours, but 20 years on, subsequent life events may have upset their hold on emotional stability and undermined the interest they used to take in their work. Divorce, the death of a parent, illness – these and other things may plunge them into a desperate psychological state where they find it difficult to tackle pressures with which they had become used to thinking they could cope. Adam has treated a couple of patients who had been seduced by their therapists. 'The way they report what went on indicates,' he says, 'that there was some basic area of insecurity in the therapist that the therapist did not know about and did not want to know about – areas which these therapists had chosen to avoid having analyzed. I guess no analysis can ever be perfect. There are always areas left unexamined.'[12]

Therapists who find themselves on the verge of committing malpractice need to undergo further analysis, seek supervision or quit the profession. They have to know that the batterings they take through life will impact on their practice and that they will need help to deal with them. 'I think it is very important,' one therapist said, 'to stay in psychotherapy, or at least to go back every few years. It is like maintaining your car. I am not necessarily in distress, but I am a growing person and my life is changing. We are always developing or dealing with something. If the self is the instrument, then that self must be taken care of. I do not think one can do an analysis and then finish.'

But it is, of course, precisely when one's emotional balance is disturbed, when life is getting one down, that the temptation is strongest simply to soldier on and ignore one's desperate condition. One patient has written of his analysis with someone whom he later discovered to be severely depressed because of a divorce from his wife. 'I can truthfully say,' he reports, 'that I cannot think of one good facet of my personality that came out in my gloomy analysis with this gloomy man, anything in me worth giving to the world or to others close to me. There was no fun or joy, only the gradual process of being ground further and further down into an all-consuming awareness of my weaknesses and inadequacies.'[13] All the signs were there that the analyst needed help but, it seems, he did nothing about it.

There has been much discussion in recent years about what the therapeutic profession can do to limit abuse and clean up its image. Attention has focused on training. How many hours of analysis should people have been through to earn the title 'therapist'? How many training patients should they have had, and for how long? How much psychoanalytic theory should they know? Additionally, detailed codes of ethics have been outlined, to which, it is suggested, every therapist should be required to declare allegiance. And consideration has also been given to the balance of lay and professional members on a properly constituted ethics tribunal.

But these measures, although important, do not touch the heart of the problem. However carefully conceived the training, some inadequate therapists will get through, and some who seemed set for a sound career at graduation will go bad thereafter. The therapist whose emotional life is in disarray, who starts to find it difficult to cope with the pressures that the job presents, will not pay much attention to any ethical code. And there will always be too few patients who can face the shame and embarrassment of hanging out their emotions in front of an ethical tribunal, and who fear that, however careful its constitution, they will never receive a fair hearing from such a body.

The dangers of therapy are so great, the temptations it offers so considerable, that only regular monitoring will tackle the problem. Therapists should be required regularly to give an account of themselves. How often do they take their cases into supervision? Do they attend lectures and conferences? With whom do they discuss their most problematic cases? What is the condition of their emotional life?

Are they in need of further analysis? And when they hear of colleagues whose methods give reason for serious concern there should be some forum in which they bring their anxieties out into the open and call that person to account, rather than simply brushing the matter to one side. There is no call for an inquisition, for the codifying of analytic technique into rigid rules and regulations. But any analyst who cannot convince his colleagues that what he is doing is justifiable may well be harming his patients. Most analysts are good at self-analysis. But psychoanalysis needs to become a self-analytic profession.

Conclusion

I HAVE found evidence to convict therapists of many of the charges which have been laid against them by Jeffrey Masson and other critics. Some sleep with their patients. Some bully their patients. Some continue with treatments long after the patient has ceased to secure any benefit. They do all these things and many more. Given such evidence of impropriety, how can one challenge Masson's suggestion that this is a profession which should be abolished?

One line of defence would be to say that such malfeasance is inevitable in any situation where one individual has influence over others. Some parents torture and murder their children. One does not immediately propose that all children should be bundled off to communal nurseries. Some teachers work out their sadistic impulses on their luckless pupils and send them away, after 11 years of education, knowing nothing of science, history, literature or art. One does not propose the abolition of schools. Some doctors misdiagnose their patients' symptoms and leave them to an unnecessary death. Some psychiatric nurses let their charges live in horrible squalor. The list of malpractices is endless. To defend psychotherapy with this argument is legitimate, but hardly sufficient.

People brought into intimate contact with each other become subject to enormous pressures and temptations. The viciousness that results has to be written off against human fallibility and weakness. So much is inevitable. It is when the percentage of bad cases is statistically significant that it becomes relevant to talk about abolition rather than vigilance and reform. There is no evidence in Masson's writings or elsewhere that therapeutic abuse is as common as he seems to suggest. He talks about trained practitioners and untrained charlatans, about the eccentric founders of movements and run-of-the-mill therapists as if they were all the same. His is an idealistic fantasy that has no space for the good that most psychotherapists undoubtedly do, and no sympathy or understanding for those who fail.

Masson believes in a natural law whereby even the kindliest people who become therapists turn into demons when they put on their analytic mask. But many of those who make their patients suffer do so not out of some evil intent, but out of confusion and misplaced kindliness. A silent stare may stir anger, but for some patients a word out of place can stimulate fury and a held hand can arouse confusion and panic. One of the paradoxes of therapy is that niceness may be counterproductive and gentleness may not produce results. Masson has published accounts of glaring abuses of therapeutic responsibility in institutional settings, but these do not really tell us much about what happens in consulting rooms all around the world. He does not seem to appreciate the subtlety and complexity of the therapeutic endeavour, and the very real dilemmas it presents to practitioners.

The practice of therapy is always precarious. It is when they are ambitious that therapists put their own personalities under the most extreme pressure. If they avoid the risk of being unsettled by their patients, they also miss out on the possibility of making genuine contact with their pain and bringing some measure of understanding. If they stick to the rules and lose the courage to dare, the experience they provide will be too stiff and formal to be of use to anyone. And if they always keep their distance, so as to avoid any risk of entanglement, they may end up causing an explosion that wreaks havoc of enormous dimensions. The risks of therapy are an inevitable part of the benefit.

Psychotherapists are no more or less human than the rest of those in the 'caring' professions. However, like the monks of medieval Europe, they are seen as living by a higher ideal. They say they can take patients' messy, muddled stories and show them a way to resolve their problems. They say they can receive a continuous bombardment of hate, viciousness and anger, and respond only with kind words and understanding sentiments. They say they can feel 'love' for all their patients and see the goodness concealed by their cruel, manipulative or psychopathic outer crust. They are people who once were sick and have now become whole. They have a message to bring to the whole of mankind. Maybe what troubles their observers most is that they charge for their services, rather than living on alms and kind thoughts.

The analytic ideal is one that can only occasionally be attained. Therapists cannot really raise themselves on to some lofty plane where, untouched by life's storms, unaffected by the tales of horror that their patients bring to their private rooms, undisturbed by the challenges their patients present, they always stand as perfect models of equanimity and kindness. They must stumble and fall. And outside their consulting rooms, they may show a completely other side of their natures. They may take the wear-and-tear of the daily sessions back home with them and give hell to spouse and children. They may let off steam in furious encounters with others at their workplace. Or they may start to behave with their patients in ways that are unbecoming, inappropriate and untherapeutic.

It is because therapists set themselves so far above the rest of humanity that many exult when they are brought low. At the same time, though, the sceptics want them to be more perfect than they are because they want to believe in their own possibilities for perfection. And they mock them also as a way to avoid the pain of acknowledging that they need them.

Behind the argument that therapy should be abolished is the assumption that it is something that people do not, or should not, need. People's refusal to accept the necessity for a profession to cure our psychological ills is rooted in a reluctance to acknowledge that society produces emotional casualties and lacks any others resources to heal them. While I was researching this book, I was constantly being told how 'sad' it was that people did not have enough good friends to dispense with the need for therapists.

There are people who talk proudly of their weekly visits to see their therapists. They want to show that they are aware of their own failings and are doing something about them. But for many others it is something that they keep very much to themselves. But where is the shame in acknowledging that the personality you developed to endure the vicissitudes of parenting is no longer adequate to the strains and stresses of life? That people need help to develop, to form relationships, to enjoy work and play? That they actively seek to increase their understanding of themselves?

Shame if the therapist reinforces society's assumption that people in need of help are truly sick and pathetic. Shame if therapy becomes a way of avoiding life, substituting the secure analytic relationship for the rough-and-tumble of reality. Shame if the therapy is indefinitely prolonged, absorbing all the individual's resources of time, energy and money. Shame if therapy becomes a quest for perfection that can never be attained. But no shame if therapy enables individuals to come to terms with their past and to live a more fulfilled life in the future as a result.

For many it is only when disaster strikes that they find out how much their defences against anxiety have crippled them inside. When cancer starts to ravage their body, when a child is lost in a car accident, or when a spouse decides he or she has had enough of the emotionally starved atmosphere, then people feel licensed to acknowledge the weakness of their coping mechanism. It is then that many begin to question the values they live by, the adjustments they have made, the devastation they have wreaked. It is an awful paradox that many find a new purpose to their lives in the wake of devastation.

When people talk about coping, not needing, not collapsing, it is often an indication that they are finding it hard to sustain a self that is no longer true to what they feel or want. There is a need to assure one's employers and colleagues that one is more organized, more dynamic, more motivated than may really be the case. One needs to attend to one's outer presentation, making sure that the suit, the hairstyle and the colours are creating the right image. For some the gap between exterior polish and the isolated grieving inside can become intolerable. They have pursued their ambitions, gratified their impulses and enjoyed material prosperity, but they wake up one day and say, 'I am empty.'

Then they may reach out to friends and find they were 'friends' who came along only for the good time. They may look to a spouse for support and find that he or she only liked the efficient, dynamic and successful part of the self, its outward manifestation, and not its pathetic, childlike core. Then they truly need a psychotherapist to offer them a setting to pour out their life story in a climate of emotional honesty. There they can tell others how they felt as children growing up with parents, and how they feel now – in the office, with their children, in the marriage bed. There they can find the deeper levels of their being, what they really want to be, where they really want to go.

Unlike so many others, psychotherapists do acknowledge their weaknesses and failings as individuals. They do so by going into therapy themselves. If people could learn from them to accept that everybody is damaged, that everybody needs to be cared for, respected and looked after, if they could learn to listen to the pain that is expressed in words of reproach and anger, rather than take it as a narcissistic slight on themselves, if they could learn that advising and preaching is much less use than listening to the individual's inner voice, then perhaps people truly would not need to rely upon psychotherapists for help. But life is not like that. Most people have too much on their own agenda. Tossed around on the waves of life's misfortunes, mishaps and accidents, they have too little space to think of others.

SHRINKS

Far better, then, to acknowledge that psychotherapists are imperfect like everybody else, than to dismiss the whole profession as a bunch of inadequate cheats. People need to learn from psychotherapists where they have discovered how to achieve good things, and to encourage their organizations to help or repudiate those who do harm. Therapy is dangerous, but then so is life. Therapy is not so frightening when you understand the way it works. And perhaps it is not such a bad thing to acknowledge that therapists provide an invaluable resource for those who live in the modern world.

References

Preface
1 Jeffrey Masson, *Against Therapy*, p. 24
2 Christopher Bollas, *Forces of Destiny*, p. 176

Chapter 1
1 Thomas Maeder, *The Children of Psychiatrists and Other Psychotherapists*, *passim*

Chapter 2
1 Stephen Mitchell, *Relational Concepts in Psychoanalysis*, p. 2
2 Robert S. Wallerstein, 'One Psychoanalysis or Many', *International Journal of Psychoanalysis*, no. 69, pp 5–19
3 Nini Herman, *My Kleinian Home*, p. 100
4 Melanie Klein, *The Psychoanalysis of Children*, p. 32
5 Nini Herman, op. cit., p. 63
6 R. D. Hinshelwood, 'Questions of Training', *Free Associations*, no. 2, p. 12
7 Patrick Casement, *Further Learning from the Patient*, p. 165
8 Deryck Dyne, 'Questions of "Training"?', *Free Associations*, no. 3, p. 94
9 Mitchell, op. cit., p. 90
10 Wallerstein, op. cit., pp 5–19

Chapter 3
1 Quoted by Ernest Gellner, *The Psychoanalytic Movement*, p. 174
2 B. A. Farrell, *The Standing of Psychoanalysis*, p. 214
3 Casement, *On Learning from the Patient*, p. 95
4 Phyllis Grosskurth, *Melanie Klein*, Alfred A. Knopf, New York, 1986
5 Masson, *The Final Analysis*
6 Farrell, op. cit., p. 214

Chapter 4
1 Arnold M. Cooper, 'Some Limitations on Therapeutic Effectiveness: The "Burnout Syndrome" in Psychoanalysis', *Psychoanalytic Quarterly*, vol. 55, p. 585

2 Casement, *Further Learning from the Patient*, p. 70
3 Atwood and Stolorow, *Structures of Subjectivity: Explorations in Psychoanalytic Phenomenology*, Analytic Press, Hillsdale, 1984, quoted Mitchell, op. cit., p. 191
4 Ralph R. Greenson, *The Technique and Practice of Psycho-Analysis*, p. 212
5 Suzie Mackenzie, the *Guardian*, 30 January 1991
6 It may be that the patient here had noticed, but could not say that he had noticed. Rachael acknowledges that it was partly her problem, finding an opening to talk about her pregnancy. The pregnant therapist, she says, feels in a very vulnerable position.
7 Sophie adds, 'It would not be accurate to claim the session referred to as "usual". It was unusual in that I was 15 minutes late and I cannot recall any other occasion when I would have been more than four or five minutes late. Then I always apologize and make up the lost time. In the example of being 15 minutes late, the session was affected by my lateness and the patient spent much time expressing anger about that and the inconvenience caused. This particular patient was not disposed to feel concern about the reason for my lateness: some others might have been.'
8 Robert Lindner, *The Fifty-Minute Hour*, pp 51–83

Chapter 5

1 Joseph Sandler, 'Reflections on Some Relations Between Psychoanalytic Concepts and Psychoanalytic Practice', *International Journal of Psychoanalysis*, 1983
2 Casement, *On Learning from the Patient*, p. 172
3 Casement, *Further Learning from the Patient*, p. 107
4 Michael Eigen, 'Boa and Flowers', delivered to the National Psychological Association for Psychoanalysis, 2 May 1990
5 Peter Lomas, *The Limits of Interpretation*, p. 78
6 Margaret I. Little, 'Winnicott Working in Areas Where Psychotic Anxieties Predominate', *Free Associations*, no. 3, pp 9–42
7 Quote taken from original lecture by Roderick Peters published as 'The Therapist's Expectations of the Transference', *Journal of Analytical Psychology*, issue 36, pp 77–92
8 More often, Charles says, they lead to investigation. (E.g., 'How come I get the impression of fear in the room?')
9 Charles says: 'As a corporate man, it was easier to be open about feelings and use them successfully. As an analyst, I must often tolerate, observe and suppress (not repress) expression. Silence is the usual mode.'

Chapter 6

1 Christopher Bollas, *Forces of Destiny*, p. 62
2 Nina Coltart, 'Slouching Towards Bethlehem', in G. Kohon, *The British School of Psychoanalysis*, pp 185–99

3 Paula Heimann, 'On Counter-transference', *International Journal of Psychoanalysis*, no. 31, pp 81–4
4 Casement, *On Learning from the Patient*, p. 4
5 Issues and fantasies touched on included ideas around knowledge, power, competence, 'text-book interpretations' and intellectual versus emotional contact.
6 Adam adds: 'I would *never* deal with such a situation in this way unless I had been seeing the patient for a long time and knew him or her well. Also, I would have built up a good deal of understanding with the patient, based on previous experiences, that the patient would be inclined to use the reporting of such an incident in a particular, symbolic way. In this case, the interpretation was based upon the idea that the patient already knew, but avoided, the knowledge that she avoids any live interaction and kills it off, then becomes distressed about the death of any live contact.'
7 Alice Miller, *Thou Shalt Not Be Aware, passim*
8 Masson, *The Assault on Truth, passim*
9 Zvi Lothane, 'Love Seduction and Trauma', *Psychoanalytic Review*, vol. 74, issue 1, pp 84–95
10 Mitchell, op. cit., p. 43
11 Masson, *The Final Analysis*, p. 91

Chapter 7
1 Neville Symington, 'The Analyst's Act of Freedom as Agent of Therapeutic Change', *International Journal of Psychoanalysis*, no. 10, p. 783
2 Sheila Ernst and Marie Maguire, *Living with the Sphinx*, p. 62

Chapter 8
1 Judy L. Kantrowitz, Ann L. Katz and Frank Paolitto, 'Followup of Psychoanalysis Five to Ten Years after Termination. 1. Stability of Change', *Journal of the American Psychoanalytic Association*, vol. 38, no. 2, p. 489
2 Hinshelwood, op. cit.
3 Nora adds: 'But I am usually somewhere near the truth at the end of a long consultation. A much more frequent experience is that my *immediate* overall impression of a patient at the very beginning of a consultation is very different from what I think by the end. My first impressions, which analysts are meant to be good at, are about 75 per cent wrong.'
4 Charles adds: 'Had this occurred in the midst of ongoing therapy, I would have worked to resolve my problems in supervision or personal analysis.'
5 Casement, *Further Learning from the Patient*, p. 182
6 Herman, op. cit., p. 108

Chapter 9
1 Masson, *Against Therapy*, p. 15
2 Paul clarified this paragraph: 'I was not interested in my own madness, or

crazy parts of myself. These are writ large in the world, whether we want to look at them or not. And they emerge in all aspects of psychotherapeutic work and are therefore unavoidable.'

3 D. W. Winnicott, 'Hate in the Counter-transference', *International Journal of Psychoanalysis*, vol. 30, p. 70

Chapter 10

1 Masud Khan, *When Spring Comes*, p. 90
2 Khan, op. cit., p. 198
3 Joel Kovel, *A Complete Guide to Therapy*, p. 296
4 Cooper, op. cit.
5 Casement, *On Learning from the Patient*, p. 145
6 Coltart, op. cit.
7 Peter Rutter, *Sex in the Forbidden Zone*, p. 97
8 *New York Times*, 6 April 1989
9 Jeremy Holmes, 'Sexualized Relations in Psychotherapy', delivered at Manchester University, 3 November 1990
10 Holmes, op. cit.
11 Holmes, op. cit.
12 Adam adds: 'In the case of therapists having sex with patients that I have heard about or which have been reported to me, it seems nearly always to be non-psychoanalytically-trained therapists who do this, *even though they may be part of an organization which has a code of ethics.*'
13 *New Society*, 18 December 1987

Bibliography

Benjamin, Jessica, *The Bonds of Love*, Pantheon, New York, 1988

Bettelheim, Bruno, *Reflections and Recollections*, Thames & Hudson, London, 1990

Bollas, Christopher, *The Shadow of the Object*, Free Association Books, London, 1977

Bollas, Christopher, *Forces of Destiny*, Free Association Books, London, 1989

Casement, Patrick, *On Learning from the Patient*, Routledge, London, 1985

Casement, Patrick, *Further Learning from the Patient*, Routledge, London, 1990

Copans, Stuart and Singer, Thomas, *Who's the Patient Here? Portraits of the Young Psychotherapist*, Oxford University Press, New York, 1978

Dryden, Windy (ed.), *Individual Therapy in Britain*, Open University, Milton Keynes, 1984

Dryden, Windy, *Therapists' Dilemmas*, Harper & Row, London, 1985

Dryden, Windy and Spurling, Laurence, *On Becoming a Psychotherapist*, Tavistock/Routledge, London, 1989

Eagle, Morris N., *Recent Developments in Psychoanalysis*, McGraw Hill, New York, 1984

Ernst, Sheila and Maguire, Marie (eds), *Living with the Sphinx: Papers from the Women's Therapy Centre*, The Women's Press, London, 1987

Farrell, B. A., *The Standing of Psychoanalysis*, Oxford University Press, Oxford, 1981

France, Ann, *Consuming Psychotherapy*, Free Association Books, London, 1988

Frosh, Stephen, *Psychoanalysis and Psychology*, Macmillan, London, 1989

Gellner, Ernest, *The Psychoanalytic Movement*, Paladin, London, 1985

Greenson, Ralph R., *The Technique and Practice of Psycho-Analysis*, Hogarth Press, London, 1967

Grosskurth, Phyllis, *Melanie Klein*, Alfred A. Knopf, New York, 1986

Guy, James D., *The Personal Life of the Psychotherapist: The Impact of Clinical Practice on the Therapist's Intimate Relationships and Emotional Well-Being*, John Wiley & Sons, New York, 1987

Havens, Leston, *A Safe Place*, Ballantine, New York, 1989

Herman, Nini, *My Kleinian Home*, Free Association Books, London, 1988

Herman, Nini, *Why Psychotherapy?*, Free Association Books, London, 1987

Holmes, Jeremy and Lindley, Richard, *The Values of Psychotherapy*, Oxford University Press, Oxford, 1989

Johnson, Lucy, *Users and Abusers of Psychiatry*, Routledge, London, 1989

Khan, Masud, *When Spring Comes: Awakenings in Clinical Psychoanalysis*, Chatto and Windus, London, 1988; published in the US as *The Long Wait*, 1988

Klein, Melanie, *The Psychoanalysis of Children*, Hogarth Press, London, 1976

Knight, Lindsay, *Talking to a Stranger*, Fontana, London, 1986

Kohon, G., *The British School of Psychoanalysis*, Free Association Books, London, 1985

Kopp, Sheldon, *Back to One: A Practical Guide for Psychotherapists*, Science and Behavior Books, Palo Alto, 1977

Kovel, Joel, *A Complete Guide to Therapy: From Psychoanalysis to Behavior Modification*, Pantheon, New York, 1976

Lindner, Robert, *The Fifty-Minute Hour*, Delta, New York, 1954

Littlewood, Roland and Lipsedge, Maurice, *Aliens and Alienists*, Unwin Hyman, London, 1989

Lomas, Peter, *The Limits of Interpretation: What's Wrong with Psychoanalysis?*, Penguin, London, 1987

Lomas, Peter, *The Case for a Personal Psychotherapy*, Oxford University Press, Oxford, 1981

Maeder, Thomas, *Children of Psychiatrists and Other Psychotherapists*, Harper & Row, New York, 1989

Malan, David, *Individual Psychotherapy and the Science of Psychodynamics*, Butterworths, London, 1979

Malcolm, Janet, *In the Freud Archive*, Cape, London, 1984

Malcolm, Janet, *Psychoanalysis: The Impossible Profession*, Pan Books, London, 1982

Masson, Jeffrey, *Against Therapy*, Fontana/Collins, London, 1989

Masson, Jeffrey, *The Assault on Truth*, Farrar, Straus & Giroux, New York, 1984

Masson, Jeffrey, *The Final Analysis*, Addison Wesley, New York, 1990

Miller, Alice, *Thou Shalt Not Be Aware*, Pluto Press, London, 1985

Mitchell, Stephen, *Relational Concepts in Psychoanalysis: An Integration*, Harvard, Boston, 1990

Orbach, Susie, *Hunger Strike*, Avon Books, New York, 1986

Rayner, Eric, *The Independent Mind in Psychoanalysis*, Free Association Books, London, 1991

Reppen, Joseph (ed.), *Analysts at Work: Practice, Principles and Techniques*, Analytic Press, New Jersey, 1985

Rowe, Dorothy, *The Successful Self*, Fontana, London, 1988

Rutter, Peter, *Sex in the Forbidden Zone*, Mandala/Unwin Hyman, London, 1990

Smail, David, *Taking Care: An Alternative to Therapy*, J. M. Dent & Sons, London and Melbourne, 1987

Storr, Anthony, *The Art of Psychotherapy*, Heinemann Medical Books, London, 1990

Torrey, E. Fuller, *Witchdoctors and Psychiatrists*, Harper & Row, New York, 1986

Yalom, Irvin, *Love's Executioner*, Bloomsbury, London, 1989

Index

Frederick, 49, 56, 65, 67, 82, 120, 131, 132
frequency of sessions, 22–3
Freud, Anna, 43, 49, 67, 175
Freud, Sigmund, 7, 11, 26, 41–2, 44, 54, 62, 84, 97, 106, 132, 135, 185
Freudian technique, 132
Freudian theory, 125, 128
Freudian theory and feminism, 151
Freudian tradition, 42, 50
Freudians, 40, 41, 43, 44, 47, 48, 49, 51, 53, 54, 69, 93, 99, 133, 151, 153, 158
friendship, 5, 21, 74, 199
friendship, dangers of – within therapy, 189
frustration in therapy, 93, 108

Gavin, 56, 117, 168, 183, 185
George, 85, 103, 110, 144
Gill, Merton, 93
Gloria, 138, 160, 186, 187
Grosskurth, Phyllis, 62
Gulf War, 87
gurus, danger of therapists becoming, 51, 62, 129, 188

Harold, 74, 97, 98, 101, 114, 177
Harvard University, 49
hatred
    felt by patients for therapists, 109, 110, 187–8
    provoked in therapists by patients, 177
Heimann, Paula, 120
Henrietta, 48, 93, 153
Herman, Nini, 47, 51, 52, 166
Hilda, 150
Hinduism, 146
Hispanic cultures, 145
Hitler, Adolf, 179
holiday breaks, 92
Holmes, Jeremy, 191, 192
homelessness, 148
humour, analysis of, 100
Huxley, Aldous, 8

Ian, 69
ideal, analytic, 197
idealization of therapists, danger of, 59–60, 63, 64, 189

ignorance, therapists' admission of, 75, 115, 139
illness, therapists', 184
Independents, 43
India, British occupation of, 31, 146, 148
Indian culture, 146
individualism, association of psychoanalysis with, 147
indoctrination of therapists, 59–60
inexperience, dangers of, 77
infancy, significance of, 51
infantile sexuality, Freudian theory of, 54, 135, 136, 152
infantilization of trainee therapists, 60
inhibitions in training therapists, 60
inhumanity of therapists, 79
insensitivity of therapists, 132
Institute of Psychoanalysis (London), 26, 43, 53, 60, 68
intercultural therapy, 148–9
International Psychoanalytic Association (IPA), 35
interpersonal approach to therapy, 132
interpretation, 21, 45, 48, 49, 53, 55, 75, 102, 115, 124, 125
interpretation, tentative, 125
intimacy, therapists' desire for, 32, 33
Irene, 44, 166

Jack, 95, 96, 109, 124, 132, 150, 185
Jane, 27, 29, 76, 191
Japanese culture, 146
Jim, 171
Jo, 74, 102, 119, 128
John, 51, 89, 122, 154, 183
Judaism, 122, 145, 155
Judith, 68
June, 73
Jung, Carl, 7, 11, 45, 172
Jungian theory, 50, 51, 52, 53
Jungians, 40, 43, 44, 50, 51, 52, 53, 54, 158

Kafka, Franz, 26
Kareem, Jafar, 148
Keith, 36
Kernberg, Otto, 80, 83
Khan, Masud, 180–81
Klein, Melanie, 7, 42, 43, 62, 83, 136
Kleinian technique, 46, 48–50, 80